TECHNICAL HANDBOOK

INDEX

		Page
1.	**OUTSTANDING FEATURES OF BRIDGESTONE 175 DUAL TWIN**	
	1.1 Main Features of Engine	1
	1.2 Main Features of Frame	2
2.	**SPECIFICATIONS**	3
3.	**PERFORMANCE**	6
4.	**ENGINE**	
	4.1 Dismounting and Mounting Engine on Frame	
	A. Care to be observed	8
	B. Dismounting Engine	8
	C. Mounting Engine	11
	4.2 Disassembling and Assembling Engine	
	A. Matters that require special attention	11
	B. Dismounting Engine	12
	C. Inspection	15
	D. Assembling Engine	15
5.	**CRANKSHAFT AND ROTARY DISC VALVES**	
	A. Construction and Operation	16
	B. Inspection	17
6.	**CYLINDERS AND PISTONS**	
	A. Construction and Operation	18
	B. Disassembling	18
	C. Assembling	19
	D. Cleaning	19
	E. Inspection	19
7.	**CLUTCH**	
	A. Construction	21
	B. Operation	21
	C. Clutch Adjustment	22
	D. Disassembling Clutch	22
	E. Assembling	23
	F. Inspection	23
8.	**TRANSMISSION**	
	A. Construction	24
	B. Operation	24
	C. Disassembling	29
	D. Inspection	29

9. KICK STARTER

    A. Construction ··· 31
    B. Operation ··· 32
    C. Disassembling and Assembling ·· 32
    D. Inspection ·· 32

10. CARBURETORS

    A. Construction and Operation ··· 33
    B. Functions of Various Parts ·· 35
    C. Adjustment ·· 37

11. OIL INJECTION SYSTEM

    A. Construction ·· 40
    B. Operation ·· 40
    C. Adjusting Oil Volume ·· 42
    D. Disassembling and Installing ·· 42
    E. Inspection ·· 42

12. CHASSIS SECTION

12.1 Frame

    A. Construction ·· 43
    B. Inspection ·· 43
    C. Disassembling ·· 43
    D. Assembling ··· 43

12.2 Front Fork

    A. Construction ·· 44
    B. Operation ·· 44
    C. Disassembling ·· 45
    D. Inspection ·· 45

12.3 Handlebar

    A. Construction ·· 46
    B. Removing ·· 46
    C. Assembling ··· 47
    D. Inspection ·· 47

12.4 Rear Suspension

    A. Construction ·· 47
    B. Operation ·· 48
    C. Disassembling ·· 49
    D. Inspection ·· 49

12.5 Rear Frame

    A. Construction ·· 49
    B. Disassembling ·· 49
    C. Inspection ·· 49
    D. Assembling ··· 49

TECHNICAL HANDBOOK

BRIDGESTONE 175
Dual Twin
Hurricane Scrambler

BRIDGESTONE TIRE CO., LTD.

TOKYO, JAPAN

INTRODUCTION

Welcome to the world of digital publishing ~ the book you now hold in your hand, was printed using the latest state of the art digital technology. The advent of print-on-demand has forever changed the publishing process, never has information been so accessible and it is our hope that this book serves your informational needs for years to come. If this is your first exposure to digital publishing, we hope that you are pleased with the results. Many more titles of interest to the classic automobile and motorcycle enthusiast, collector and restorer are available via our website at www.VelocePress.com. We hope that you find this title as interesting as we do.

NOTE FROM THE PUBLISHER

The information presented is true and complete to the best of our knowledge. All recommendations are made without any guarantees on the part of the author or the publisher, who also disclaim all liability incurred with the use of this information.

TRADEMARKS

We recognize that some words, model names and designations, for example, mentioned herein are the property of the trademark holder. We use them for identification purposes only. This is not an official publication.

INFORMATION ON THE USE OF THIS PUBLICATION

This manual is an invaluable resource for those interested in performing their own maintenance. However, in today's information age we are constantly subject to changes in common practice, new technology, availability of improved materials and increased awareness of chemical toxicity. As such, it is advised that the user consult with an experienced professional prior to undertaking any procedure described herein. While every care has been taken to ensure correctness of information, it is obviously not possible to guarantee complete freedom from errors or omissions or to accept liability arising from such errors or omissions. Therefore, any individual that uses the information contained within, or elects to perform or participate in do-it-yourself repairs or modifications acknowledges that there is a risk factor involved and that the publisher or its associates cannot be held responsible for personal injury or property damage resulting from the use of the information or the outcome of such procedures.

WARNING!

One final word of advice, this publication is intended to be used as a reference guide, and when in doubt the reader should consult with a qualified technician.

12. 6 Front and Rear Wheels

    A. Description 50
    B. Removing Front Wheel 51
    C. Removing Rear Wheel 51
    D. Inspection 52
    E. Assembling 52
    F. Removing Tire 52
    G. Mounting Tire on the Rim 52
    H. Caution 53

12. 7 Brakes

    A. Construction 53
    B. Description 53
    C. Disassembling 54
    D. Inspection 54
    E. Assembling 54

12. 8 Fuel Tank and Seat

    A. Description 54
    B. Removing 55
    C. Inspection 55
    D. Assembling 55

12. 9 Air Cleaner

    A. Construction 55
    B. Description 55
    C. Removing 55
    D. Inspection 56
    E. Installing 56

12. 10 Exhaust System

    A. Construction 57
    B. Removing 57
    C. Inspection 57
    D. Installing 57

12. 11 Footrest and Stands

    A. Removing 58
    B. Inspection 58
    C. Installing 58

13. ELECTRICAL EQUIPMENT

13. 1 Generator

    A. Construction 59
    B. Description 59

13. 2 Selenium Rectifier 59

13. 3 Ignition System 63

- A. Contact Breakers ... 63
- B. Condensers ... 64
- C. Spark Plugs ... 65
- D. Ignition Coils ... 65

13. 4 **Battery** ... 65

13. 5 **Lights** ... 66

14. INSPECTION AND MAINTENANCE

- A. Daily Check Procedure ... 67
- B. Periodic Checking ... 67
- C. Periodic Greasing ... 68
- D. Inspection and Maintenance During Storage ... 69

15. TROUBLE SHOOTING ... 74

1. OUTSTANDING FEATURES OF BRIDGESTONE 175 DUAL TWIN

The Bridgestone 175 DT was perfected by concentrating the know-how and technical skills of Bridgestone's engineers, with their long years of rich experience and plentiful experiments. The high engine performance and excellent steering and stability of this 175 cc motorcycle matches that of machines with engines of 250 cc or even larger. The Bridgestone 175 DT is earning a good reputation as a remarkable motorcycle not only in the domestic market but in overseas areas as well.

1.1 Main Features of Engine:

Tremendous Acceleration:
The two cylinder engine, incorporating dual carburetors and dual rotary disc valves, has tremendous acceleration. The Bridgestone 175 DT is the only production model in the world which has these unique engine features. The engine earns a high reputation wherever it is sold.

Exclusive Sportshift Transmission
Gear changes are smooth with either the four speed rotary or five speed return shift. A simple lever allows the unique gearbox, the only one in the world, to be used as a four speed rotary shift system for riding adout town or switched to a five speed return shift system with stopper incorporating an overdrive fifth gear for sports riding.

Tremendous Top Speed
Bridgestone 175 DT riders can enjoy the thrills of 130 kmph (80 mph) speeds with the overdrive fifth gear in addition to the convenience of the rotary shift system for town riding.

Primary Kick Starter
The kick starter is installed in the transmission instead of working through the clutch, so the engine can be started with the transmission in any gear simply by pulling in the clutch lever. This eliminates the trouble of finding neutral before starting the engine.

Oil Injection System
A separate lubrication system is used for the engine so that a fuel mixture of oil and gasoline is not necessary. This is particularly handy where pre-mixed fuel is not readily available. The Bridgestone Oil Injection System always makes the ideal mixing ratio regardless of engine speed, so that oil consumption is reduced, engine performance is increased, care is easier and the machine is more economical.

Fully Enclosed Carburetors
Both carburetors are fully enclosed under covers so that the areas around the carburetors is always kept clean and danger of soiling the rider's clothing is eliminated.

1.2 Main Features of Frame

A Cradle Type Pipe Frame
A single cradle type frame of light and strong steel pipe holds the engine, giving the motorcycle excellent steering and stability even on rough roads and decreasing vibration. This makes the Bridgestone 175 DT a most reliable motorcycle.

B Sporty Telescopic Fork
A hydraulically damped telescopic front fork gives a sporty appearance and with its superior rigidity reduces the change of trail when stroking, so that the motorcycle gives extremely high performance when ridden on rough roads or at high speeds.

C Powerful Brakes
Large brake drums, 180 mm (7 inches) in diameter, are mounted on both the front and rear wheels and a racing type double leading shoe brake is installed on the front to guarantee brakes so powerful the rider can enjoy high speeds safely without worries about braking power.

D Dynamic Style, Fine Finish
The powerful layout of the engine, balanced appearance of the motorcycle and fine finish of all parts of the Bridgestone 175 DT combine to fascinate the rider so he wants to get on it and take a ride as soon as he sees this motorcycle.

2. SPECIFICATIONS

*Engine

- (1) Type : 2-stroke, Dual Cylinders
- (2) Piston Displacement : 177 cc. (10.8 cu-inch)
- (3) Bore & Stroke : 50 mm × 45 mm (1.97 × 1.77 inch)
- (4) Compression Ratio : 9.5 : 1
- (5) Max. Brake Horsepower : 20 HP/8,000 rpm
- (6) Max. Torque : 1.9 kg-m/7,500 rpm
- (7) Air Intake System : Rotary disc valve
- (8) Starting System : Kick Starter
- (9) Charging System : A.C. Generator
- (10) Ignition System : Battery
- (11) Ignition Timing : $\left(21 \begin{smallmatrix}+1\\-2\end{smallmatrix}\right)$ degrees before T.D.C.
- (12) Spark Plugs : N G K B-8 H
- (13) Carburetors : AMAL Type. VM 17 SC
- (14) Engine Lubrication : 2 cycle engine motor oil
- (15) Fuel : Gasoline
- (16) Transmission oil : 0.8 litre (0.21 US gal.) in transmission case
  SAE No. 10 W/30 in all seasons or
  SAE No. 30 in summer and SAE No. 20 in winter

*Performance

- (1) Max. Speed : Over 130 km/h (80 mph)
- (2) Climbing Gradient : 1 in 3
- (3) Fuel Consumption : 55 km/l (129 mpg) at 40 km/h (25 mph) on paved flat test road
- (4) Min. Turning Radius : 1.95 m (76.8 inch)
- (5) Acceleration :
  (Standing Start 1/4 mile) Under 18 sec (0-400 m)
- (6) Braking Distance : Less than 6 m at 35 km/h (20 feet, at 22 mph).

*Frame & Suspension

- (1) Frame Type : Pipe Frame, Cradle Type
- (2) Front Suspension : Telescopic Fork with Hydraulic Damper
- (3) Rear Suspension : Swinging Arm with Hydraulic Damper

*Transmission

(1) Clutch : Manual, Multiple discs in oil bath.
(2) Transmission : Dual Transmission, selective 4-speed constant mesh-rotary or 5-speed constant mesh-return by shifting "sportshift" lever
(3) Gear Ratios : Primary (Helical gear) : 1 : 3.41
　Gear Box :　　　1 st　1 : 2.61
　　　　　　　　　2 nd　1 : 1.67
　　　　　　　　　3 rd　1 : 1.24
　　　　　　　　　4 th　1 : 1.00
　　　　　　　　　5 th　1 : 0.85
　Secondary (Chain) :　　1 : 2.37
　Total Gear Ratio : 1 st　1 : 21.19
　　　　　　　　　2 nd　1 : 13.50
　　　　　　　　　3 rd　1 : 10.03
　　　　　　　　　4 th　1 : 8.10
　　　　　　　　　5 th　1 : 6.86

*Dimensions and Weight

(1) Overall Length : 1,885 mm (74.2 inch)
(2) Overall Width : 750 mm (29.5 inch)
　　　　　　　　　with Standard Western type Handlebar
(3) Overall Height : 1,020 mm (40.2 inch)
(4) Saddle Height : 780 mm (30.7 inch)
(5) Wheelbase : 1,235 mm (48.6 inch)
(6) Road Clearance : 150 mm (5.9 inch)
(7) Tire Size　　(Front) : 2.50-18 4 ply
　　　　　　　　(Rear) : 2.75-18 4 ply
(8) Tire Pressure　(Front) : 1.6 kg/cm^2 (22 lbs/in^2)
　　　　　　　　(Rear) : 2.0 kg/cm^2 (28 lbs/in^2)
(9) Caster : 64°
(10) Trail : 83.5 mm (3.29 inch)
(11) Banking Angle : 45°
(12) Net Weight : 123 kg (271 lbs)
(13) Fuel Tank Capacity : 10 L (2.64 US gal.)
　　　　　　　　　Including 1.2 litre (0.317 US gal.) reserve
(14) Oil Tank Capacity : 1.8 L (3.8 pint)
(15) Front Brake : Right Hand Operated
(16) Rear Brake : Right Foot Operated

*Electrical Equipment

(1) Head light : 12 V − 35/25 W
(2) Tail light : 12 V − 8 W
(3) Stop light : 12 V − 25 W
(4) Speedometer lamp : 12 V − 3 W
(5) Third gear indicator lamp : 12 V − 2 W
(6) Neutral indicator lamp : 12 V − 2 W
(7) Battery : 12 V − 6 AH

Side, front and back views of "BRIDGESTONE 175 DUAL TWIN"
Dimensions in Millimeters (inches)

3. PERFORMANCE

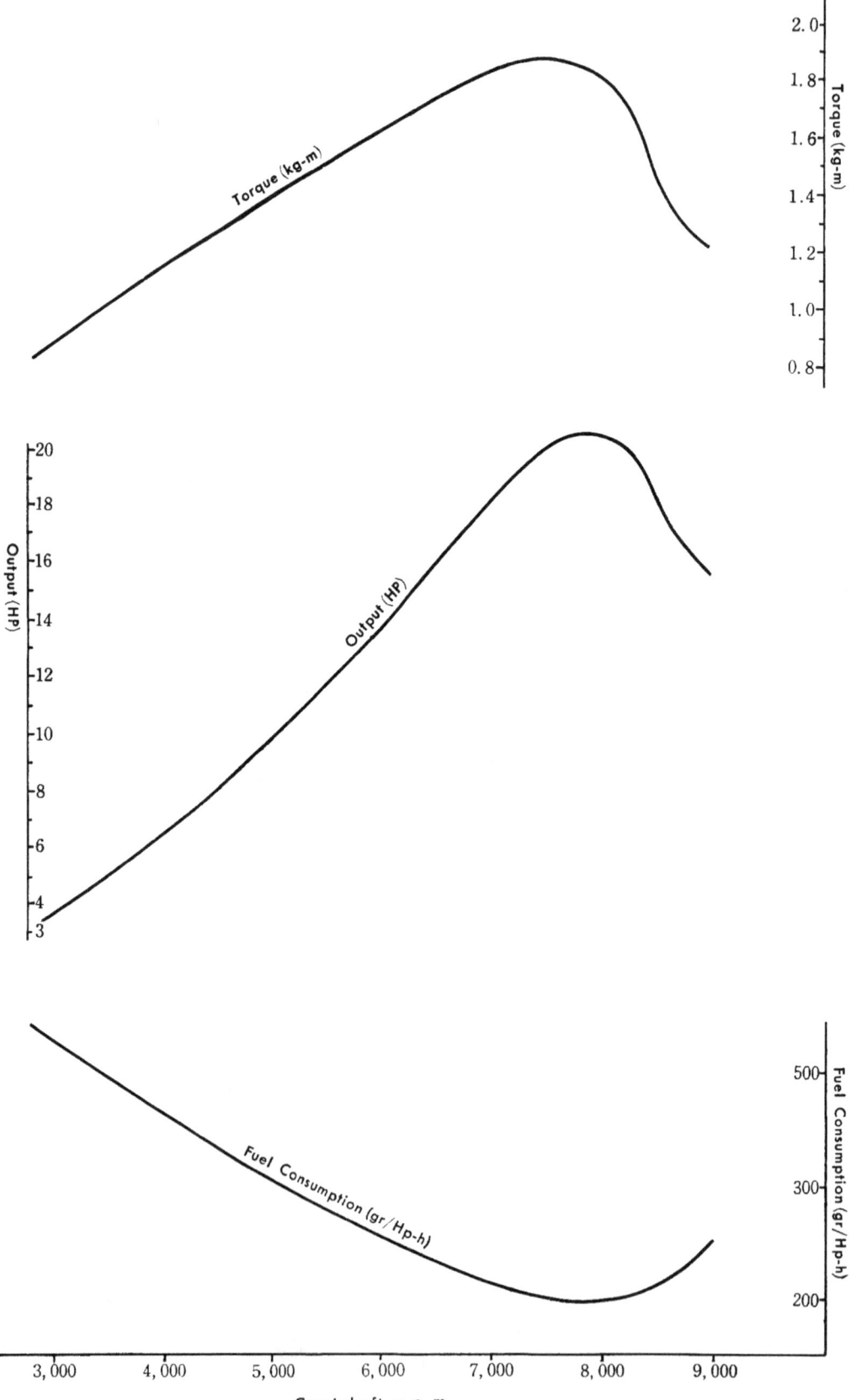

ENGINE/ROAD SPEED

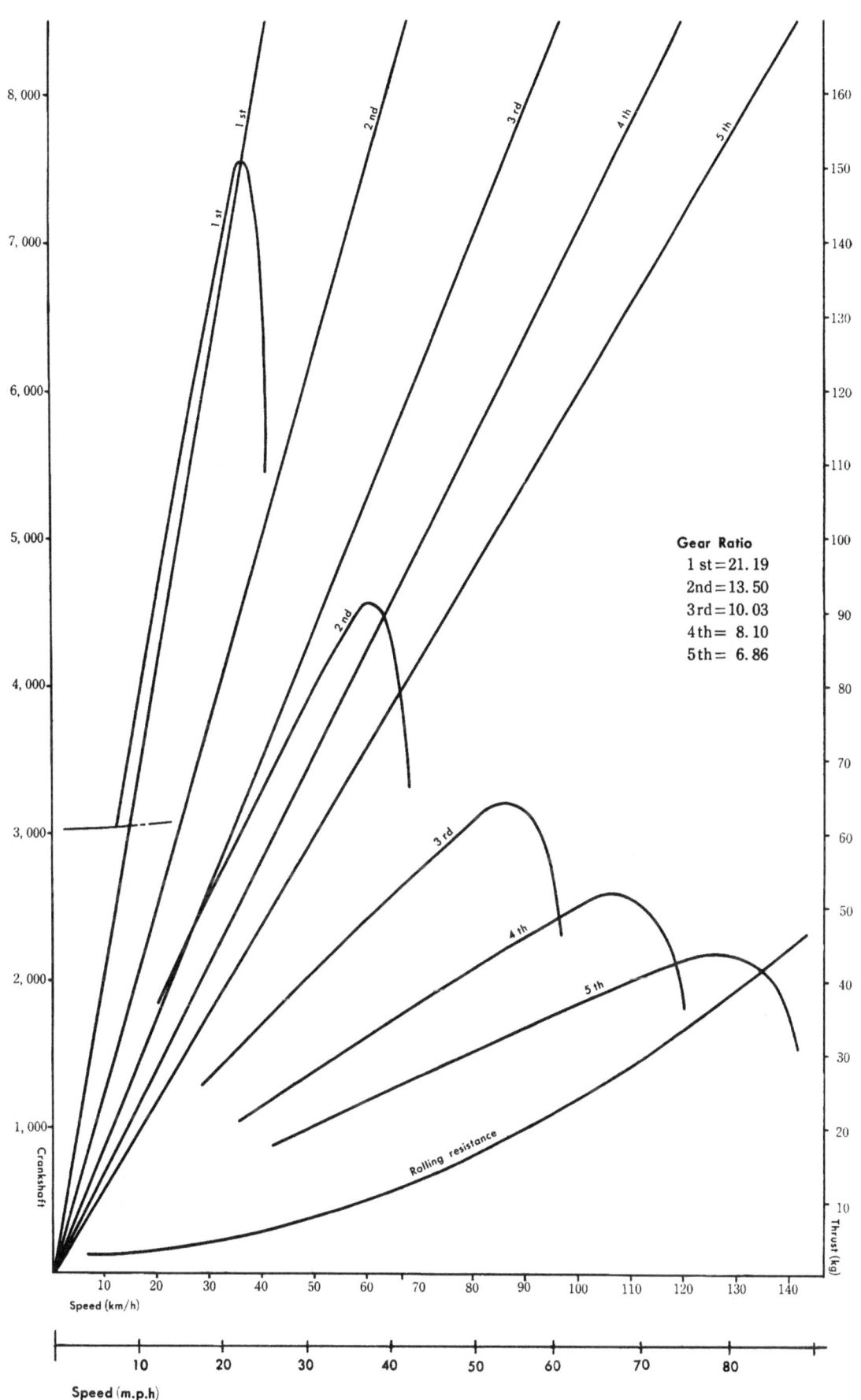

4 ENGINE

4.1 Dismounting and Mounting Engine on Frame:

A. Care to be observed

(1) Be careful not to damage the insulation of the various electrical wires.

(2) Be careful not to damage the frame or engine when handling bolts and nuts by tools.

(3) The chain connector should be linked with slotted end pointing in the reverse direction of the regular motion of chain.

Fig. 1.   Fig. 2.

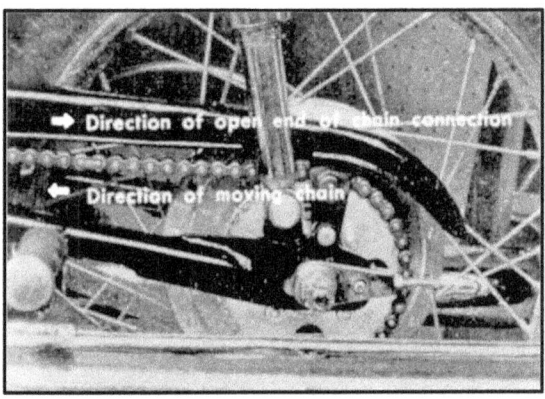 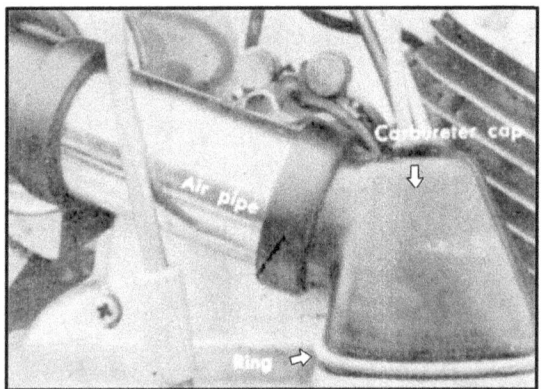

B. Dismounting Engine:

(1) Tools necessary (Fig. 3).

(2) Place oil receiver with capacity of more than 1 litre (0.26 U.S. Gal.) under engine and drain out transmission oil by removing drain cock.

(3) Loosen the clutch cable with wire adjuster and remove the cable from the clutch lever (Fig 4).

(4) Remove the rubber caps mounted on the transmission case after the air pipes and rubber cap setting bands are removed.

(5) Close fuel by turning fuel cock lever to "O" position.

(6) Remove air cleaner by removing two (6×25) air cleaner bolts.

(7) Remove carburetor covers (R) & (L) by removing three (6×20) and one (6×25) screws on the right and pull out rubber plugs, three (6×20) and one (6×35) screws on the left.

Fig. 3. Tools necessary   Fig. 4. Clutch

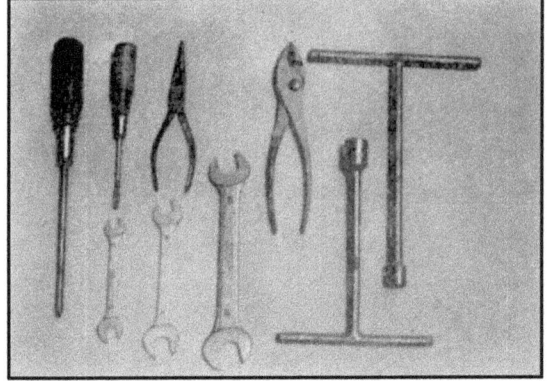 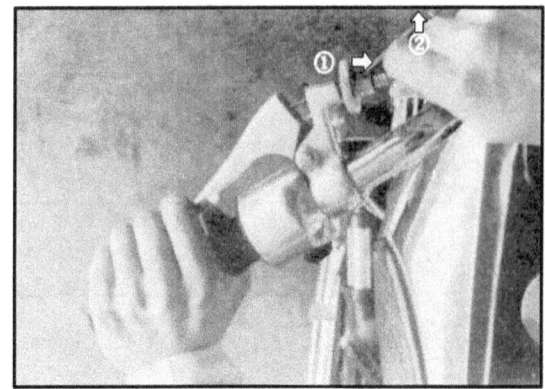

(8) Pull out dual carburetors by using a ⊖ driver. (Fig. 5)

(9) Remove hexagonal bolt (6×25) of kick arm and detach kick arm. (Fig. 6)

(10) Remove both exhaust pipes by removing two bolts. (Fig. 7)

(11) Take off footrest (L) by removing hexagonal bolt of footrest. (Fig. 8)

(12) Remove change pedal by removing hexagonal bolt (6×20). (Fig. 9)

(13) Remove crankcase cover (L) by removing two (6×20) and two (6×30) screws of crankcase cover (L)

(14) Remove dust cover by removing two (6×30) and one (6×20) screws of dust cover (Fig. 10)

Fig. 5. Pulling out carbureter

Fig. 6. Removing kick arm

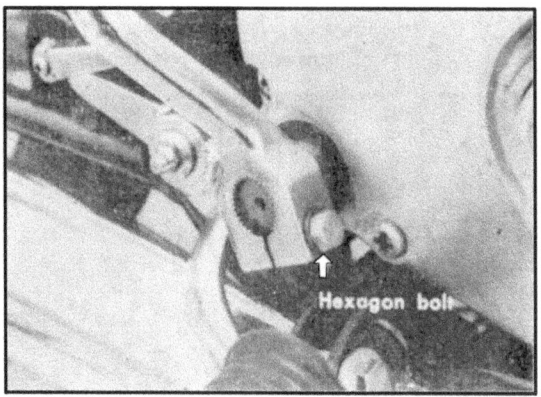

Fig. 7. Removing exhaust pipe

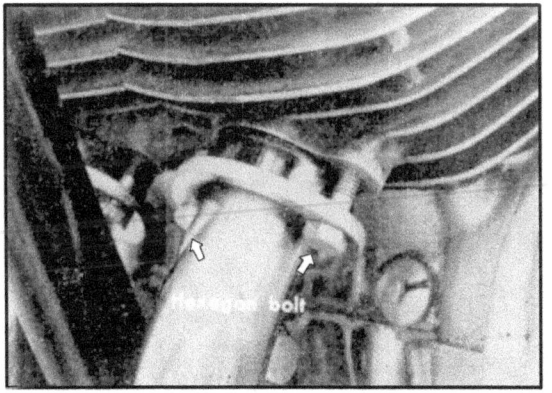

Fig. 8. Removing footrest (L)

Fig. 9. Removing change pedal

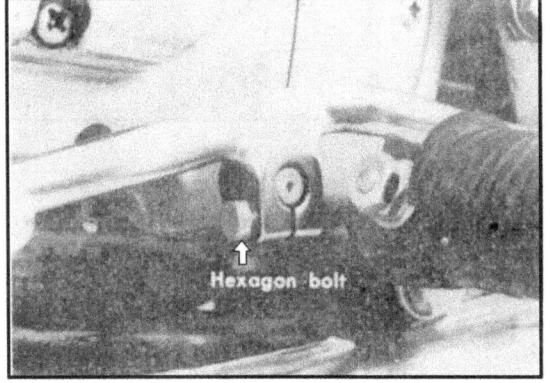

Fig. 10. Removing dust cover

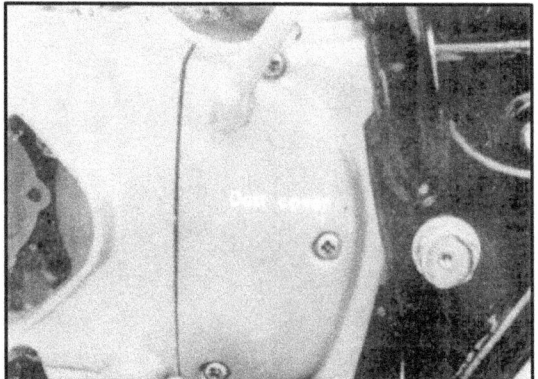

(15) Remove two hexagonal bolts (6×10) on the drive sprocket to remove the drive sprocket set plate by removing it on left or right side, and then remove drive sprocket and chain. (Fig. 11)

(16) Disconnect main switch wires and A.C. generator wires from the terminals. (Fig. 12)

Coloring of wires

$\begin{cases} \text{White} : \text{from contact breaker} \\ \text{Black} : \text{from ignition coil} \end{cases}$

$\begin{cases} \text{Yellow} : \text{Selenium rectifier} \\ \text{Blue} : \text{A.C generator} \end{cases}$

$\begin{cases} \text{Brown} : \text{A.C generator} \\ \quad\quad\quad\ \text{Main switch} \end{cases}$

(17) Remove high-tension terminal plug cap from spark plug.

Fig. 11. Removing drive sprocket

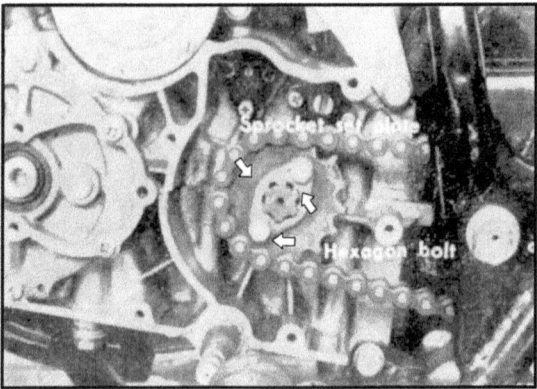

Fig. 12. Disconnecting wires

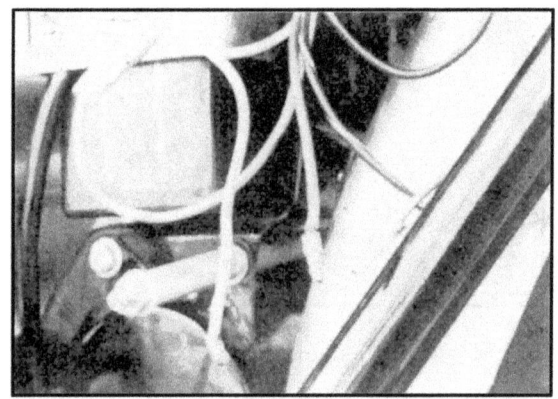

Fig. 13. Removing engine bracket

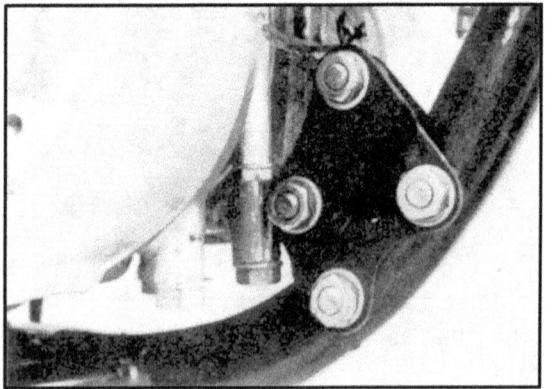

Fig. 14.

(18) Remove engine bracket by taking off four hexagonal bolts, two (8×45 mm) and two (8×50 mm). (Fig. 13)

(19) Remove two (8×108) engine mounting bolts and then lift out engine from the left side of the frame.

* **Be careful not to damage fuel cock ass'y.**

C. **Mounting Engine:**

(1) The engine should be installed in the reverse order of removal.

* **Be careful of the following points:**

a) The chain connector should be linked with the open end pointing in the reverse direction of the moving chain.

b) Chain adjustment is correct when chain slack is approximately 10 mm (3/8") up or down. (Fig. 15 Fig. 16)

Fig. 15. Adjusting chain by chain adjuster

Fig. 16. Chain adjustment

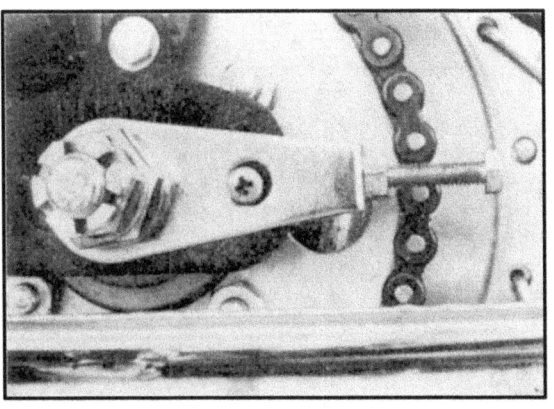

c) Mount the carburetors securely.

d) See that the throttle valves work properly.

e) Set the clutch wire correctly.

f) See that the clutch works properly.

g) See that gas does not leak from the exhaust pipes and muffler joints.

h) See that all nuts, bolts and screws are tightened firmly.

i) See that the transmission is filled with the proper amount (0.8 litre = 0.91 U.S. quarts) of oil, and check the amount by pulling out the oil level screw.

4.2 **Disassembling and Assembling Engine:**

A. **Matters that require special attention.**

(1) When removing or installing the engine, use a wooden or plastic hammer and tap it lightly and uniformly so as not to strain any part. (4.2B. 20–25)

(2) When handling bolts, nuts, screws, tools, etc., exercise great care so that the component of gear, case, piston, cylinder etc. are not damaged or lost.

(3) When disassembling, take careful note of the position of the meshing gears and location of the many washers, and lay the parts out in an orderly manner, so that they may not get mislaid or confused when assembling.

(4) Be careful not to damage the case to prevent leakage of oil.

(5) Handling of the respective parts should be carried out carefully and neatly.

(6) The parts should be carefully cleaned.

(7) When assembling transmission gears, set the timing mark or notch of crankshaft-pinion gear, pinion gear-driven gear, driven gear-timing gear respectively.

B. Dismounting Engine:

(1) Mount the engine on an engine repair stand.

(2) Loosen and remove diagonally four nuts of the cylinder head, spring washers and remove cylinder head and gasket.

(3) Remove piston pin by taking off piston pin circrips and detach piston from connecting rod. (Fig. 17)

Then take off needle bearing from connecting rod small end.

(4) Turn crankcase cover (R) section upward and remove casecover (R) by removing casecover (R) screws, three (6×65), two (6×40), four (6×35). (Fig. 18)

Fig. 17. Taking off piston circlip   Fig. 18. Removing crankcase cover (R)

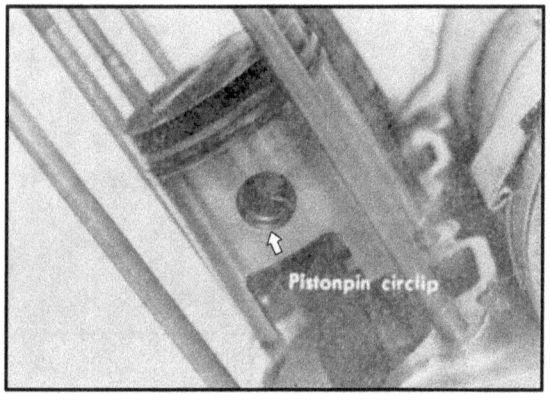
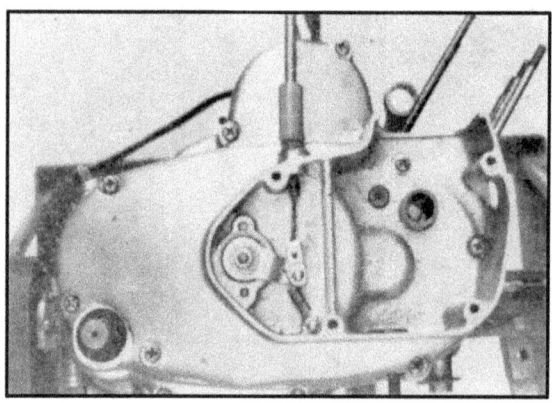

(5) Remove clutch set plate and clutch springs by removing diagonally and evenly the six (5×12) hexagonal bolts of the clutch set plate.

(6) Remove clutch hub nut (16mm) with clutch hub stopper, and then remove clutch hub and driven gear complete.

(7) Remove timing gear fitting bolt (6×12) and then remove timing gear with special tool. (Fig. 19)

(8) Place the "piston seat" to the connecting rod, remove the left-hand threaded pinion gear by removing pinion gear nut. (Fig. 20)

Fig. 19. Removing timing gear   Fig. 20. Removing pinion gear

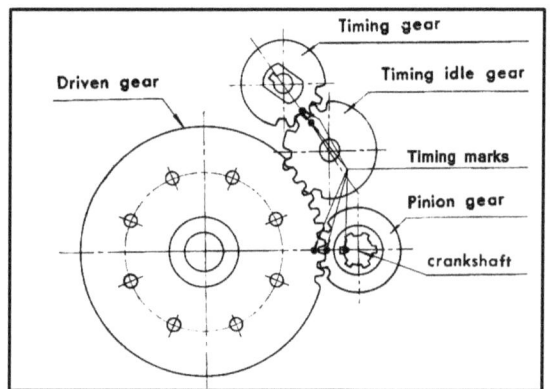

(9) Remove kick return spring holder and take out kick return spring.

(10) Remove two drum guide screws (6×14), detach drum guide plate.

(11) Remove drum stopper arm by removing drum stopper bolt.

(12) Remove drum shifter from shift drum, and pull out change shaft assembly. (Fig. 21)

(13) Take off bearing holder for countershaft by removing three bearing fitting screws (6×14).

(14) Take off rotary valve cover (R) by unscrewing six screws (6×20) of valve cover. (Fig 22)

Fig, 21.　Removing drum shifter

Fig. 22.　Rotary valve cover (R)

(15) Remove rotary disc valve.

(16) Remove crankshaft collar and valve guide.

(17) Turn A.C. generator section to the top, remove generator stud nut and generator band. (Fig. 23)

(18) Take off timing adjusting screw (5×12) for A.C. generator, removing A.C. generator by pushing it from right side.

(19) Pull out oil pump by removing oil pump screws. (Fig. 24)

Fig. 23.　Removing generator band

Fig. 24.　Pulling out oil pump

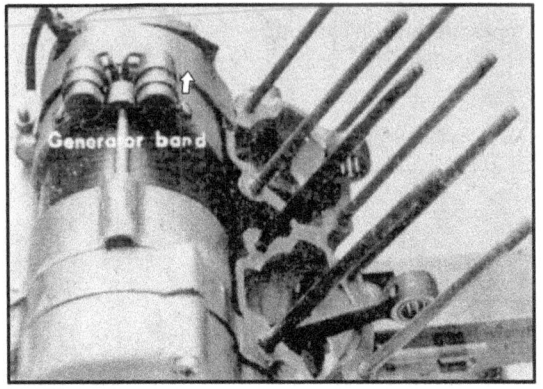

(20) Take off rotary disc valve cover (L) by unscrewing six (6×20) screws of valve cover. (Fig. 25)

(21) Remove rotary disc valve.

(22) Put the engine upside down, remove eleven lower crankcase hexagonal bolts, two (6×90), three (6×50), one (8×100), four (8×80) and one (8×62), and then take off lower crankcase. (Fig. 26)

Fig. 25. Taking off rotary disc valve cover (L)

Fig. 26. Transmission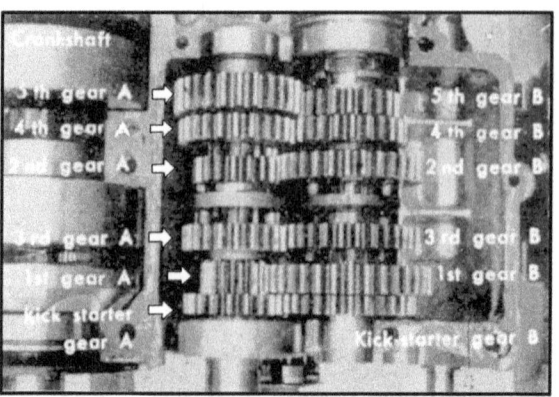

(23) Remove crankshaft comp., countershaft and driveshaft together with gears.

(24) Pull out kick starter shaft by taking off 16B circlip on the kick starter shaft and then remove kick starter gears C, kick starter ratchet arm. (Fig. 27)

Fig. 27. Taking off 16B circlip

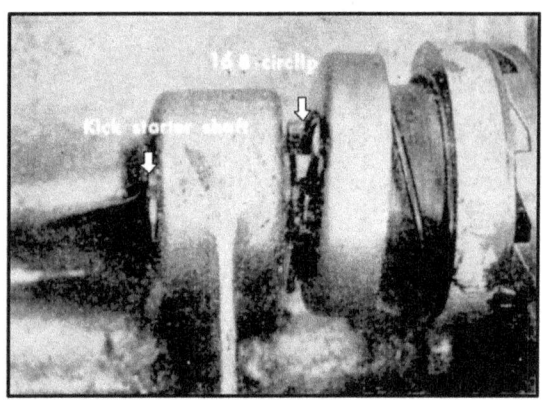

(25) Remove shift drum from upper case.

(26) Remove gears and thrust washer from countershaft and driveshaft.

(27) Remove gasket of each case.

Fig. 28 Transmission gears

C. Inspection:

After dismantling, inspect each part comparing it with servicing standards.

D. Assembling Engine:

(1) The engine should be assembled in the reverse order of disassembling.

(2) Be careful to set gears and thrust washers correctly. (Fig. 28)

(3) When assembling lower crankcase, insert 8 mm hexagonal bolt first and then 6 mm hexagonal bolt.

(4) When fitting bolts, bolts should be fitted from center part of case. (Fig. 29)

Fig. 29. Crankcase fitting

Timing gear setting

When assembling engine, fit Pinion gear, Driven gear, Timing idle gear and Timing gear to meet the "Timing Mark" together as shown in the following figure.

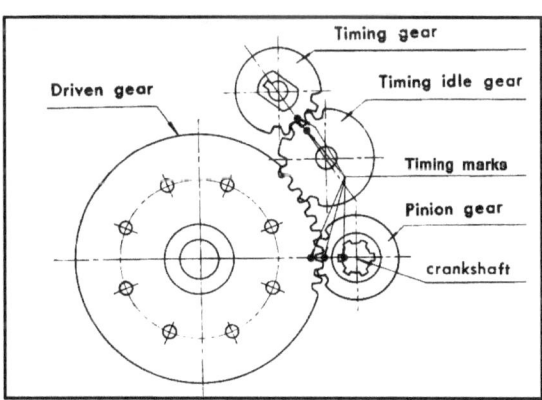

5. CRANKSHAFT AND ROTARY DISC VALVES

A. Construction and Operation:

Dual cylinders, dual carburetors and dual rotary disc valves are incorporated in the Bridgestone 175 DT engine. Rotary disc valves are spline fitted on each end of the crankshaft of this parallel twin.

(1) When the pistons move up and down in the cylinders from the force of the explosion of fuel/air mixture gas, the crankshaft converts this reciprocating movement to rotary motion and supplies power to the rear wheel through the clutch and transmission. The crankshaft must endure the impact of explosive force and the high temperatures of combustion.

Crankshaft strength and precision are required to endure continuous high speed operation for long times.

Crankshaft materials must be selected carefully and machined exactly to prevent twisting, cracking, off-centering, etc. The amount and direction, vertical or horizontal, of engine vibration has extreme affect on riding comfort and fatigue of the rider. The crankshaft is one source of vibration. If the crankshaft is not balanced properly, engine vibration will increase. Following research and experiments by Bridgestone engineers, the crankshaft of the Bridgestone 175 DT is designed to give smooth rotation and balanced operation with a minimum of vibration.

(2) Rotary disc valves are installed between the carburetors and the crankcase and control the supply of fuel/air mixture from the carburetors to the crankcase. In conventional two-stroke engines, the fuel/air mixture is controlled by the skirt of the piston and port timing, the opening and closing of inlet and exhaust ports, is limited to before top dead center and after top dead center so that fuel mixture supply is not efficient. By using a rotary disc valve, however, the best timing for engine operation can be determined by altering the cutaway of the valve disc, so that fuel supply and engine power are increased. Carburetor blow-back and fuel loss can also be eliminated and engine performance increased tremendously.

Fig. 30. Crankshaft

Fig. 31. Port timing

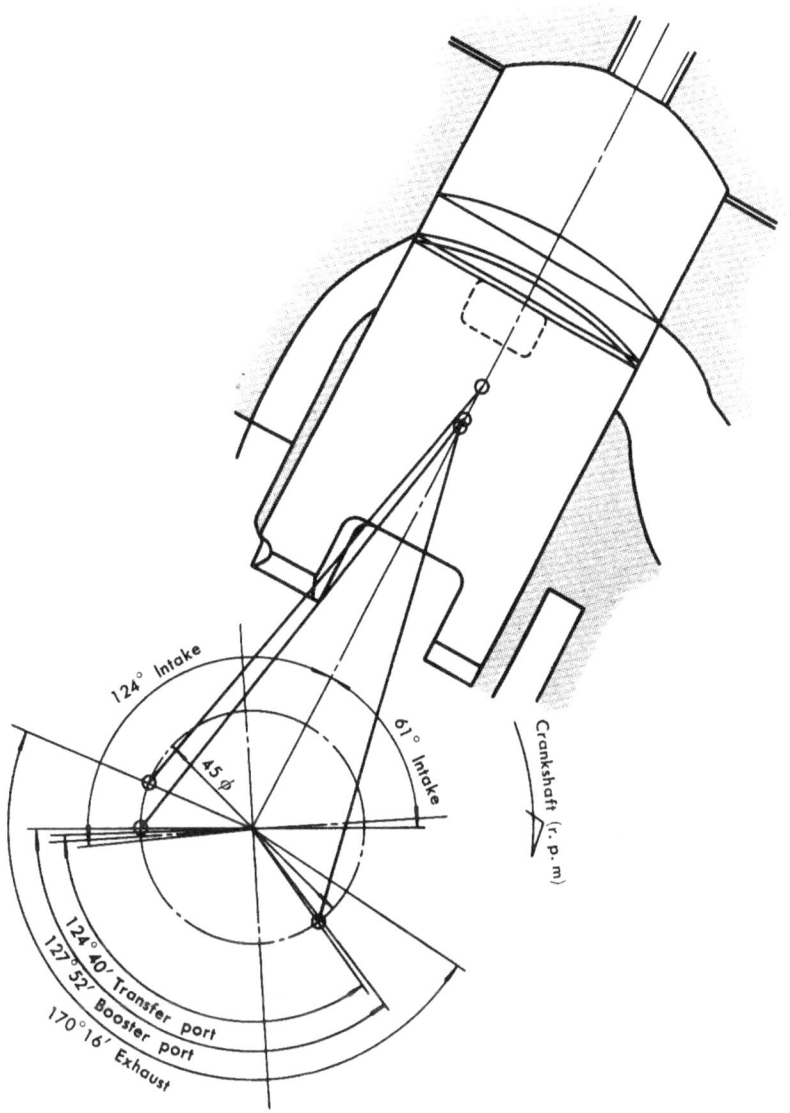

B. Inspection:

(1) Measure crankshaft shake with a dial guage and act in accordance with Maintenance Standards.

(2) Inspect the part of the crankshaft where bearings are fitted for wear and excess play. If abnormal noise is produced or there is excessive play, replace the crankshaft with a new one.

(3) If the connecting rod lower end bearing is worn or damaged, replace the crankshaft with a new one.

(4) If an oil seal lip is damaged or deformed, replace the oil seal with a new one.

(5) If a disc valve is damaged, replace with a new one.

(6) If an O-ring is damaged or worn, replace with a new one.

6. CYLINDERS AND PISTONS:

A. Construction and Operation:

(1) The cylinders of the Bridgestone 175 DT are made of aluminum alloy. Cylinder walls are honed after hard chromium plating and then porous treated.

When the engine is running, the cylinder wall must endure high temperatures of combustion and friction of the moving piston. In porous treatment numerous oil retainers are created on the cylinder wall and these lubricate the cylinder and piston with oil which is contained in the fuel mixture inhaled into the crankcase.

The aluminum alloy cylinder has excellent cooling efficiency and as the heat expansion coefficient of the cylinder and piston is the same, the piston/cylinder clearance can be kept to a minimum and quiet engine operation is possible.

The alminum alloy cylinder has a longer life than a cast iron cylinder. When the aluminum alloy cylinder becomes worn, the cylinder wall can be replated.
In addition to these features, the alminum alloy cylinders reduce the weight of the engine.

As aluminum alloy cylinders are used, take care not to use chromium plated piston rings. Always use only ferox treated piston rings.

(2) Construction of the cylinder is shown in Fig. 32. The exhaust port is located in the forward part and the transfer ports in the right and left sides and rear part of the cylinder. The transfer port in the rear part of the cylinder is called the booster port. The booster port expells exhaust gas and induces fresh fuel/air mixture into the combustion chamber, increasing scavenging efficiency.

Fig. 32. Cylinder

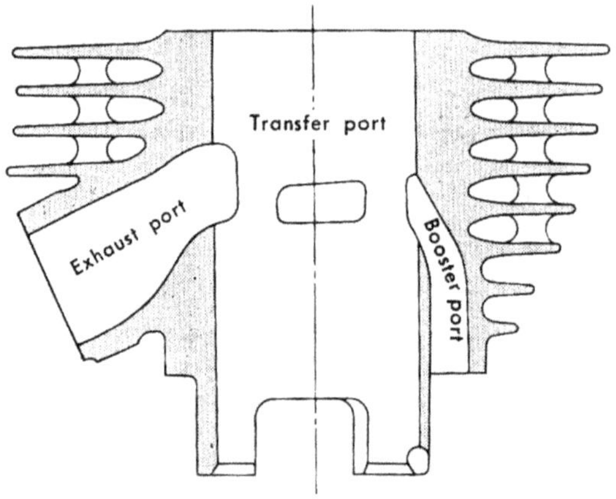

(3) The pistons in the Bridgestone 175 DT engine are Lo-Ex pistons, and identical to that used in the Bridgestone 90 engine. These pistons have a lower heat expansion coefficient than normal aluminum alloy pistons and low specific gravity, so the pistons resist wear yet maintain excellent mechanical property at high temperatures.

B. Disassembling:

(1) The cylinder head and pistons can be taken off without removing engine from the frame.

Disconnect high tension terminals and plug caps from spark plugs and detach exhaust pipes by removing exhaust pipe clamp nuts with a special tool.

(2) Take off eight cylinder head nuts and remove cylinder head and gasket.

(3) Before removing pistons, remove cylinder and cover the crankcase with cloth to prevent dirt from entering into the crankcase and then remove piston pin circlips.

Fig. 33. Removing circlip   Fig. 34. Removing pistons

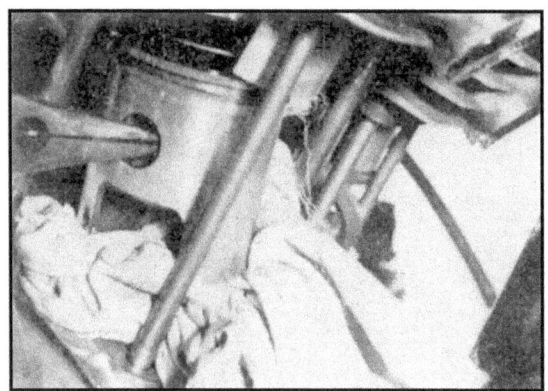
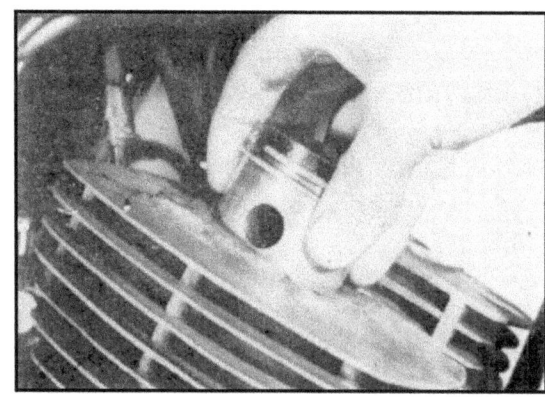

Be careful connecting rod is not forced left or right.)

(4) Cylinder should be removed after engine is dismounted.

C. Assembling:

(1) The piston and cylinder head should be assembled in the reverse order of disassembling.

(2) Fit piston rings to the piston before inserting piston in the cylinder.

D. Cleaning:

Throughly scrub pistons. piston rings and cylinders with gasoline or cleaning solvent to remove carbon deposits.

Pay particular attention to the cylinder intake and exhaust ports.

Where carbon deposit is heavy or hard, it is advisable to scrape it before cleaning. Use extreme care to avoid scratching the walls of the cylinders.

Clean piston ring grooves. After the parts are throughly washed, dry with compressed air. Force air through all passages in cylinder.

E. Inspection:

E-1. Insufficient Power:

(1) Check the compression pressure with compression guage after warming up engine by opening throttle grip fully and if very little compression is felt, the cause may be either wear of piston rings or cylinder. Replace parts where necessary. (Refer to Service Standards Manual.)

(2) Check side clearance between piston and cylinder and see whether any part is damaged (such as burnt spots, stiff rings or scratches).

(Refer to Service Standards Manual.)

(3) Check for gas leakage through cylinder gasket and cylinder packing. Replace with new ones if unsatisfactory.

E-2. Knocking:

(1) Check clearance between piston skirt and cylinder wall. (Refer to Service Standards Manual).

(2) Check for tightness of piston pin. (Refer to Service Standards Manual).

SERVICE MEMO:

7. **CLUTCH:**

   A. **Construction:**

   The clutch is located between the engine and transmission and transmits or cuts off engine power to the transmission and rear wheel. Engine power is transmitted from the drive pinion on the crankshaft through the driven gear on the clutch housing. Shocks are absorbed by six rubber dampers installed between the driven gear and the clutch housing. The clutch housing rotates the clutch friction plates.

   In addition to transmitting engine power, the clutch has a large affect on riding comfort, so smooth operation of the clutch is necessary for comfortable riding.

   If the clutch drags, gear shift operation becomes faulty and gears or the gear change arm can be damaged.

   If the clutch slips, poor acceleration, engine overheating, loss of engine power and uncomfortable riding will result.

   Clutch Friction Plate ……6   Clutch Spring…………6
   Inner Plate……………………5   Fitting Tension ………57~63 kg (126~139 lbs)

   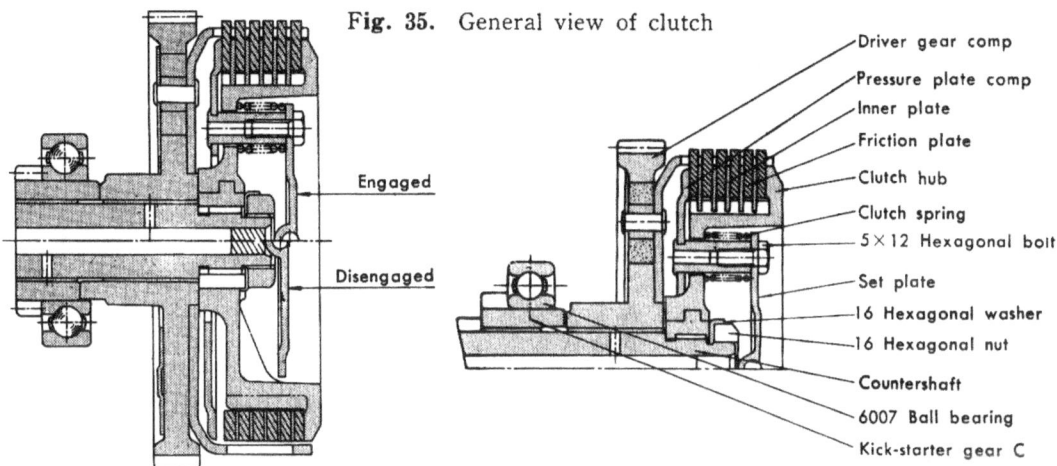

   Fig. 35. General view of clutch

   B. **Operation:**

   (1) Transmitting Engine Power.

   Engine power is transmitted through the drive pinion on the crankshaft and the driven gear. The driven gear is attached to the clutch housing with six rubber dampers. Clutch friction plates are fitted inside the clutch housing with six teeth so that they turn together with the clutch housing and driven gear. Clutch friction plates and inner plates are fitted alternately, with the inner plates fitted to the clutch hub with teeth. The clutch hub, friction plates and inner plates all fit inside the clutch housing and are pressed together tightly by the clutch springs. The clutch hub is spline fitted to the transmission countershaft, which turns the transmission gears.

   (2) Engine Power Cut Off.

   When the clutch lever is pulled, the clutch wire turns the clutch release arm so that the adjusting screw pushes the roller and depresses the clutch set plate ball. The clutch springs are then compressed so that they do not press the clutch friction plates against the inner plates. As the friction plates and inner plates separate, the inner plates cease to turn so that engine power is cut off from the clutch hub and transmission countershaft.

C. Clutch Adjustment:

(1) Adjustment is easily carried out with the cable adjuster.

(2) When satisfactory adjustment cannot be made in this way, remove rubber cap from carburetor (R), loosen lock nut with 10 mm box spanner in the tool set, and adjust by holding down the lock nut and turning adjustment screw.

The play of the lever is lessened by turning the screw right and increased by turning left.

Fig. 36. Wire adjuster   Fig. 37. Cable adjuster

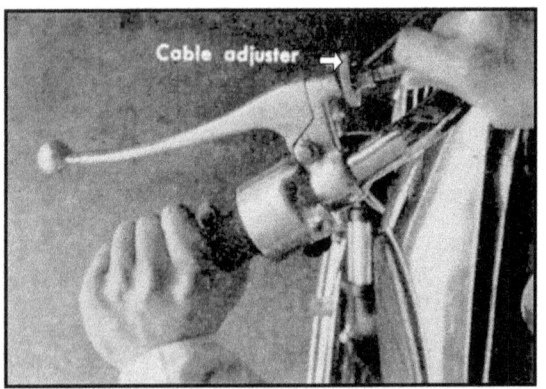 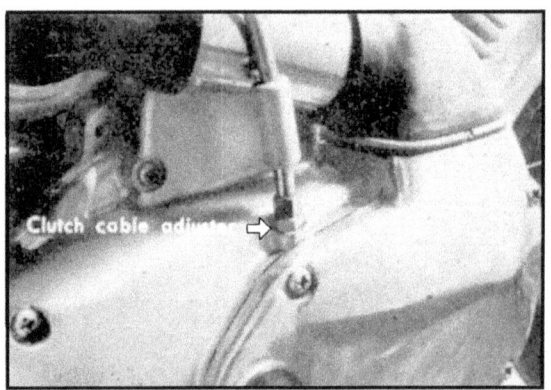

Fig. 38. Clutch Adjustment

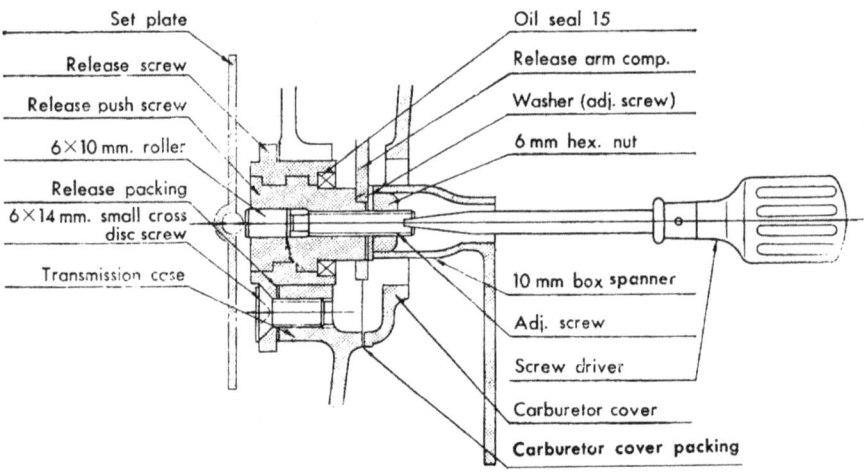

Fig. 39. Clutch release screw

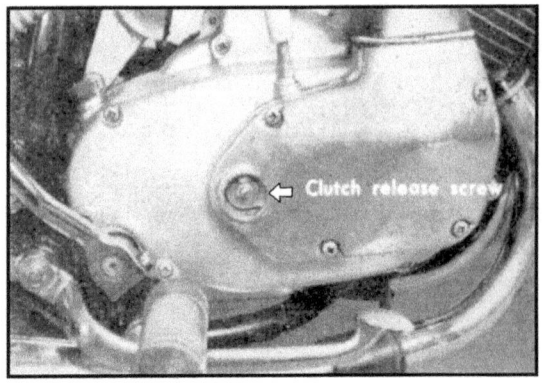

D. Disassembling Clutch:

(1) Follow procedure described on page 9 for removing crankcase (R). (This work can be done by removing kick pedal, air pipe, carburetor cover and carburetor, without dismounting the engine.)

(2) Remove six (5×12) hexagonal clutch set plate bolts.

(3) Fix clutch hub with clutch hub stopper, remove clutch nut and then remove clutch hub and driven gear comp. (Fig. 40, 41)

Fig. 40. Removing clutch fitting nuts.

Fig. 41. Removing clutch hub stopper

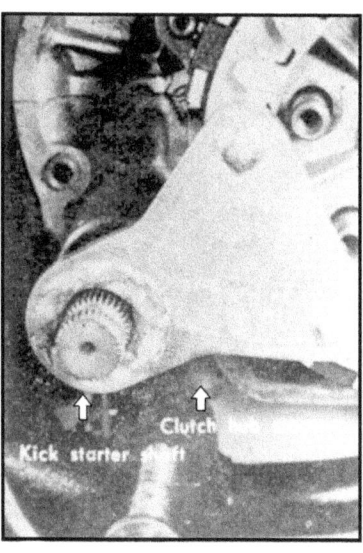

E. Assembling:

(1) Assembling can be done in the reverse order of disassembling.

(2) The facings and inner plates alternately contact with each other. The outer plate is thicker than the other plates. [Thickness 3 mm (0.12″)].

(3) Set circlip after assembling friction plates and inner plates to clutch hub and clutch housing connectly.

F. Inspection:

(1) See if there are any damaged serrations on the inner plates, and worn or uneven plates.

(Refer to Service Standard Manual.)

(2) Check for damaged arms on facings, worn on uneven.

(3) Check for irregularities in set plates, looseness of set bolts or weakened tension or breakage of return springs.

Adjust or replace any that are found to be unsatisfactory.

(4) Check release arm for wear, release screw, release push screw and 7/32″ ball.

Replace where necessary.

Fig. 44. Check clutch release screw

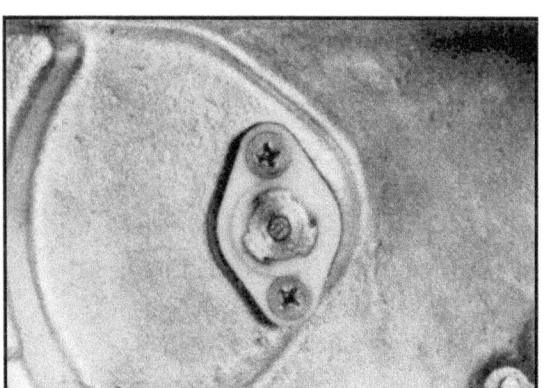

Fig. 42. Check friction plate

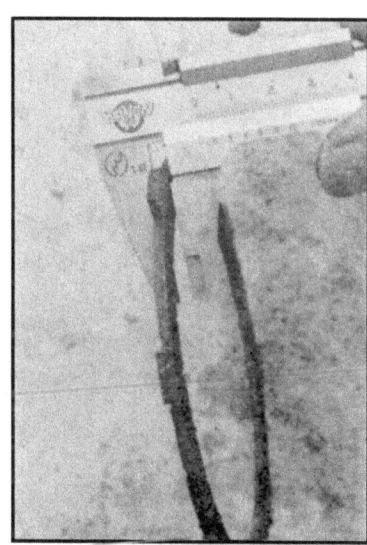

Fig. 43. Check Inner plate

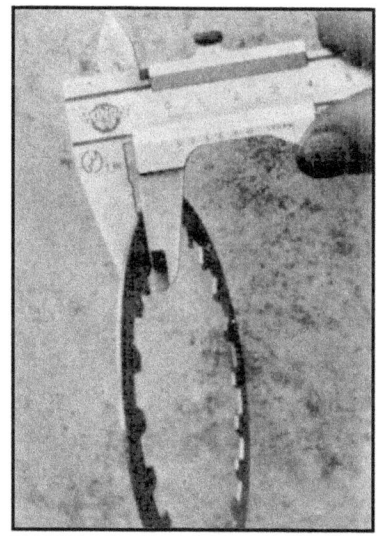

8 TRANSMISSION:

A. Construction:

The Bridgestone 175 Dual Twin has a transmission which can easily be switched from a rotary change type four speed to a return change type five speed with overdrive by simply moving a sportshift lever. The gear change system components are installed in the left crankcase cover so that maintenance, disassembling and inspection are easy.

Fig. 45. 4-Speed constant mesh-rotary   Fig. 46. 5-Speed constant mesh-return

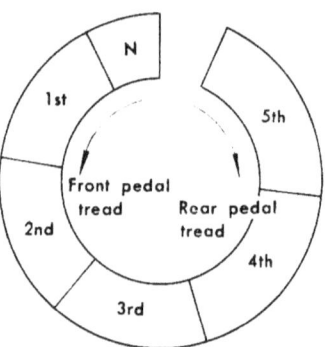

Faulty gear changing or missed gear changes can change a good handling motorcycle into a bad handling one. Also, the gear shift pedal must be located in an easily operated position so that gear changes can be made smoothly and lightly by feel. The Bridgestone 175 Dual Twin satisfies these requirements. When gears are changed into a higher gear with a rapid motion, the gear shift drum tends to turn excessively because of the heavy pressure on the gear shift pedal, causing missed gear shifting. The gear shift drum of the Bridgestone 175 Dual Twin firmly turns only a determined angle even if the gear change pedal is depressed too strongly, so that it is impossible to miss a gear.

B. Operation:

(1) Shifting Operation

When the front part or the rear part of the gear shift pedal is depressed, the shift drum is turned by the shifter fixed on the gear shift shaft. Three shifting forks are fitted to the shift drum and travel along three grooves on the drum when it turns. The gear shifting forks move the gears on the countershaft and driveshaft.

The operating angle of the gear shift pedal is 11 degrees and the gear shift drum turns 72 degrees for each gear change.

Fig. 47. Neutral Gear 4 Speed Rotary

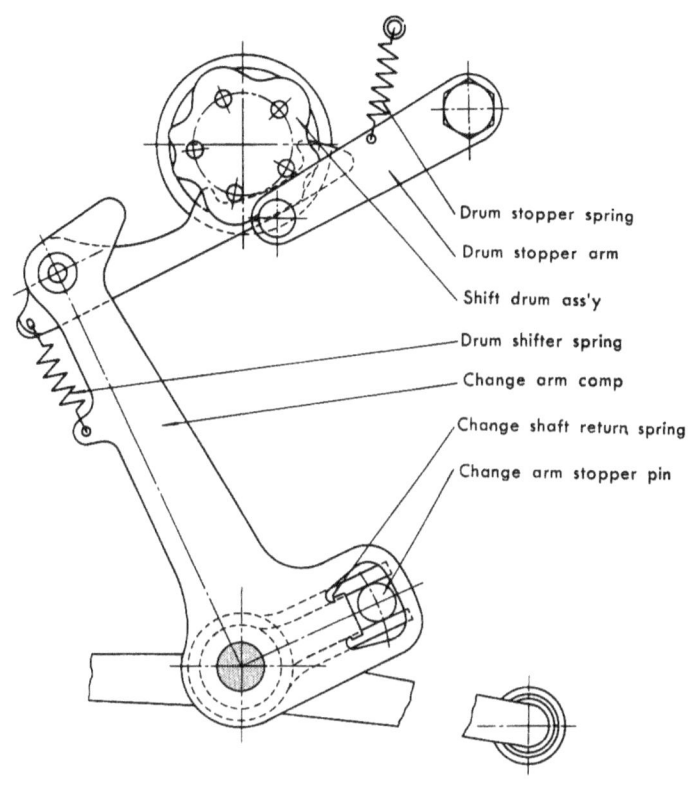

- Drum stopper spring
- Drum stopper arm
- Shift drum ass'y
- Drum shifter spring
- Change arm comp
- Change shaft return spring
- Change arm stopper pin

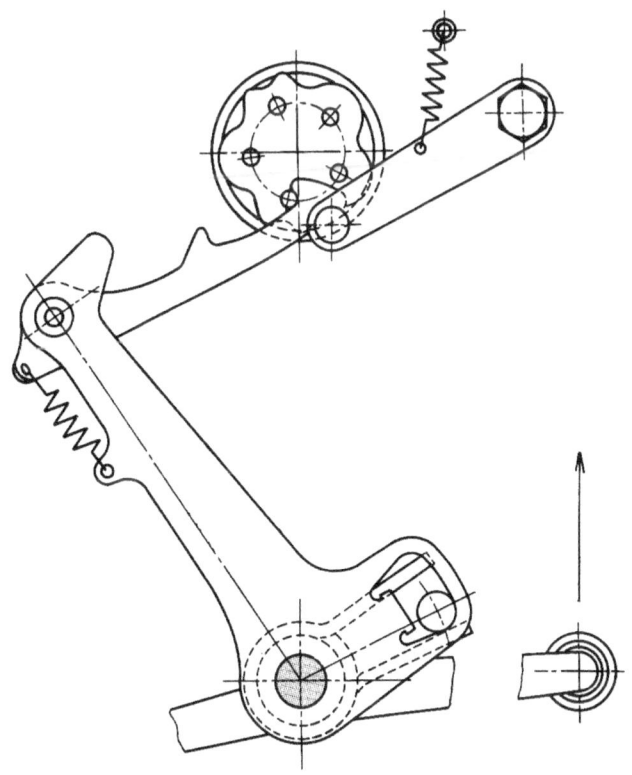

Fig. 48. Neutral Gear (5 Speed Return)

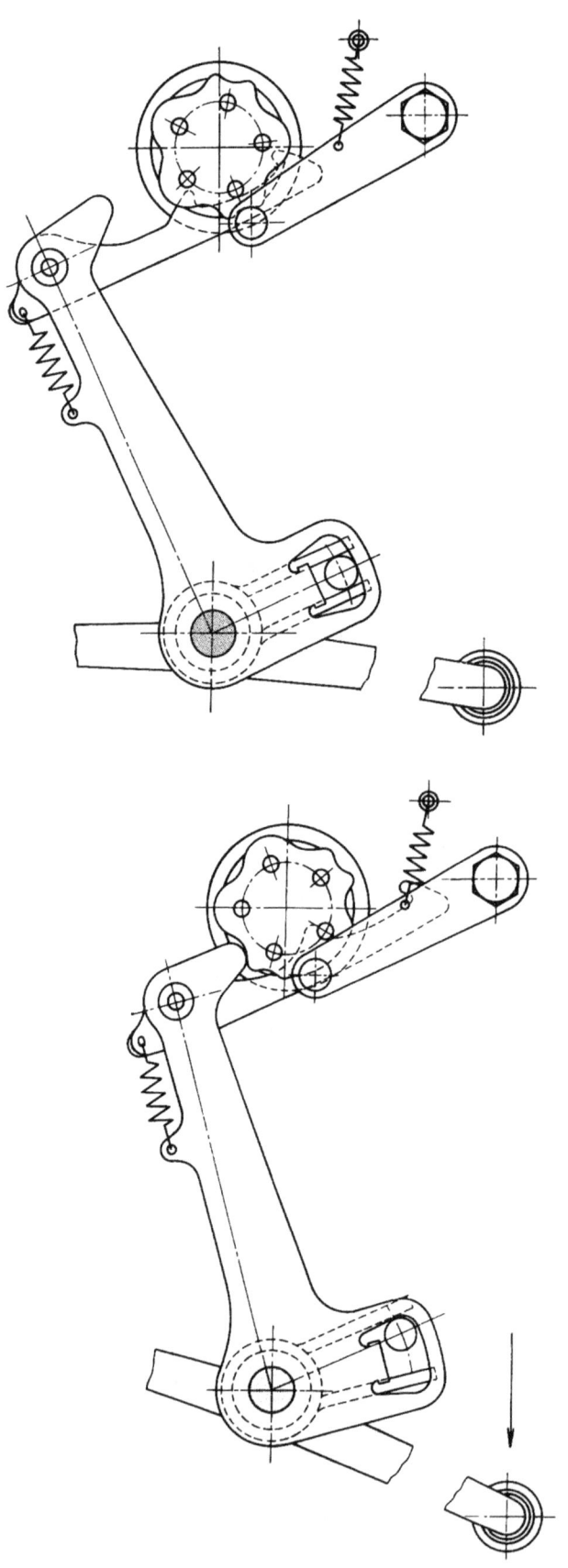

Fig. 49. "Sportshift" lever mechaninsm

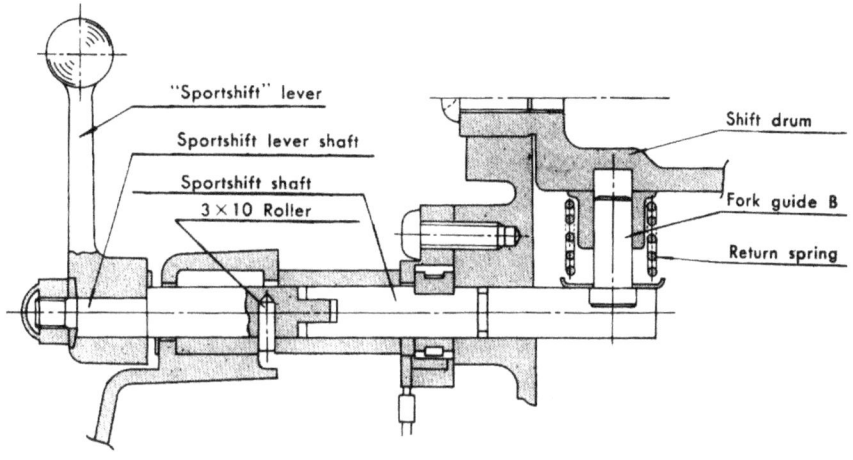

(2) Gear Operation and gear ratios.

KINDS OF GEARS	NUMBERS OF TEETH "A" GEARS TRAIN (COUNTERSHAFT)	"B" GEARS TRAIN (DRIVESHAFT)	TRANSMISSION GEAR RATIO
First gear (Low gear)	13	34	2.61
Second gear	18	30	1.67
Third gear	21	26	1.24
Fourth gear	24	24	1.00
Fifth gear	26	22	0.85

The countershaft and First Gear A act as a unit, and Second Gear A slides on the countershaft spline. The Third Gear A and Fourth Gear A turn freely on the countershaft. The second Gear A engages with the dog claws on the Third Gear A and also with the Fourth Gear A which has oval holes to engage the claws on the Second Gear.

The Fourth Gear B is spline fitted on the driveshaft. The Third Gear B slides on the driveshaft spline, the Second Gear B, First Gear B and Fifth Gear B turn freely on the driveshaft, and only Third Gear B slides both ways and engages with First Gear B or Second Gear B with claws.

Fig. 50. Transmission Mechanism in Neutral Gear Position.

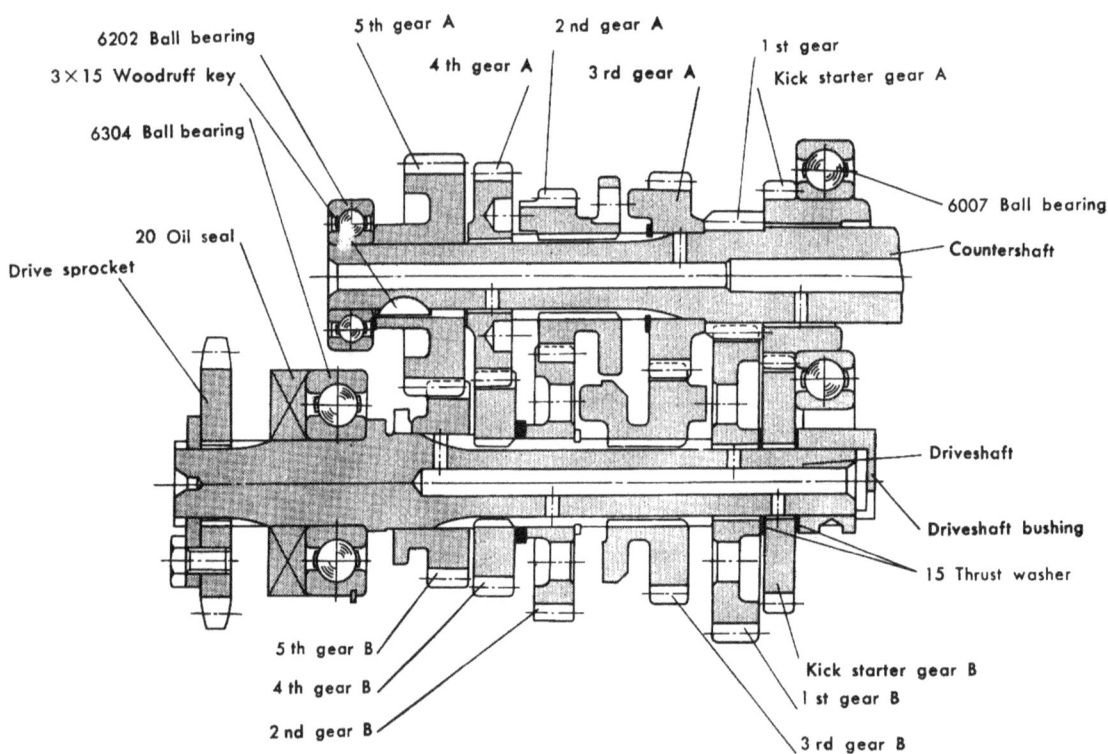

First Gear:

With the First Gear A on the countershaft remaining in position, the Third Gear B on the driveshaft slides to the right and the claws engage with the First Gear B.

Engine power is transmitted in the order of driven gear—clutch—countershaft—First Gear A—First Gear B—Third Gear B—driveshaft and drive sprocket.

Fig. 51. In First Gear Position

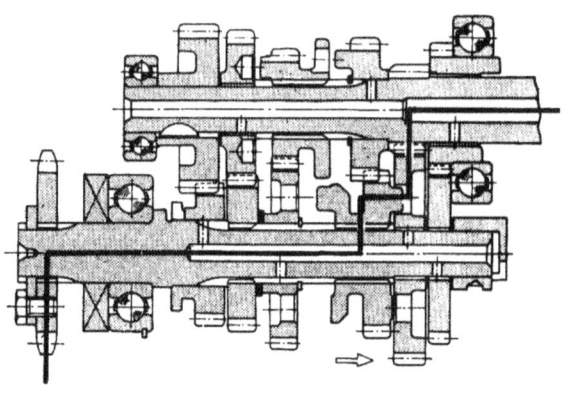

Second Gear:

The second Gear A remaining in position, the Third Gear B slides to the left and the claws on this gear engage with the Second Gear B.

The engine power is transmitted in the order of driven gear—clutch—countershaft—Second Gear A—Second Gear B—Third Gear B—driveshaft and drive sprocket.

Fig. 52. In Second Gear Position

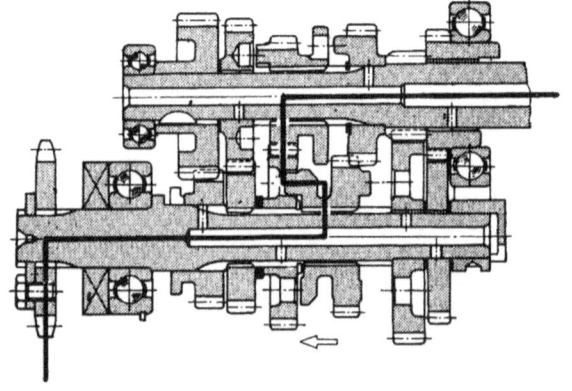

Third Gear:

With the Third Gear B on the drive shaft remaining in position, the Second Gear A slides to the right and engages with the claws on the Third Gear A.

The engine power is transmitted in the order of driven gear—clutch—countershaft—Second Gear A—Third Gear A—Third Gear B—driveshaft and drive sprocket.

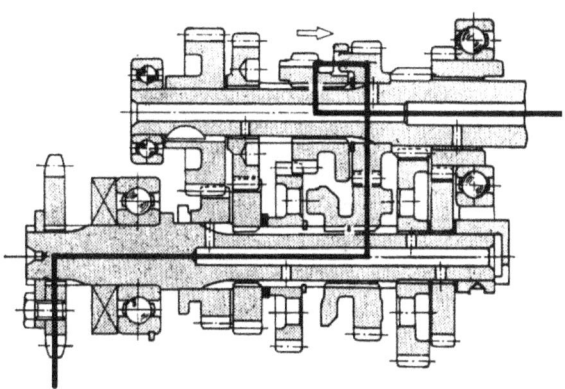

Fig. 53. In Third Gear Position

Fourth Gear:

The Third Gear B remaining in position, the Second Gear A slides to the left and the dog teeth engage with the Fourth Gear A.

The engine power is transmitted in the order of driven gear—clutch—countershaft—Second Gear A—Fourth Gear A—Fourth Gear B—driveshaft and drive sprocket.

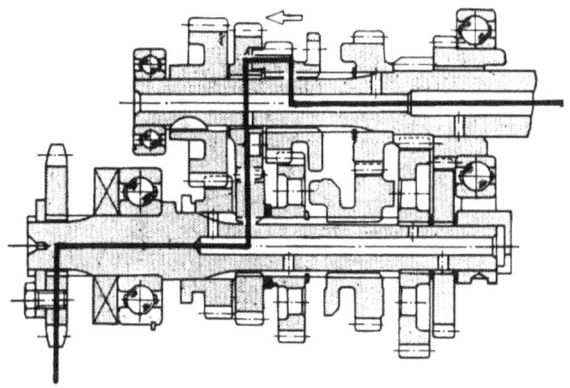

Fig. 54. In Fourth Gear Position

Fifth Gear:

The Fifth Gear B is engaged with driveshaft by shifting "Sportshift" lever.

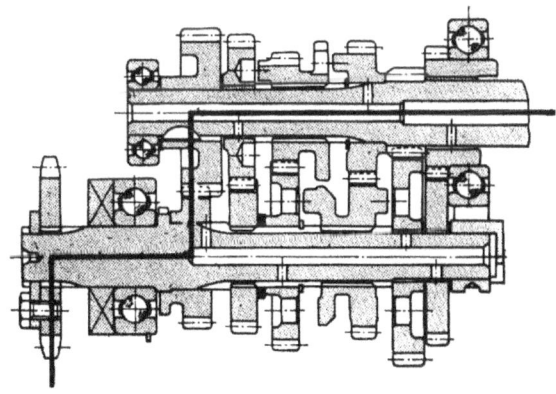

Fig. 55. In Fifth Gear Position

C. Disassembling:

Disassembling and assembling procedures are carried out in accordance with paragraph 4-2-B Pg.12.

D. Inspection:

(1) Check for worn or damaged gears, splines, bearings and shafts.
    (Refer to Service Standards Manual.)

(2) Inspect shift fork and drum grooves.
    (Refer to Service Standards Manual)

Fig. 56. Checking shift fork

Fig. 57. Checking drum shift arm

SERVICE MEMO:

9. KICK STARTER:

A. Construction:

A primary kick starter system such as is installed on other Bridgestone models is used on the Bridgestone 175 DT. As the kick starter does not operate through the clutch the engine can be started even if the transmission gears are engaged by simply pulling in the clutch lever.

This is a very convenient system which has earned a good reputation and eliminates the need for finding neutral, allowing quick starting of the engine.

In the conventional kick starter, the kick gear engages with one of the transmission gears, but in the primary type kick starter three kick starter gears are installed independently in the transmission.

Fig. 58. Kick Mechanism

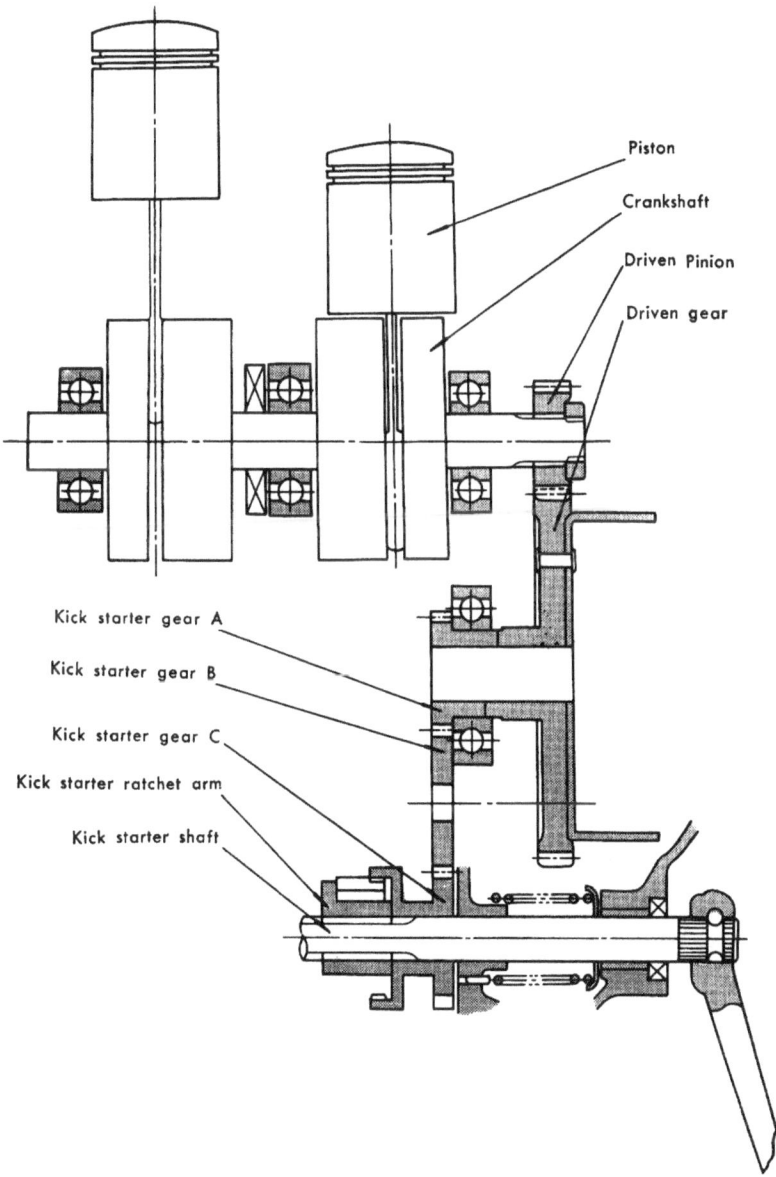

B. Operation:

B-1. In Cruising:

(1) Ratchet arm is turned counterclockwise, as shown, by the kick return spring.

(2) Ratchet is kicked up by the ratchet arm stopper counterclockwise as shown by arrow in Fig. 59, and ratchet and kick gear are held apart.

Fig. 59. In cruising position   **Fig. 60.** In kicking poition

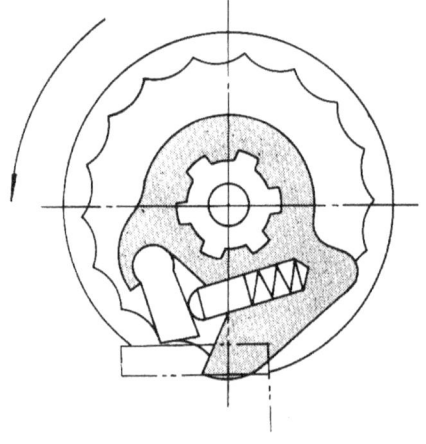

B-2. To start:

(1) Kick down kick-arm

(2) Kick shaft and rachet arm turn counter clockwise as shown by arrow in Fig. 60.

(3) Ratchet turns counterclockwise as shown by arrow in Fig. 60, resulting from the pressure of rachet spring, and meshes with the kick gear.

(4) Ratchet, which is in mesh, turns kick gear clockwise as shown by arrow in Fig. 60.

(5) Since kick gear is always in mesh with kick idle gear the force created by turning the kick pedal is transmitted from kick gear, through kick idle gear kick idle gear driven gear and pinion gear, to the crankshaft and starts the engine.

(6) When the kick pedal is released, it is returned to its original position by the return spring and the ratchet is released automatically from the kick gear, and the kick gear rotates freely.

C. Disassembling and Assembling:

Performed according to procedure described in earlier paragraph.

D. Inspection:

Check for worn or damaged gears and kick return spring.

10. CARBURETORS:

A. Construction and Operation:

Two 17 mm carburetors supply a mixture of fuel and air to the engine. Either a too rich or too lean mixture lowers engine performance, so it is necessary that the proper mixture be supplied to the engine at all times.

Different parts of the carburetors control the fuel/air mixture for low speeds, medium speeds and high speeds. Instructions for each follow:

Fig. 61. Carburetor

(1) Slow Channel (mainly for idling)

The suction stroke of the piston induces air at the pilot outlet of the carburetor so that gasoline is metered through the pilot jet and air is drawn through the pilot air hole and metered by the air adjusting screw. The gasoline and air make a rich fuel mixture which jets from the pilot outlet into the main bore where it mixes with a small amount of air and is supplied to the engine, along with a correct amount of oil injected into the intake between the carburetor and the engine.

(2) Main Channel (mainly for medium and high speeds)

Air entering the carburetor from the air cleaner passes under the throttle valve and is inhaled into the engine as the main air flow. Induction is created at the needle jet by this main air flow and gasoline in the float chamber is metered by the main jet and enters the needle jet. This gasoline passes through the gap between the needle jet and jet needle and flows into the main bore of the carburetor. The gap between the needle jet and jet needle is controlled by the throttle grip, so that when it is opened the gap increases and the flow of gasoline increases and when it is closed the gap decreases and the flow of gasoline also decreases.

Air which enters through the air jet mixes with the gasoline from the main jet in the needle jet and it is atomized when mixed with the main air flow and flows into the engine.

(3) Starter System

When the carburetor starter lever on the handlebar is pushed the starter plunger is raised by the starter wire.

When the kick starter lever is depressed with the throttle valve closed, air induction is generated behind the throttle valve by the engine suction. This condition is similar to that created when the choke of a conventional carburetor is fully closed. As the throttle valve is closed, air is inhaled only through the starter air channel. Strong

Fig. 62. Carburetor.

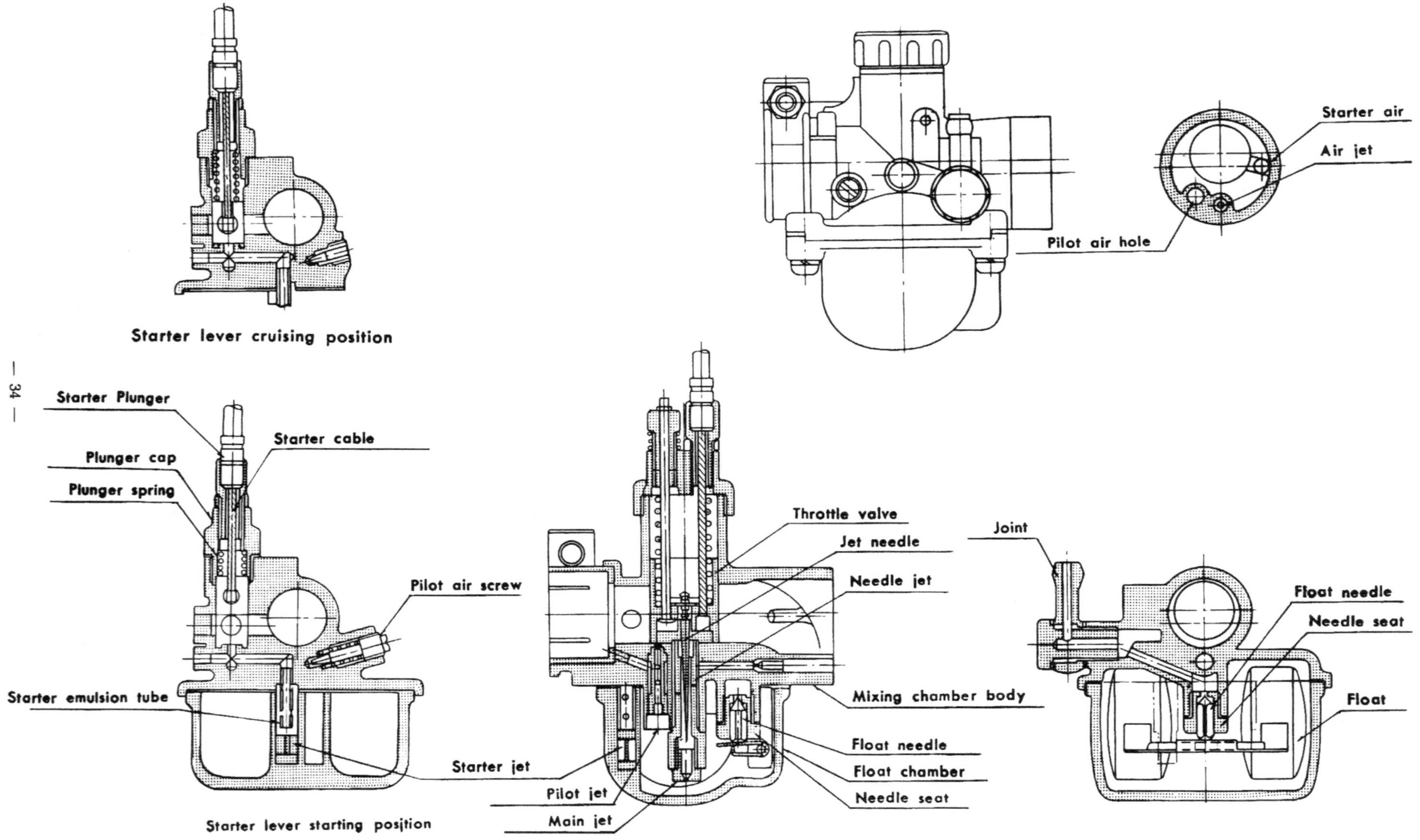

air induction is generated at the fuel jet located at the narrow starter plunger. Fuel in the float chamber is metered by the starter jet and moves up the emulsion tube.

Air is inhaled from the wall of the tube and a rich mixture of air and gasoline is made. When secondary air is added to this mixture a correct rich mixture for starting a cold engine is inhaled into the engine through the nozzle located behind the main bore.

(4) Float Chamber

The carburetor makes a proper gasoline/air mixture according to the throttle opening and engine speed. To create this proper gasoline/air mixture, the supply of gasoline must remain constant. The float chamber supplies a constant flow of gasoline to the carburetor.

Gasoline flows from the tank through the pipe to the carburetor banjo bolt and be tween the valve seat and valve to enter the float chamber. When gasoline enters the float chamber, the float moves up to stay on top of the gasoline and pushes the valve closed with the valve arm. When the valve touches the valve seat the flow of gasoline stops. When gasoline in the float chamber is consumed and the level lowers, the float moves down and the float arm no longer presses against the valve, allowing it to move away from the valve seat and gasoline to enter the float chamber between the valve and valve seat. These procedures are repeated and a constant level of gasoline is kept in the float chamber.

B. Functions of Various Parts:

(1) Main Jet (M.J. 90)

The main jet controls the fuel supply when the throttle is more than three-quarters open, but at smaller throttle openings although the fuel passes through the main jet the amount is diminished by the tapered needle jet.

Fig. 64. Air Jet.

Standard number of the main jet of this machine is No. 90. (Fig. 63)

Fig. 63. Main Jet.

(2) Air Jet (A.J. 0.5)

The air jet controls the flow of air entering the needle jet. The fuel passing through the needle jet mixes with the air coming in from the air jet. (Fig. 64)

(3) Needle jet (N. J. 0-0)

At full throttle or at medium speeds, the fuel is first regulated by the main jet and the needle jet acting simultaneously (Fig. 65)

Fig. 65. Needle Jet

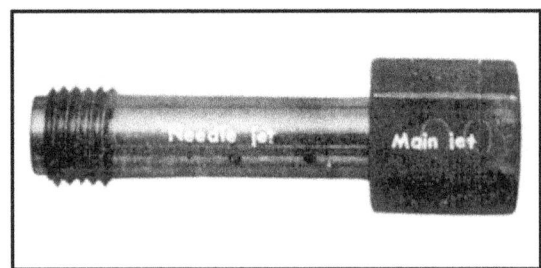

(4) Jet Needle (J.N.)

The tapered jet needle attached to the throttle valve works in the needle jet and adjusts the air-fuel ratio at medium (1/4 to 3/4) throttle openings. (Fig. 66)

(5) Throttle Valve (C.A. 2.0)

The throttle valve is cut away on the inlet side and controls the flow of main fuel supply from 1/8 to 1/4 throttle opening.

The extent of cut away is marked on the valve, viz. 2.0 for 2.0 m/m cut away. (Fig. 67)

Fig. 67. Throttle Valve

Fig. 66. Jet Needle

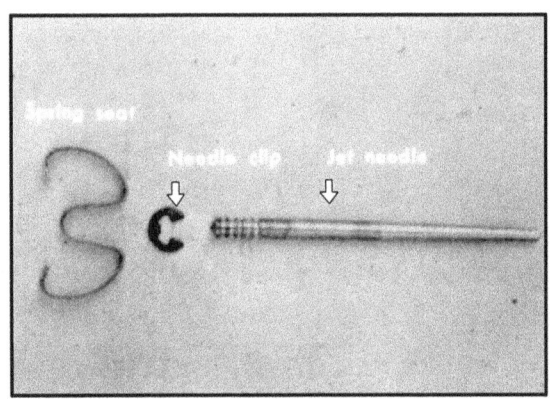

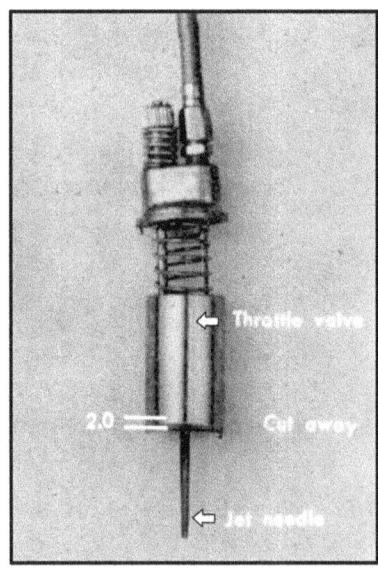

(6) Pilot Jet (P.J. 20)

At idling speed or small throttle openings, the pilot jet controls the flow of fuel mixed with air which enters through the air jet, and atomizes the mixture. (Fig. 68)

(7) Air Screw (A.S.)

Fig. 69. Air Screw

The air screw controls the flow of air which mixes with the fuel passing through the pilot jet. (Fig. 69)

Fig. 68. Pilot Jet

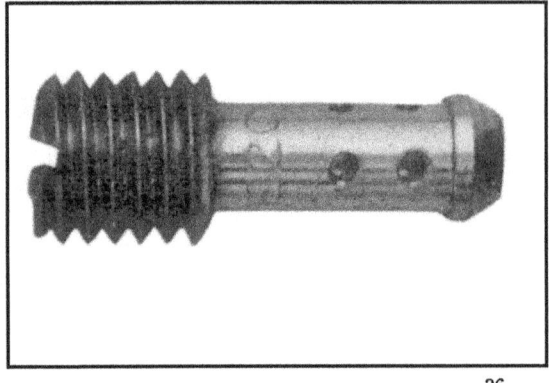

The standard adjustment of screw position is 1-1/2 turn back.

C. Adjustment:

Engine performance is mainly dependent on the proper functioning of the carburetors, i. e. the ability to adjust to the supply of the most suitable air-fuel mixture at any speed, from idling to the maximum engine speed. Through experiments and tests have been conducted by the carburetor maker and Bridgestone technicians to produce the efficient carburetors fitted to the Bridgestone 175 DT. As all the component parts have been correctly set by experts at the factory, it would be unwise to make casual adjustments.

In the event, however, of adustment being inevitable, a careful check of the engine and component parts should be first made as indicated.

(1) Look for possible air leakage from carburetor adaptor connections.

(2) Replace all worn parts.

(3) Warm up the engine for 2 to 3 minutes before adjusting.

a. Synchronizing Carburetors.

1) Turn the cable adjuster and slow adjuster in to lower the throttle valve.

2) Insert the throttle valve adjuster (special tool) between the mixing chamber top and the throttle valve. (Fig. 70)

Fig. 70.

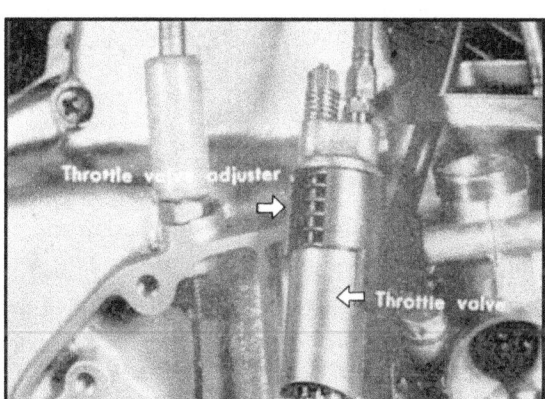

3) Turn the throttle cable adjuster out and raise the throttle valve until it touches the throttle valve adjuster.

4) Tighten the cable adjuster lock nut and remove the throttle valve adjuster.

5) Adjust the throttle valve in both right and left carburetors in the same manner.

Fig. 71.   Fig. 72.

 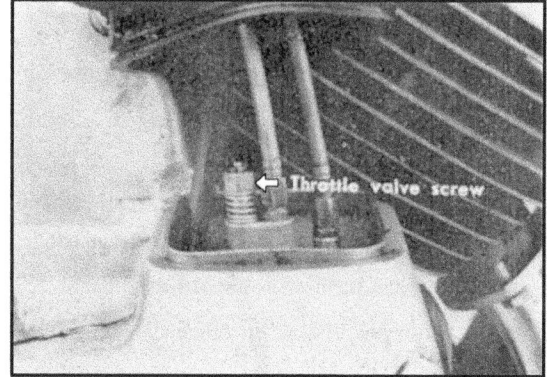

b. Idling Adjustment.

1) If the engine stops when idling, start the engine and turn the slow adjuster on both carburetors out until the engine runs smoothly while controling engine speed with the throttle grip.

2) Turn the pilot air screws on the carburetors alternately. Both screws must be turned an equal amount. Set the screws at the point where the engine runs the most smoothly. When the pilot air screw is turned clockwise, the gasoline/air mixture becomes richer and when it is turned counterclockwise the mixture becomes leaner.

3) When turning the pilot air screw, consider not only smooth operation at idling but also as a slightly higher engine speed with the throttle opened just a little.

4) If engine speed cannot be adjusted with the pilot air screw at over 1/8 throttle opening, engine speed can be adjusted with the throttle valve cutaway.

When the gasoline/air mixture is too rich, use a throttle valve with a higher number and when the mixture is too lean use a smaller numbered throttle valve.

Conditions to be checked before inspection.

Too Lean Mixture	Too Rich Mixture
1. Engine runs smoothly when carburetor is choked.	1. Engine runs smoothly when carburetor cover is removed.
2. Exhaust fumes are light blue or colorless.	2. Exhaust fumes are white or grey.
3. Engine turns smoothly when starter is used.	3. Sparks plugs are wet or dirty.

c. Medium Engine Speeds Adjustment.

The gasoline/air mixture can be adjusted by raising or lowering the jet needle at 1/8~3/4 throttle openings for medium engine speeds. Standard setting is in the third groove from the top. The throttle valve cutaway also affects engine operation at below 1/8 throttle opening, so do not change throttle valve cutaway for only medium speeds adjustment.

It is recommended to raise or lower the jet needle for medium engine speeds adjustment within the range where acceleration is not adversely affected.

Conditions to be checked before inspection.

Too Lean Mixture	Too Rich Mixture
1. Engine overheats.	1. Engine does not run smoothly.
2. Engine speed fluctuates at constant throttle opening.	2. Exhaust fumes are white or grey.
3. Acceleration of motorcycle is bad.	3. Acceleration of motorcycle is bad.
4. Exhaust fumes are light blue or colorless.	
5. Engine runs smoothly when carburetor starter is used.	

d. High Engine Speeds Adjustment.

The gasoline/air mixture can be adjusted by the main jet at 3/4~full throttle openings. Check conditions before inspection in the same manner as medium engine speeds adjustment.

SERVICE MEMO:

11. OIL INJECTION SYSTEM:

A. Construction:

In the conventional two-stroke engine, a fuel mixture of gasoline and lubricating oil is used so that parts inside the engine are lubricated by oil contained in the fuel mixture. In the Bridgestone Oil Injection System, a pre-mixed fuel is not necessary and gasoline and oil are supplied separately to the engine. Gasoline is supplied through a carburetor as in the conventional system.

Lubrication oil is supplied by an oil pump installed in the left crankcase cover. Oil pump gear A, fitted on the left crankshaft, turns oil pump gear B. The pump drive shaft is fitted to pump gear B and teeth in the shaft engage with teeth on the plunger so that the plunger turns in accordance with crankshaft revolutions. (Fig. 73. Fig. 74)

Fig. 73.

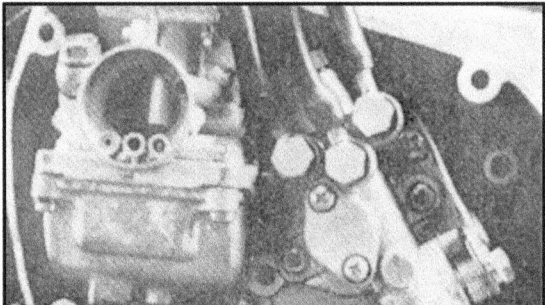

B. Operation:

The plunger turns in accordance with crankshaft speed. One end of the plunger is held by a spring and the other end is tapered. The plunger is held by a plunger guide and moves up and down inside the pump body.

Oil Intake:

The plunger moves in the direction indicated by the arrow in the illustration and rotates. An induction is generated at the sides and top of the differential plunger, the oil intake port opens and oil is sucked into the oil pump.

Fig. 74.

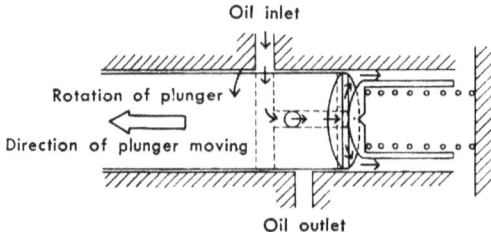

Oil Discharge:

When the plunger moves in the direction indicated by the arrow in the illustration while

Fig. 75. Oil Injection System

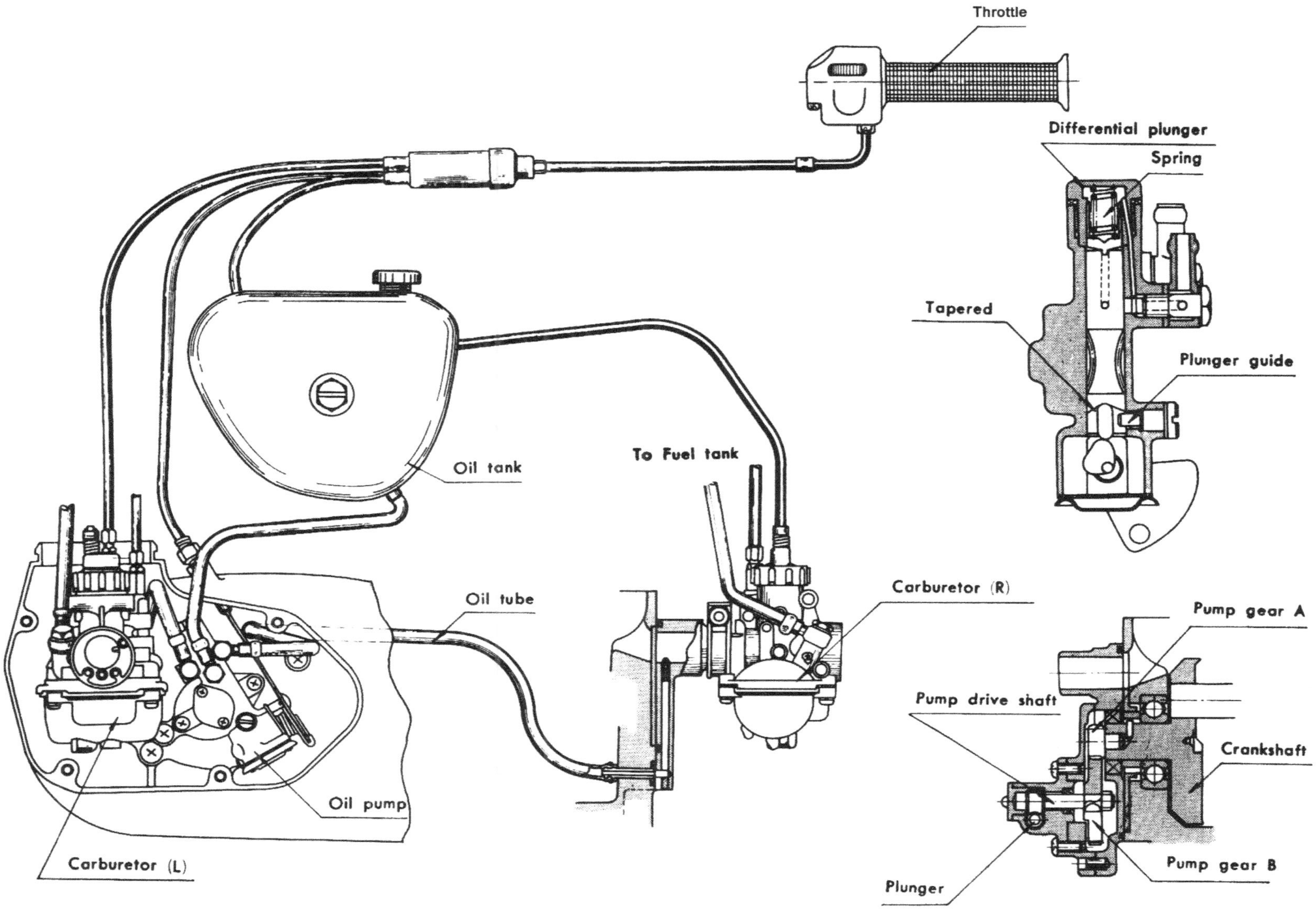

rotating, the intake valve is closed and compression is generated at the sides and top of the differential plunger, the oil discharge port opens and oil is discharged.

Fig. 76.   **Fig. 77.**

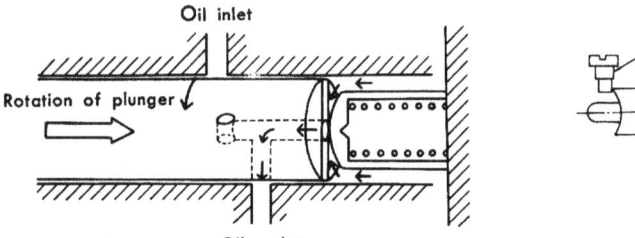
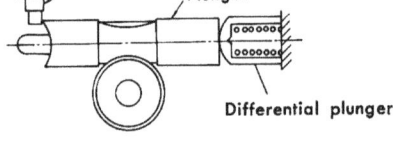

C. Adjusting Oil Volume:

(1) Oil intake and discharge volume can be increased or decreased by changing the size of the differential plunger. A differential plunger with a smaller outside diameter increases oil volume and one with a larger outside diameter decreases oil volume.

(2) Oil volume is also changed according to the turning of the throttle grip. Turning the throttle grip moves a cam at the bottom of the plunger, so that the more the throttle is opened the longer the plunger stroke becomes and the larger the volume of oil supplied to the engine.

D. Disassembling and Installing:

Remove the left crankcase cover to take out the oil pump. Oil pump gear A is pressed onto the left crankshaft and it cannot be removed. The oil pump wire play can be adjusted outside the case without removing the left crankcase cover.

E. Inspection:

(1) Check oil pump gear A and gear B teeth for wear. If worn, act in accordance with Service Standards Manual.

(2) If the oil pipe is damaged or clogged, repair or replace with a new one.

12. CHASSIS SECTION:

12.1 Frame:

A. Construction:

The single cradle type tubular frame of the Bridgestone 175 DT motorcycle is light in weight, flexible, not brittle and has excellent handling performance.

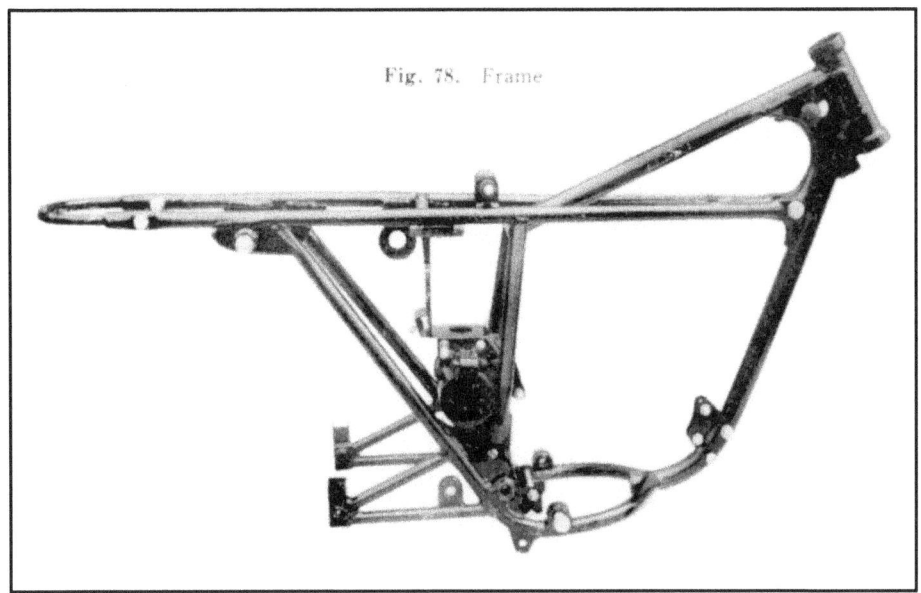

Fig. 78. Frame

Many parts and components are mounted on the frame and if its rigidity is not sufficient, handling and stability when turning corners becomes bad and dangerous. Sufficient tests and research have been conducted so that the frame of the Bridgestone 175 DT motorcycle is very reliable.

B. Inspection:

(1) Inspect welded parts for cracks. If cracked, repair or replace the frame with a new one.
(2) If the frame becomes out of center as the result of a collision, replace the frame with a new one. If the frame is out of center, handling and stability become extremely bad.
(3) If engine mounting brackets are damaged or the welding is cracked, repair or replace the frame with a new one.
(4) If any section of the frame is damaged, replace the complete frame with a new one.

C. Disassembling:

Disassemble the frame by removing engine as explained in section 3, handlebar, front fork, front wheel, rear wheel, rear swinging arm, seat, fuel tank, muffler and exhaust pipe, stands, rear fender, air clerner, etc.

D. Assembling:

Assemble in the reverse order from disassembling.

12. 2 Front Fork:

A. Construction:

Shocks received by the front wheel while running are absorbed by the front fork and those received by the rear wheel by the rear shock absorbers so that riding is comfortable.

In addition to this damping operation, the front fork must hold the front wheel and steer the motorcycle, keeping its rigidity and strength during operation.

Fig. 79. Front Fork

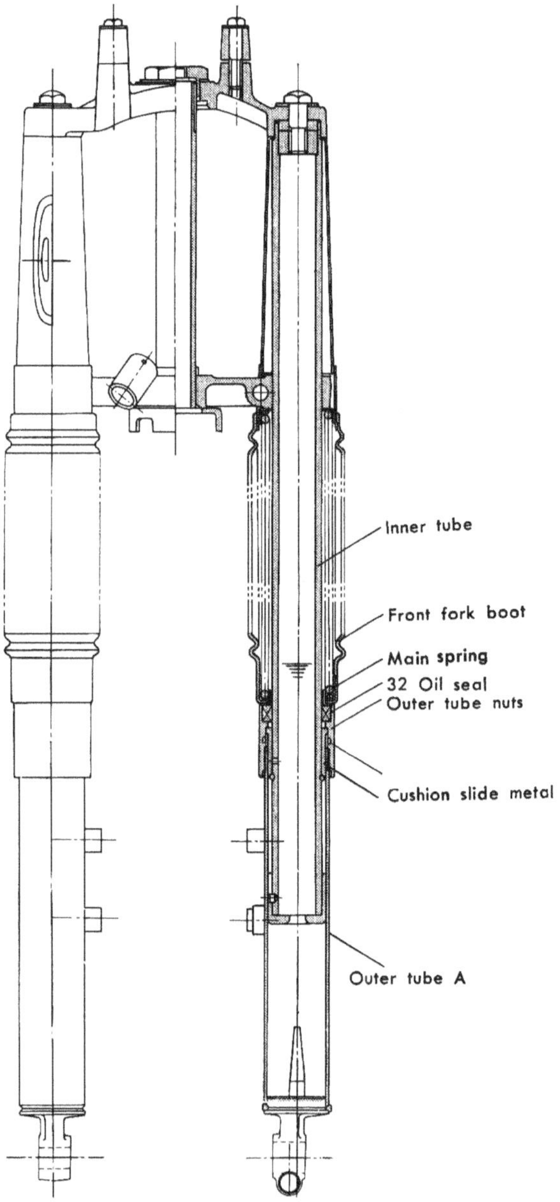

- Inner tube
- Front fork boot
- Main spring
- 32 Oil seal
- Outer tube nuts
- Cushion slide metal
- Outer tube A

Fig. 80. Compressed position

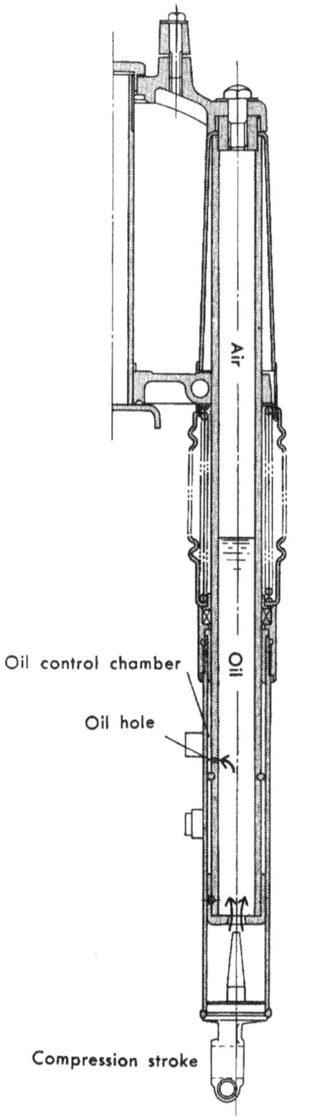

- Air
- Oil
- Oil control chamber
- Oil hole
- Compression stroke

B. Operation:

When a load is applied to the front fork, the load is received by the fork springs. At the same time, oil in the oil chamber flows into the oil control chamber and the load is held by resistance of the compressed oil and air and the shock is absorbed.

Oil lock bars are installed inside the bottom of the lower fork legs to prevent the fork from bottoming when receiving severe shocks. When oil moves through the gap between the piston oil hole and the oil lock bar, shock is absorbed by the resistance of the oil. The oil lock bar is tapered so that oil resistance increases as the front fork shortens.

When the fork lengthens, rebound is damped by oil resistance generated by the oil flow from the oil control chamber through the oil hole to the oil chamber and by the oil flow through the gap between the oil lock bar and the piston oil hole.

C. Disassembling:

(1) Stand up the mainstand of the machine and place a supporting block under the engine before disassembling front fork and front wheel.

(2) Front wheel should be disassembled according the procedure described on page 51.

(3) Handlebar should be disassembled according the procedure described in "Removing Handlebar" (page 46).

(4) Take off front fender by loosening four hexagonal bolts (8×12) and then turning fender outer tube. (Fig. 81)

(5) Front fork is removed separately by removing upper bracket bolts and lower bracket bolts.

Fig. 81. Front fender

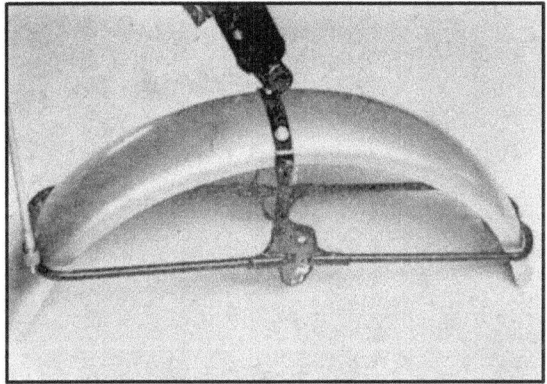

Fig. 82. Loosening lower bracket bolts

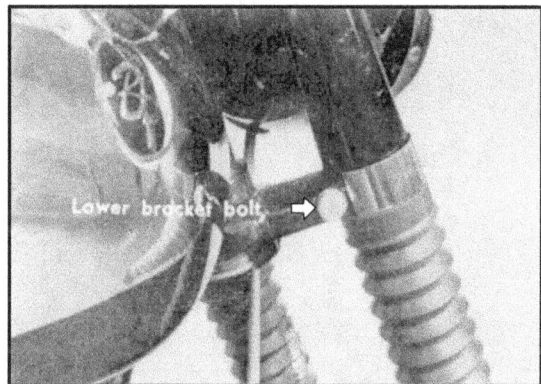

D. Inspection:

(1) Repair or replace outer tube which is bent. (Refer to Service Standards Manual.)

(2) Replace upper bracket and lower bracket which are bent or have flaws.

(3) Adjust or replace parts which are the source of oil leakage or any springs which have lost tension.

(Free length of spring 184 mm.)

Fig. 83. Checking oil level with oil level guage

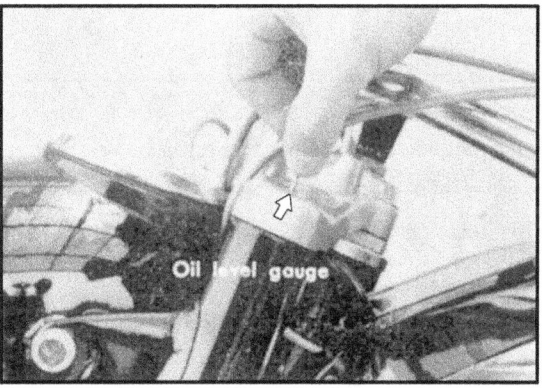

(4) Fill in the ratio of 7 and 3 with 220 c.c. fork oil in each fork tube. Mixture of S.A.E. No. 60 spindle oil (70%) and No. 30 engine oil (30%).

The fork oil can be drained from the draining hole at the bottom of fork tubes by removing screws.

12. 3 Handlebar:

A. Construction:

The handlebar should be designed for easy handling of the motorcycle, safe riding and to prevent riding fatigue. Accordingly, the length of the handlebar, height of the handlebar, diameter of the pipe, shape of the grips, etc., have an affect on handling and stability.

Fig. 84.

After long tests and research, the length of the handlebar of the Bridgestone 175 Dual Twin was determined at 1.5 times the width of the shoulders of an average man. The height of the handlebar is proper for touring for long periods of time and the handlebar grips are also comfortable, enabling riders of the Bridgestone 175 Dual Twin to enjoy comfortable touring without fatigue.

B. Removing:

(1) Tools neccessary. (Fig. 85)

(2) Loosen clutch cable to the limit of adjusting nut and remove from clutch lever.

(3) Remove adjusting nut of front brake wire and pull out of brake lever. (Fig. 86)

Fig. 85. Tools necessary   **Fig. 86.** Remove brake wire

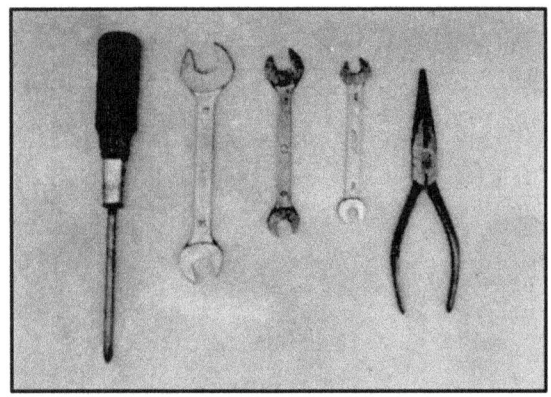
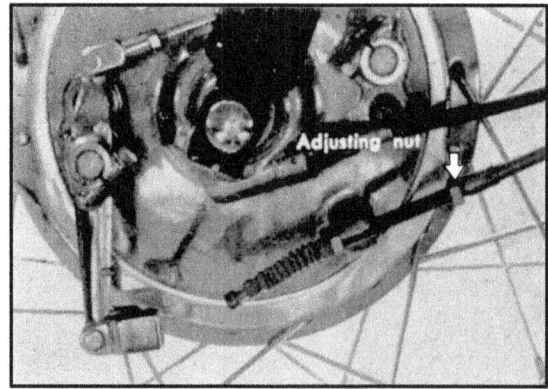

(4) Remove mixing chamber tops from carburetor bodies and remove throttle cable while pressing down throttle valve springs.

(5) Take off (5×10) hexagonal nuts of starter lever bodies and remove starter cable from lever.

(6) Unscrew head light screw (5×10) at left bottom of head light cover and light rim, and disconnect wiring harness connections from terminals. (Fig. 87 Fig. 88)

(7) Take off steering head bolts, handlebar holder and remove handlebar assembly from front fork.

Fig. 87. Unscrewing head light screw

Fig. 88. Disconnecting wires

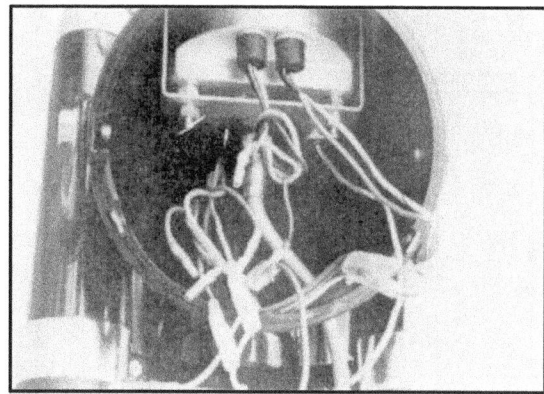

C. Assembling:

(1) Assembling is done in the reverse order of removing.

(2) Connect all wires.

(3) Connect clutch cable and front brake cable and adjusts levers.

Fig. 89. Adjustment of clutch and front brake levers

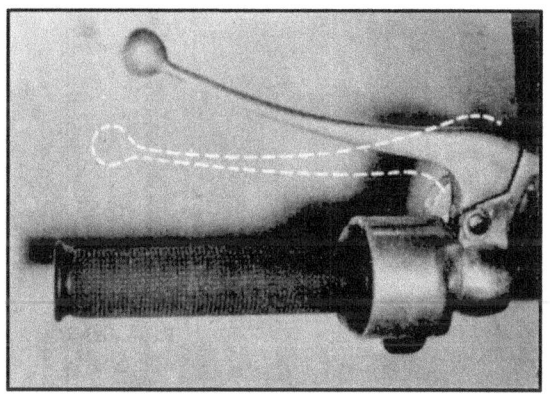
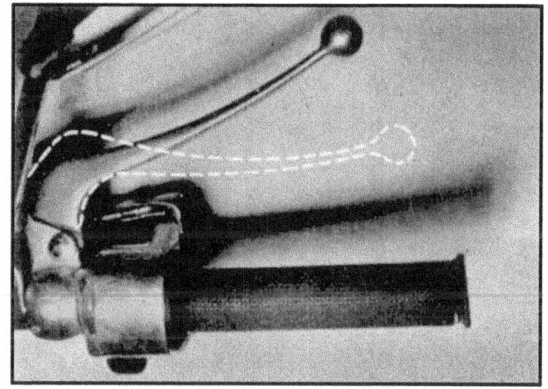

D. Inspection:

(1) Replace handlebar which is bent or cracked.

(2) Check for damaged or cracked wire and replace if necessary.

(3) Replace levers which are cracked or bent.

(4) Replace handlebar holder which is cracked.

12.4 Rear Suspension:

A. Construction:

The rear suspension system absorbs shocks in a similar manner to the front fork during running.

The rear suspension units are installed between the frame and the rear fork. The rear fork moves up and down, pivoting on a shaft which fits it to the frame.

Fig. 90. Rear suspension

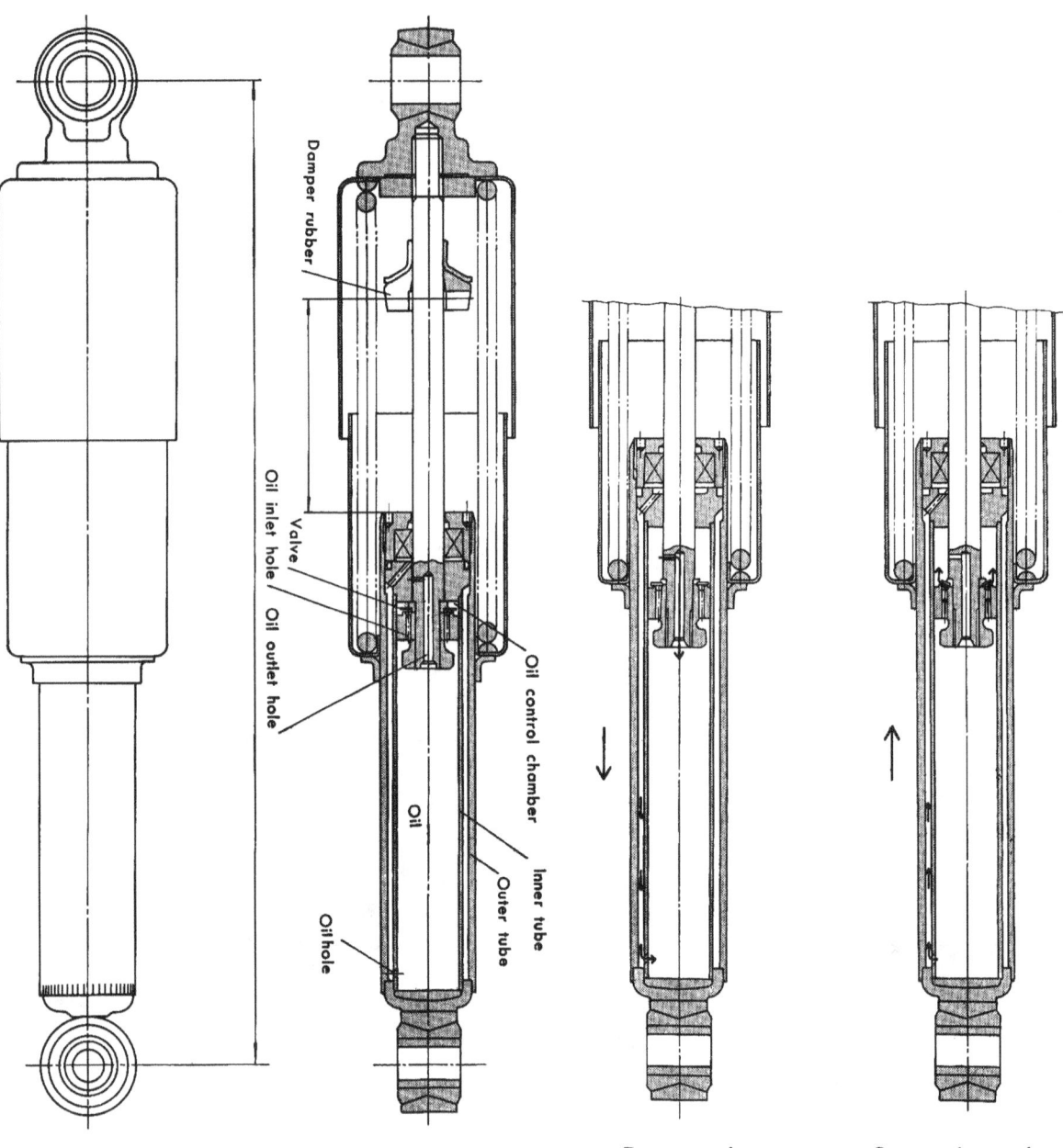

Return stroke   Compression stroke

B. Operation:

(1) When **shortening** from shock or load:

When the unit receives shock or load, the spring is compressd and the damping oil chamber becomes smaller. Damping oil enters the oil passage, pushes open the valve and flows into the oil control chamber. Oil flows through the oil hole on the inner tube into the gap between the inner tube and the outer tube. Shocks are absorbed by this oil flow and the spring action.

(2) When **lengthening**:

When the unit lengthens, the valve on the oil control chamber closes and the damping oil flows out of the oil passage. The oil meets a large resistance when it begins to flow and oil in the gap between the inner tube and the outer tube flows back into the damping oil chamber. Rebound is damped by this oil flow resistance.

C. **Disassembling:**

Rear suspension should be removed by taking off 10×32 hexagonal bolt and cap nut.

D. **Inspection:**

Check to see if rear suspension is damaged or leaking and replace if necessary.

Fig. 91. Rear frame

12.5 Rear Frame:

A. **Construction:**

The rear frame is built of tube and connected to the main frame by the rear frame shaft (bolt), and pivots on this shaft.

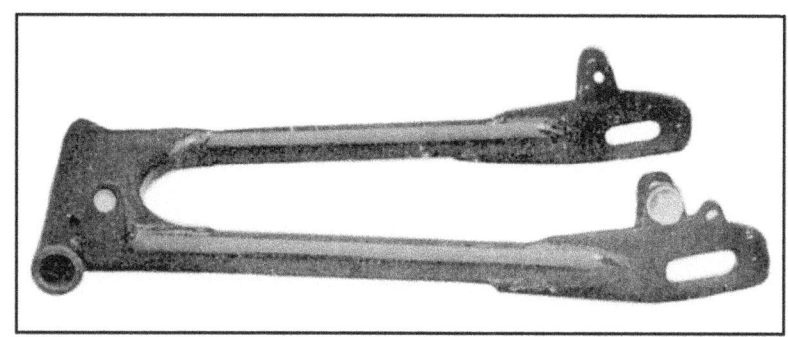

B. **Disassembling:**

(1) Tools necessary. (Fig. 92)

Fig. 92. Tools necessary

(2) Remove chain case and drive chain.

(3) Remove rear torque bar and remove rear wheel by pulling out the rear axle.

(4) Remove rear suspension by loosening four bolts.

(5) The rear frame can be detached by removing the pivot shaft nut.

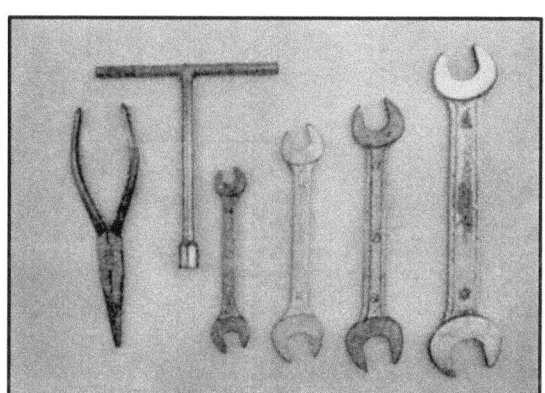

C. **Inspection:**

(1) Check for bends or damage of frame and rear frame shaft (bolt).

(2) Check to see if torsion rubber is damaged and replace if necessary.

D. **Assembling:**

(1) Assembling is carried out in the reverse order of disassembling.

Fig. 93.

Fig. 94.

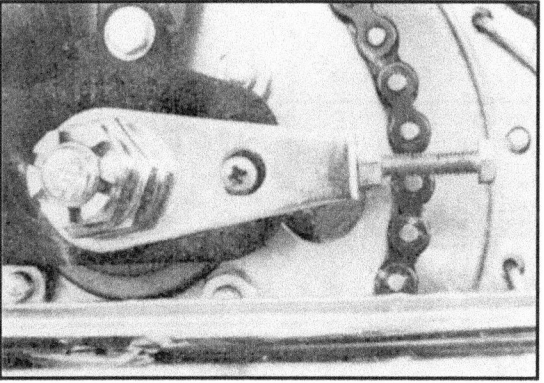
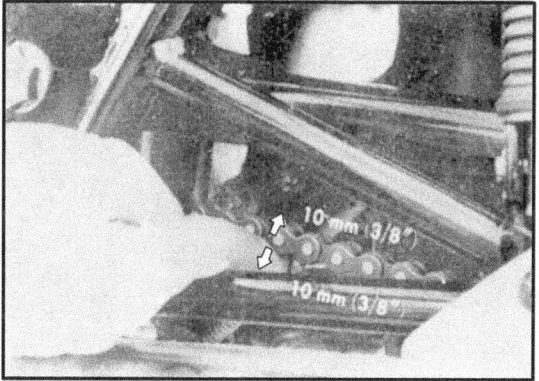

(2) Adjust chain play after assembling chain. (Fig. 93, 94)

(3) Adjust the position of rear wheel with the notch of rear frame.

12. 6 Front and Rear Wheels:

A. Description:

Tires are 2.50-18 for front, 2.75-18, 4 PR for rear, and spokes No. 10 for front and tapered type No. 9 and No. 10 for the rear.

Brake hubs are of aluminum alloy and diameter is 180 mm ϕ.

Fig. 95. Construction

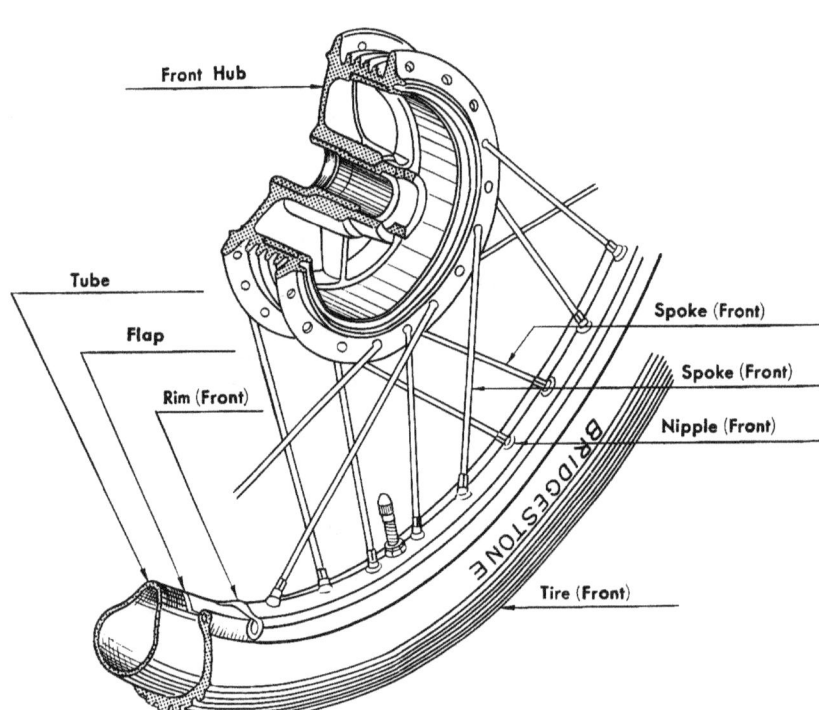

CORRECT AIR PRESSURES

No. of Passengers	FRONT	REAR
1 passenger	1.6 kg/cm² (22 lb/in²)	2.0 kg/cm² (28 lb/in²)
2 passenger	1.6 kg/cm (22 lb/in²)	2.1 kg/cm (30 lb/in²)

1. FRONT WHEEL:

The front wheel brake is installed on the right side of the machine. The speedometer unit is installed in the hub to keep out water and dust.

2. REAR WHEEL:

The rear wheel has the rear sprocket and drive flange on the left side of the machine and the brake on the right side. To absorb shocks while running, rubber dampers are installed between rear drum and drive flange.

B. Removing Front Wheel:

Place a supporting block under the engine, loosen axle bracket bolt, remove front torque bar from the hub side, remove front shaft nut, pull out front shaft, raise front fork slightly, and detach wheel.

Fig. 96.   Fig. 97. Removed hub cover

C. Removing Rear Wheel:

Lift the machine on its main stand, remove brake rod adjusting nut, remove torque bar from the side of the hub, remove rear shaft nut on left side (**the big nut need not be touched**), pull out rear shaft together with chain adjuster, and by removing rear hub collar the wheel will come off the drive flange on the right side.

Take out the wheel by leaning the machine to the left.

Fig. 98. Removing rear wheel   Fig. 99. Removing rear wheel

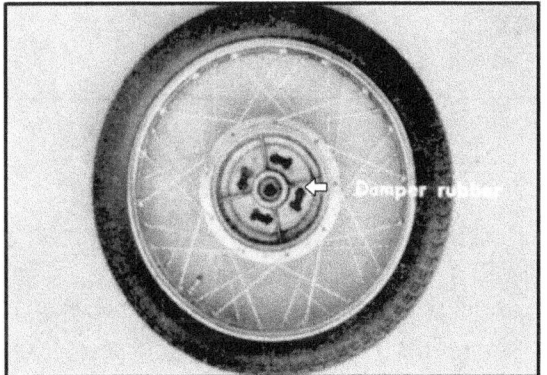 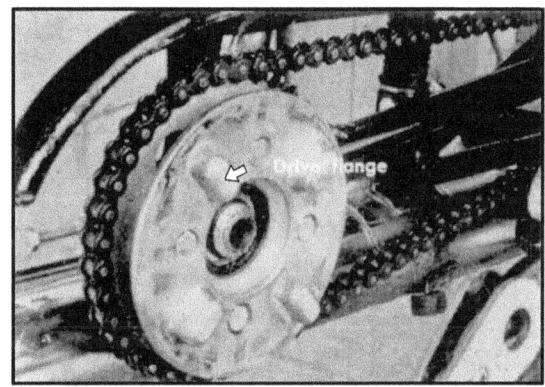

D. Inspection:

(1) Bent or deformed rim.

(2) Check to see if any spokes are loose and tighten if necessary.

(3) Check to see if tires have any bad cuts or nails embedded and if necessary make repairs or replacements.

(4) Wash ball bearing of the hubs well with gasoline and check for looseness and snatching action while idling. Make replacements if necessary.

(5) Replace bent or damaged front and rear shafts.

(6) The speedometer gear should rotate smoothly. Apply grease if necessary. Also check speedometer pinion.

(7) Check oil seal for damage, deforming or wear. Replace if necessary.

E. Assembling:

Assembling is performed in the reverse order of disassembling.

Assemble after applying sufficient grease to ball bearings.

F. Removing Tire:

(1) When removing tire to repair punctures, blowouts, etc., take off valve cap and with its top loosen valve care in the stem, to let air out.

After deflating, lay wheel on the ground as shown in Fig. 100 and press tire down with the feet. Detach bead of tire from rim, insert tire lever between rim and tire bead, and remove from rim with the tire lever.

It would be more convenient to use two levers for this purpose. When one side of the bead is completely out of the rim, push in stem of tube valve and pull out tube.

Fig. 100. Press tire down with the feet   Fig. 101. Insert tire lever

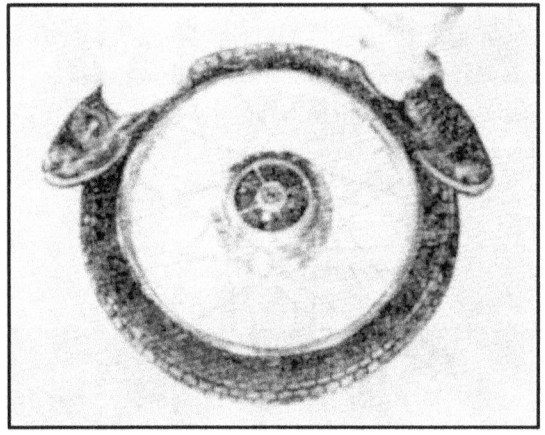 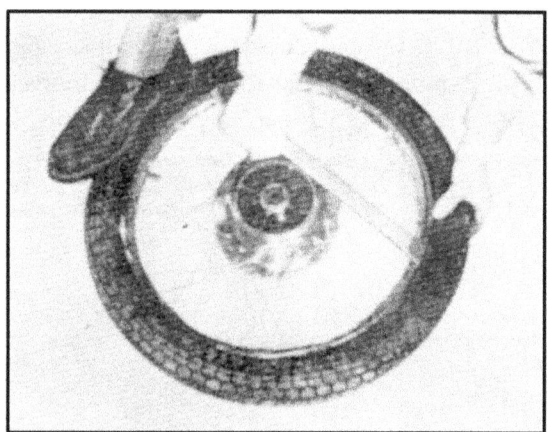

After repairing tube, replace it in the tire, being careful to see that the valve stem is exactly centered in the hole of the rim.

G. Mounting Tire on the Rim:

To lever the bead onto the rim, hook one tire lever on the rim and with the other lever gradually pull the bead over the rim.

H. **Caution:**

(1) As tire bead is a very tight fit on the rim, be careful not to put too much strain on it when mounting tire on the rim. Refer to 12.6 A on page 50 regarding correct tire pressure.

(2) Always choose the correct size tire or tube for replacement.

(3) After inflating, put soapy water on the valve tip to check for leakage of air. If it is found to be leaking, tighten valve or replace it with a new one if necessary.

(4) When removing or putting back tube, be careful not to damage stem threads,

12. 7 Brakes:

A. **Construction:**

The Bridgestone 175 DT has internal expanding type brakes on both front and rear wheels. When the front brake lever or rear brake pedal is depressed, the brake cam turns and brake shoes are expanded so that they contact the brake drum. As powerful brakes are required for motorcycles capable of high speeds, large 180 mm ϕ brake drums are fitted to the Bridgestone 175 DT motorcycle. A double leading shoe type brake is also fitted to the front wheel to increase brake power.

Fig. 102. Brake shoe and lining

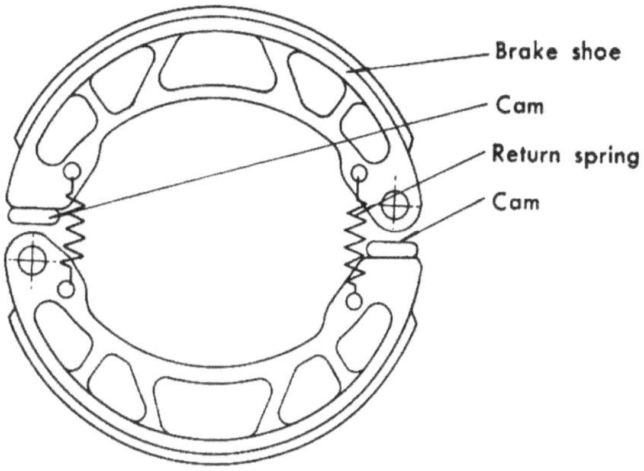

- Brake shoe
- Cam
- Return spring
- Cam

Fig. 103

Fig. 104

B. **Description:**

The front and rear brakes are of the internal expansion type and operated by a lever and pedal respectively, and the brake shoes contact the drum by cam action. The brake linings made of woven asbestine are cemented on the shoes with a special adhesive agent. (Fig. 104)

C. Disassembling:

(1) By removing the wheel according to the procedure given in 12.6 B and C, the hub cover (front or rear hub) can be detatched.

(2) Unhook springs from one shoe only, and both shoes can be detached.

Remove brake arm and cam after shoes are detached.

D. Inspection:

(1) Check brake cam for wear. (Fig. 105)

Refer to the Service Standards Manual.

(2) Check worn return springs (brake shoe) and replace if necessary.

(3) Replace shoe assembly when worn to the limit. Refer to Service Standards Manual.

(4) Replace bent or damaged oil seal.

Fig. 105

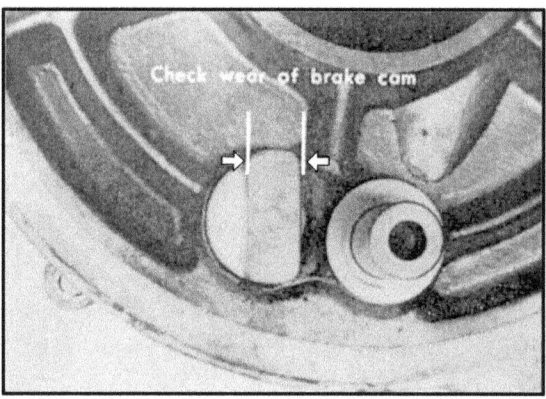

E. Assembling:

Assembling can be done in the reverse order of disassembling. When any particles are embedded in the surface of the shoe lining or if it is unevenly worn, roughen the surface with rough sandpaper.

12. 8 Fuel Tank and Seat:

A. Description:

The fuel tank is located on the frame with the rear part fastened by two hexagonal bolts and the front part insulated by rubber pads attached to the frame. (Fig. 106)

Fig. 106. Fuel Tank

The seat is hooked on to the fuel tank bracket pipe, and the brackets on the rear are fastened by two hexagonal nuts of rear suspension.

B. Removing:

Take off hexagonal nuts on the rear suspension and raise rear of seat slightly and unhook.

The fuel tank can be detached by taking off the two hexagonal bolts at the back and moving it to the rear.

C. Inspection:

(1) Replace front insulation rubber of fuel tank if it is worn or damaged.

(2) Replace fuel tank if there is any leakage.

(3) Replace tank cap packing if it is damaged or worn.

(4) Replace damaged pipe union or clips of drain pipe and fuel pipe if they are worn.

D. Assembling:

Assembling can be done in the reverse order of disassembling.

Fig. 107. Unhook seat

12. 9 Air Cleaner:

A. Construction:

The paper element air cleaner, installed to the rear and above the engine, is cylindrical in shape. An air intake is located on the lower part of the air cleaner. Air filtrated by the air cleaner element enters the carburetors through air pipes fitted to each end of the air cleaner.

B. Description:

The air cleaner is installed in front of the side covers by two screws. The air sucked in here is filtered, and flows into the dual carburetors through two air hoses. (Fig. 108)

C. Removing:

Air cleaner element can be detached by taking off joint rubber and air cleaner nut. (Fig. 109)

Fig. 108. Air Cleaner

Fig. 109. Removing Air Cleaner

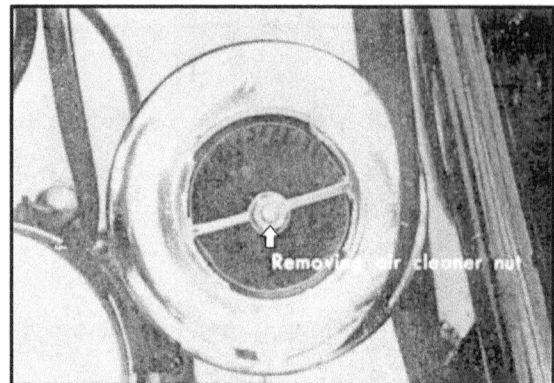

D. Inspection:

(1) Clean or replace air cleaner element periodically by compressed air or with soft hair brush. (Fig. 110)

Fig. 110

(2) Replace joint rubber if it is damaged.

E. Installing:

Install in the reverse order of removing. However, special attention should be paid when installing air cleaner to see that no air is sucked in from any source other than through the air cleaner to prevent any foreign matter entering the carburetors.

12. 10 **Exhaust System:**

   A. **Construction:**

      Exhaust fumes produced in the cylinders are expelled into the air through the exhaust pipes and mufflers. The mufflers silence exhaust noise and also increase engine performance.

   B. **Removing:**

      Remove bolt and nut on muffler brackets, and then the mufflers will come off by pulling to the rear.

      The exhaust pipes can be removed by loosening two screws.

Fig. 111	Fig. 112. Remove Muffler Inner Pipe

   C. **Inspection:**

     (1) Scrape off carbon from exhaust pipes and mufflers periodically.

     (2) When rubber joints are noticeably worn and cause gas leaks or when ring rubber joints or rings are worn, make necessary replacements.

     (3) When exhaust gaskets are noticeably worn, make necessary replacements.

   D. **Installing:**

      Installing can be done in the reverse order of removing.

12. 11 Footrest and Stands (main stand and side stand):

A. Removing:

(1) The footrest can be detached by loosening hexagonal bolt. (Fig. 113)

(2) To detach main stand, suspend motorcycle with rope or lean it against the wall with the stand in position, take out cotter pin, take off hexagonal bolts. (Fig. 114)

Fig. 113. Footrest   Fig. 114. Main stand & Brake pedal

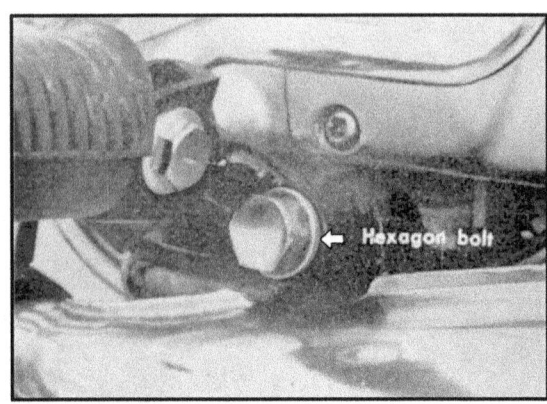 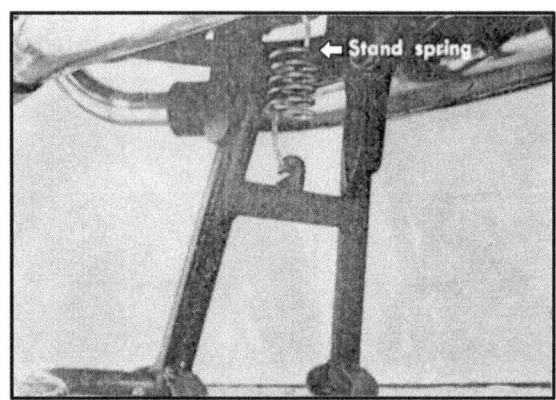

Fig 115. Main stand

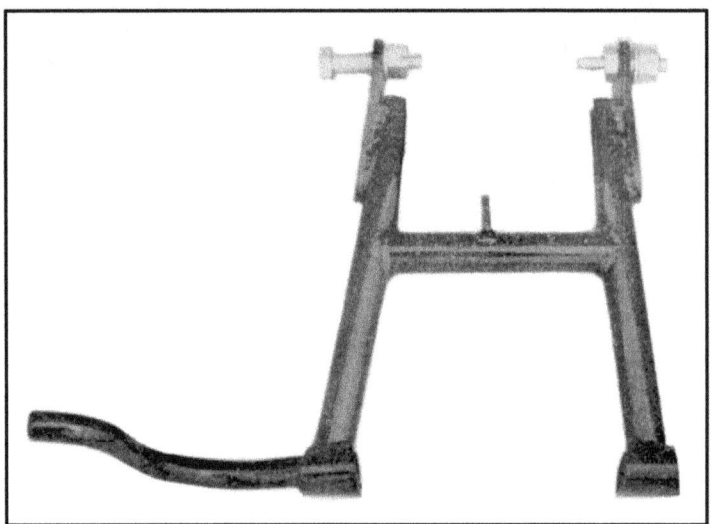

B. Inspection:

(1) Check the footrest shaft for bends, adjust or replace if necessary.

(2) Replace stretched main stand spring.

(3) Adjust or replace bent main stand.

C. Installing:

Install in the reverse order of removing, applying grease to working parts of main stand.

13. ELECTRICAL EQUIPMENT:

13. 1 Generator:

A. Construction:

The generator fitted to the Bridgestone 175 DT is a six pole, magnetic, inner rotor type AC dynamo. The dynamo consists of a rotor into which magnets are cast and a stator consisting of an iron core and wires wound around the iron core. The timing gear is fitted on one end of the rotor and a cam which operates the contact breakers is fitted on the other end. A six pole parmanent magnet is contained in the center of the rotor.

Fig. 116

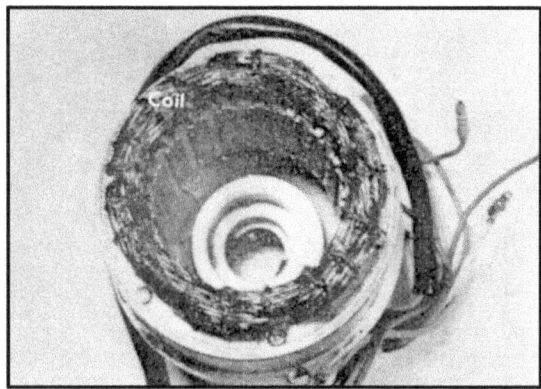

Fig. 117

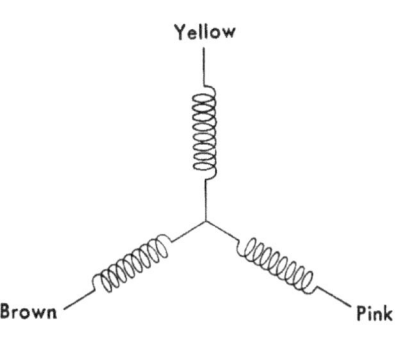

B. Description:

Outstanding features of the magneto type AC dynamo are good resistance to vibration, capability for high speed operation, etc. This type of dynamo is particularly suitable for high speed motorcycles.

To increase output, anisotripic cast magnets, which are specially treated for magnetizing, are used. The principle of the generator is the same as that of a conventional magneto, but the stator consists of three coils as shown in Fig. 117, so the dynamo generates three phase alternating current.

13. 2 Selenium Rectifier:

The selenium rectifier converts AC current generated by the coils into DC current and charges the battery.

As the dynamo mounted on the motorcycle is a six pole type AC dynamo with large output, a selenium rectifier with a large area is used. The three phase bridge all wave rectifying system is used, so that charging performance is excellent. As shown in the illustration, the charging current flows in the direction indicated by a solid arrow during half a cycle and in the next half cycle flows in the direction indicated by a broken arrow. Charging current always flows in the same direction and the AC current is rectified most effectively.

Care must be taken to prevent high temperatures in the rectifier, wetting with water and handling. No trouble from high temperatures will be experienced if the rectifier is mounted in a properly ventilated position. Take care not to wet the rectifier when washing the motorcycle.

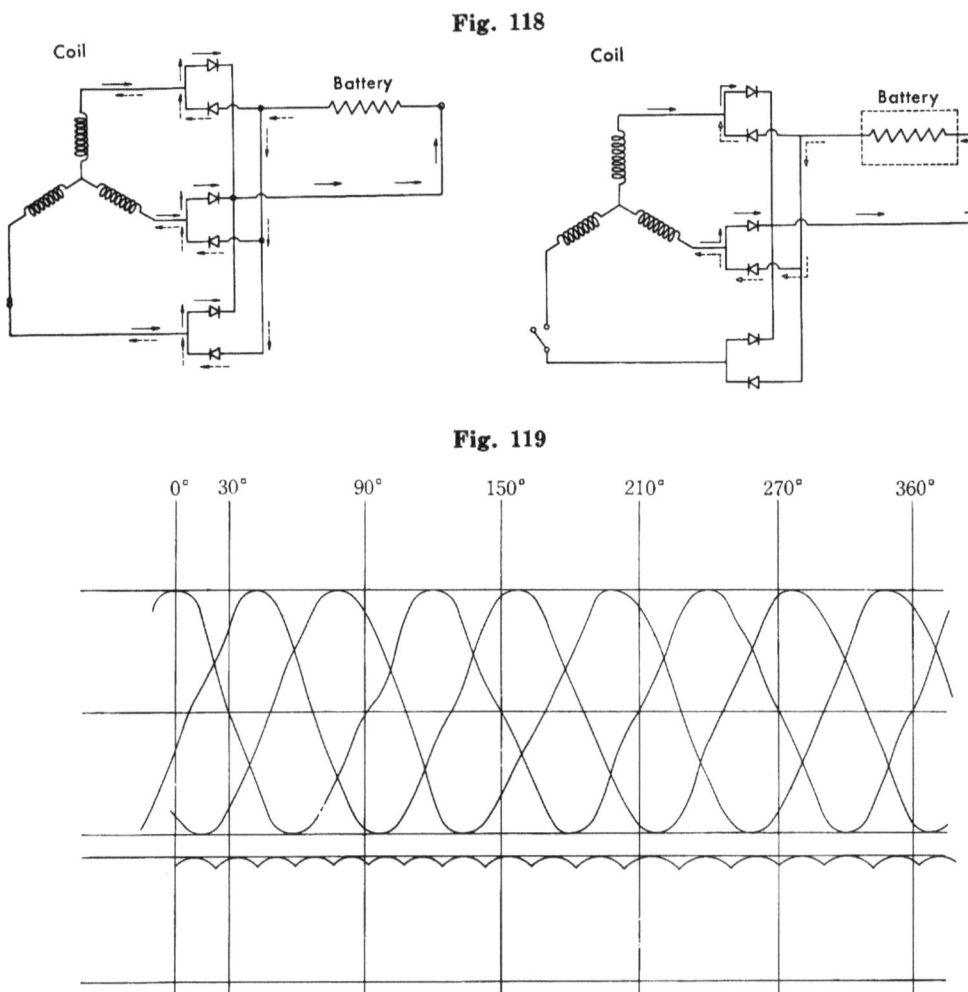

Fig. 118

Fig. 119

If the dynamo operates with the secondary circuit (DC side) of the rectifier disconnected and voltage rises too high, sparks will be generated in the synthetic materials in the layers of the selenium rectifier.

Spots where sparks are generated will be burned and electrical current will flow in the reverse direction through the burned parts so that electrical current from the battery will flow to the ignition coil when the engine stops. This will decrease the magnetic power of the generator. Take care not to run the engine with the selenium rectifer disconnected.

Fig. 120. Selenium Rectifier   Fig. 121.

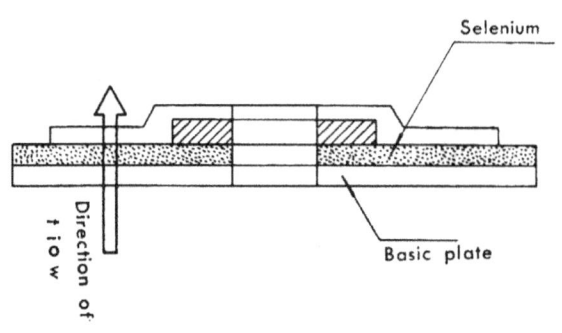

WIRING DIAGRAM

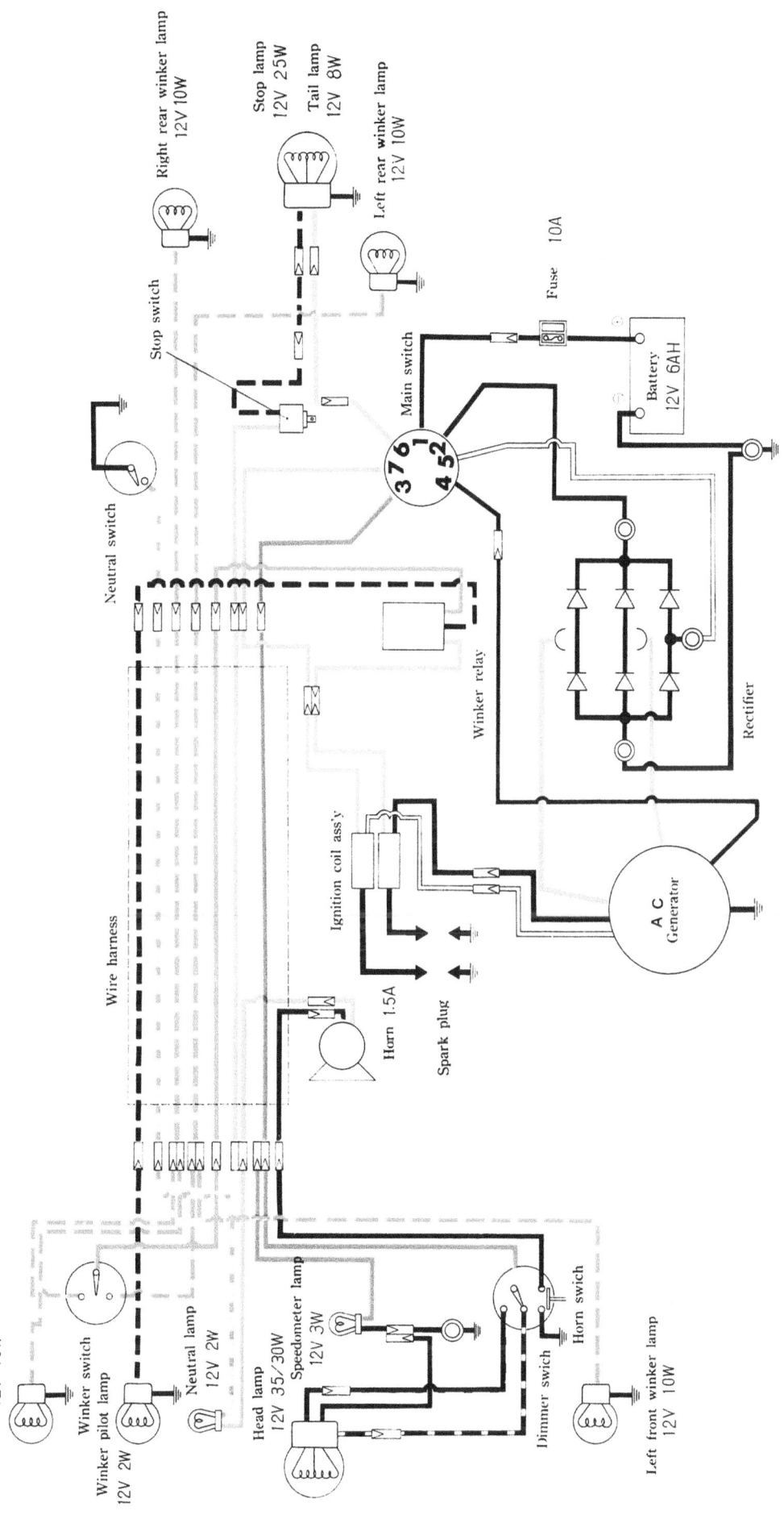

SERVICE MEMO

13. 3 Ignition System:

The igniton system consists of contact breakers, condensers, ignition coil, spark plugs, etc. Battery low voltage current is converted to high voltage current by the ignition coil. High voltage current is supplied to the spark plug and when timed by the contact breakers ignites the fuel mixture in the cylinder.

A. Contact Breakers.

Two contact breakers are fixed on the AC dynamo. The AC dynamo is turned through the Pinion gear, Driven gear, Timing idle gear and Timing gear.

The Timing gear turns one full revolution when the crankshaft turns one full revolution. Timing gear and point cam are fixed on the dynamo shaft and turn with it. The engine of the Bridgestone 175 is a two-stroke two cylinder so one explosion occurs for every cylinder when the crankshaft makes one full revolution.

Fig. 123   Fig. 124

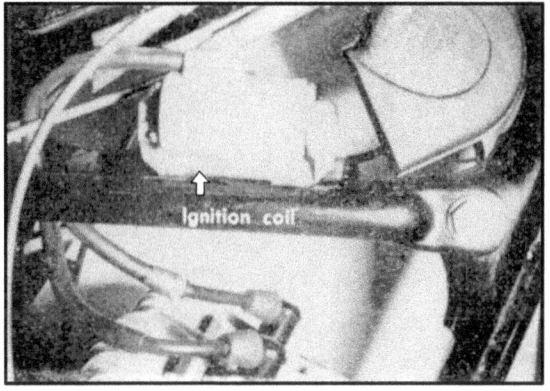 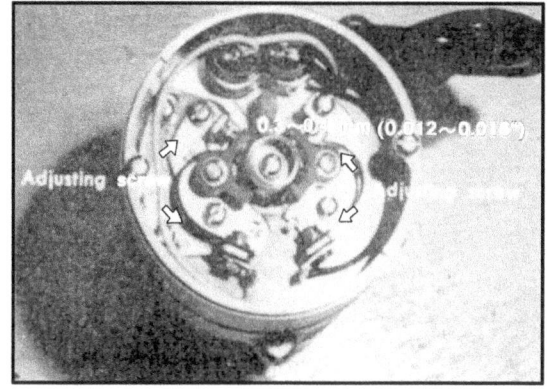

Maintenance:

Contact breaker points should be kept bright and smooth. If point surfaces are rough or pitted, polish surfaces of both points with a point file. If point surfaces are excessively rough or pitted, polish lightly and evenly on an oil stone until the surfaces are smooth. If points cannot be repaired, replace with new ones.

After polishing, wash the point surfaces with gasoline or thinner and wipe dry with a clean cloth. Reinstall the points.

Adjustment

Fit a Dial Gauge on the left cylinder head after removing the spark plug. Connect the black wire from the AC Dynamo to a timing tester and the other terminal to the contact breaker on the left.

Find top dead center with the Dial Gauge. (Fig. 125)

Put the motorcycle in gear and turn the rear wheel in reverse direction until the piston is backed to 1.44mm(0.056″) below top dead center. (Fig. 126) This is 19° before top dead center. Contact breaker points should just begin to open at this point. Permissible timing is between 1.14mm(0.045″) and 1.59mm(0.062″) piston distance below top dead center. This is 17° to 20° before top dead center.

Fig. 125. Finding top dead center

Fig. 126

When Ignition Timing Retarded.

Loosen the fittings of the AC dynamo and turn the Dynamo counterclockwise.

When Ignition Timing is Advanced.

Loosen the fittings of the AC dynamo and turn the Dynamo clockwise.

Before Top Dead Center	20	19	18	17
Piston distance (mm)	1.59	1.44	1.29	1.14
(inch)	0.06260	0.05669	0.05079	0.04488

Remarks:

Timing is checked by pushing timing push button.

When the push button is set to the hole of crankshaft, it shows 19° B.T.D.C. (above table)

Fig. 127

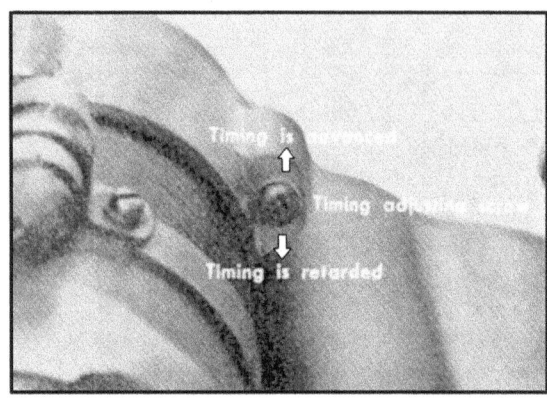

Fig. 128

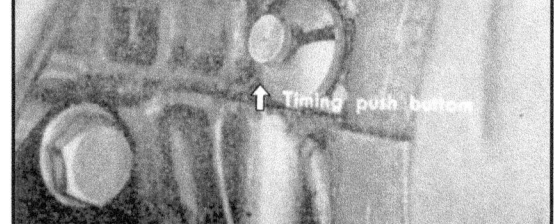

B. Condensers:

The condensers prevent sparks from jumping between the contact breaker points and pitting them.

Fig. 129

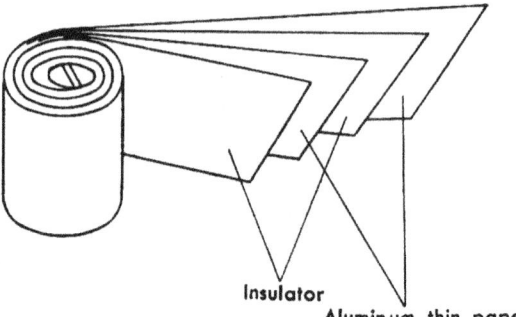

— 64 —

C. Spark Plugs:

NGK B-8H spark plugs are standard for the Bridgestone 175 DT. Be sure to use the proper spark plugs, as the engine cannot develop 100 percent performance if an incorrect spark plug is used.

Fig. 130. Plug

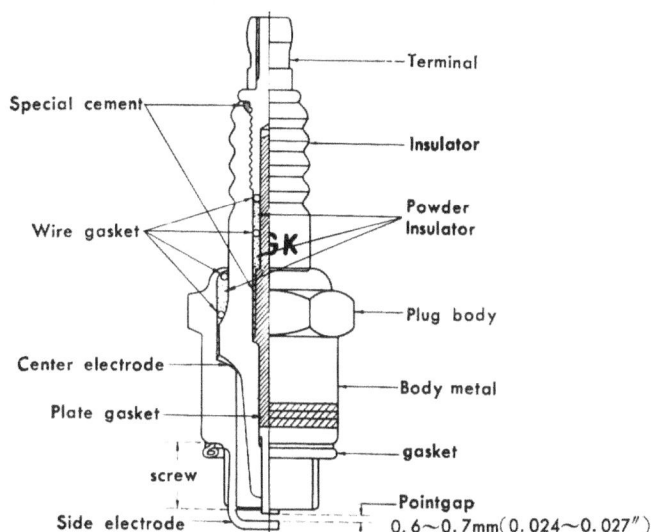

The spark plug is proper for the engine when the spark plug insulator is light brown in color. If the insulator is black or carbon accumulates on it, use a hot type of spark plug, that is one with a smaller number. If the insulator has a bleached appearance, use a cold type of spark plug, that is one with a larger number.

D. Ignition Coils:

The ignition coil induces high voltage current from low voltage current supplied by the battery by the operation of the contact breakers. The amount of high voltage current induced is determined by the ratio between the number of windings on the primary coil and secondary coil. This high voltage current is supplied to the spark plugs.

The Bridgestone 175 DT has a battery ignition system. Twelve volt battery current flows into the primary coil of the ignition coil. When this primary current is cut off suddenly by the operation of the contact breaker, high voltage current is induced in the secondary coil.

13.4 Battery:

AC current generated by the AC dynamo is rectified to DC current by the selenium rectifier and charged into the battery.

All current for operation of the motorcycle flows from the battery. The battery should be kept in good condition at all times since electricity for all electrical equipment is supplied by the battery.

The capacity of the battery is 12 V—6 AH. The battery should be checked periodically by the rider or the dealer. Check the level of the electrolyte solution and the specific gravity of the solution.

Specific gravity of the solution should be 1.260~1.280 at 20° centigrade (68° F) when the battery is fully charged.

Fig. 131. Battery

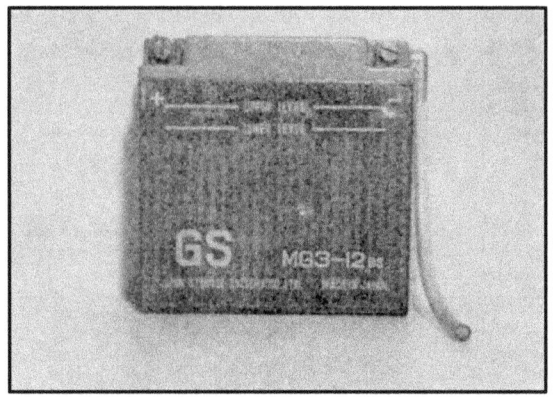

BRAND	STANDARD	IF PLUG FOULS EASILY (Slow speed)	IF PLUG BURNS EASILY (High speed)
NGK	B-8 H	B-7 H B-7 HC	B-8 HN B-9 H
CHAMPION	L-58 R	L-5	L-56 T L-55 T
KLG	F 260	F 100	F 280
LODGE	R 47	3 HN	R 49
BOSCH	W310 T16	W225 Ti W240 Ti	W340 T16

13.5 Lights:

Headlight:

The headlight includes a 12 V, 35 W main beam and a 12 V, 25 W dim beam. The battery is the electric source for the headlight. Riding will be dangerous at night if obstacles cannot be seen clearly. As the headlight of the Bridgestone DT is operated on battery current, it remains bright regardless of engine speed and riders can enjoy safe riding at night.

MAIN SWITCH

The ignition switch is combined with the lighting and horn switches and divided into four positions and operated as follows:

Position of key	Object	Use of Key
0	For parking (Entire electric circuit is opened)	Can be pulled out
1	For Daylight driving (Engine can be started and horn, stop light, neutral lamp are available)	Cannot pulled out
2	For Night time driving (Head light, tail light, stop light, neutral lamp, high beam lamp, horn are available)	Cannot be pulled out
3	For Parking (Parking light is available)	Can be pulled out

Note: The ignition key is also used for the steering lock.

14. INSPECTION AND MAINTENANCE:

A. Daily Check Procedure:

Tire Air Pressure	Front 1.6 kg/cm² (22 lbs/in²) Rear 2.0 kg/cm² (28 lbs/in²)
Front Brake	Proper adjustment (10—20 mm = 0.39~0.79 inch)
Rear Brake	Proper adjustment (20—30 mm = 0.79~1.18 inch)
Gasoline (Gasoline tank)	It is sufficient?
Oil (Oil tank)	It is sufficient?
Horn	Does it work well?
Lights	Proper operation.
Transmission Oil	Check level.
Battery	Check liquid level.

B. Periodic Checking:

400 km (250 miles)   3,000 km (2,000 miles)   6,000 km (3,500 miles)

ITEM	PROCEDURE	AFTER BREAK-IN (400 km)	ONCE EVERY 3,000 km (2,000 mile)	ONCE EVERY 6,000 km (3,500 mile)
Front & Rear Brake Play	Check	×	×	×
Chain Play	Check	×	×	×
Mufflers & Exhausts	Clean Carbon			○
Clutch Play	Check	×	×	×
Carburetor Operation	Check		○	○
Battery Liquid	Check	×	×	×
Spark Plugs	Clean		×	×
Contact Point Gap	Check	○	○	○
Air Cleaner	Clean		○	○
Cylinder Head	Clean Carbon		×	×
Bolts and Nuts	Tighten	○	○	○
Fuel Cock Filter	Clean		○	○
Transmission Oil	Replace	×		×

Items marked "O" Should be checked more frequently.

C. Periodic Greasing:

Periodic greasing with a grease gun and lubrication.

	ITEM	1ST GREASING	2ND GREASING MILEAGE INTERVAL	PROCEDURE
1.	Front Brake Cam Shaft	400 km. (250 miles)	3,000 km. (2,000 miles)	Grease
2.	Rear Brake Cam shaft	400 km. (250 miles)	3,000 km. (2,000 miles)	Grease
3.	Throttle Grip Pipe	400 km. (250 miles)	3,000 km. (2,000 miles)	Grease
4.	Speedometer Gear Box	6,000 km. (3,500 miles)	4,000 km. (2,500 miles)	Grease
5.	Front & Rear Wheel Bearings	3,000 km. (2,000 miles)	3,000 km. (2,000 miles)	Grease
6.	Steering Bearings	6,000 km. (3,500 miles)	6,000 km. (3,500 miles)	Grease
7.	Oil Felt (Magneto)	6,000 km. (3,500 miles)	6,000 km. (3,500 miles)	Oil
8.	Cables	1,500 km. (1,000 miles)	3,000 km. (2,000 miles)	Oil
9.	Chain	400 km. (250 miles)	1,000 km. (600 miles)	Motor Oil
10.	Stand Tube	3,000 km. (2,000 miles)	3,000 km. (2,000 miles)	Grease
11.	Front Fork	10,000 km. (6,000 miles)	10,000 km. (6,000 miles)	220 cc. of Hydraulic fork oil (or mixture of 70 parts of Spindle oil SAE No. 60 to 30 parts of No. 30 motor oil)

D. Inspection and Maintenance During Storage:

As new motorcycles are placed in the warehouse pending sale and delivery, the Distributor/Dealer should carry out certain inspections and certain measures for protection of the machines to avoid trouble after delivery due to rust and other causes resulting from long storage.

Safeguarding against such a possibility will save much labor and time.

I. BATTERY:

1. Inspection of specific gravity of electrolyte fluid.
2. Storage of dry charged battery.
3. Initial charging rate.

II. CARBURETORS:

1. Draining gasoline in float chamber.
2. Adjusting for slow running.

III. CONTACT BREAKER IGNITION POINTS:

1. Cleaning of points.
2. Adjustment of point gap.

IV. TRANSMISSION OIL:

1. Quantity of transmission oil.
2. Quality of oil.

V. FUEL TANK AND OIL TANK:

1. Draining.

I. **BATTERY**:

1. **Inspection of Specific Gravity**:

   The condition of the battery can be determined by measuring the specific gravity of the electrolyte solution.

   If the gravity is below 1.220, the battery should be charged without delay.

Specific Gravity at 20°C. (68°F.) (Solution Temperature)	Amount of Charge
1.260	100%
1.220	75
1.160	50
1.105	25
1.050	None

   (Caution) Take care of the following points when checking the specific gravity.

   (1) Do not let the hydrometer float touch the side of the wall.

   (2) Read the hydrometer at A (upper level of contact) instead of B (low level) as shown in Figure.

   (3) As specific gravity varies according to the temperature of the solution, apply the following conversion table based on standard 20°C. (or 68°F.) for the different temperatures.

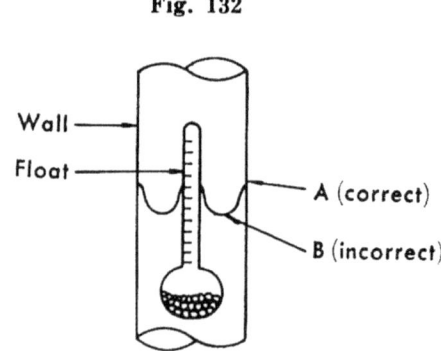

Fig. 132

Relation between Specific Gravity and Temperature of Solution

0°C 32°F	5°C 42°F	10°C 50°F	25°C 59°F	20°C 68°F	25°C 77°F	30°C 86°F	35°C 95°F	40°C 104°F	45°C 113°F
1,218	1,215	1,212	1,208	1,205	1,202	1,198	1,195	1,191	1,188
1,223	1,220	1,217	1,213	1,210	1,207	1,203	1,200	1,196	1,193
1,228	1,225	1,222	1,218	1,220	1,212	1,208	1,205	1,202	1,198
1,233	1,230	1,227	1,223	1,225	1,217	1,213	1,210	1,206	1,203
1,238	1,235	1,232	1,228	1,225	1,222	1,218	1,215	1,211	1,208
1,244	1,241	1,237	1,234	1,230	1,226	1,223	1,219	1,216	1,212
1,249	1,246	1,242	1,239	1,235	1,231	1,228	1,224	1,221	1,217
1,254	1,251	1,247	1,244	1,240	1,236	1,233	1,229	1,226	1,222
1,259	1,256	1,252	1,249	1,245	1,241	1,238	1,234	1,231	1,227
1,264	1,261	1,257	1,254	1,250	1,246	1,243	1,239	1,236	1,232
1,269	1,266	1,262	1,259	1,255	1,251	1,248	1,244	1,240	1,237
1,274	1,271	1,267	1,264	**1,260**	1,256	1,253	1,249	1,245	1,242
1,276	1,276	1,272	1,269	1,265	1,261	1,258	1,254	1,250	1,247
1,284	1.281	1.277	1,274	1,270	1,266	1,263	1,259	1,255	1,252
1,289	1,286	1,282	1,279	1,275	1,270	1,268	1,264	1,260	1,257
1,294	1.260	1,287	1,284	1,280	1,276	1,273	1,269	1,265	1,261

2. **Storage of Dry Charged Battery**:

Dry charged battery, if stored in a relatively dry place, will remain in good condition for a considerable period, but if the cells absorb moisture during storage, the negative plates will discharge slowly and the charging rate will be longer as shown in the following table.

Storage period	Decreased Capacity	Capacity	Charging Rate
One Month	0%	100%	0.6 Ampere × 10 Hour
Three months	15%	85%	0.6 ″ × 12 ″
Six months	30%	70%	6.6 ″ × 14 ″
One year	50%	50%	0.6 ″ × 20 ″

3. **Initial Charging Rate**:

(2) Leave battery from 2 to 12 hours after filling before charging. When the level of electrolyte has dropped, add more electrolyte until the proper level is reached.

(3) Charge at the proper rate as given in table below until all cells are gassing freely and cell voltage and specific gravity stop rising and remain constant.
The total charging time will be 10 hours. During charging, battery temperature should be kept below 45°C (113°F.) Should the temperature exceed 45°C., stop charging for a time until the temperature falls below 45°C.

Model	Proper Charging	Quick Charging
BRIDGESTONE 7		
Deluxe	0.6 Ampere × 12 hour	3 Ampere × 1 hour
Standard	0.2 ″ × 12 ″	1 ″ × 1 ″
BRIDGESTONE 50		
(Standard)	0.2 ″ × 12 ″	1 ″ × 1 ″
BRIDGESTONE 90	0.4 ″ × 12 ″	2 ″ × 1 ″
BRIDGESTONE 60 Sport	0.2 ″ × 12 ″	1 ″ × 1 ″
″ 50 Sport	0.2 ″ × 12 ″	1 ″ × 1 ″
″ 175 Dual Twin	0.6 ″ × 12 ″	3 ″ × 1 ″

II. CARBURETORS:

1. Maintenance:

(1) Disassemble float chamber, and clean it with gasoline.

(2) Clean hole on main jet, and needle jet with compressed air.

2. Adjusting for Slow Running:

(**Note**) Warm up the engine for 2 or 3 minutes before adjusting.

(**Adjusting**)

(1) Screw the air screw in to the limit and then unscrew;

    2 full turns for BRIDGESTONE 50 HM

    1 turn for BRIDGESTONE 90

    2 turns for BRIDGESTONE 7

    1 turn for BRIDGESTONE 50 Sport

    1 turn for BRIDGESTONE 60 Sport

    2 turns for BRIDGESTONE 175 Dual Twin

(2) Adjust the engine with the throttle stop screw to the lowest speed it will run smoothly.

(3) Turning the air screw back and forward about 1/2 turn each way, find the position where the engine fires best.

(4) Re-adjust the idling speed with the throttle stop screw.

(5) Adjust both carburetors same amount.

III. CONTACT BREAKER IGNITION POINTS:

1. Cleaning of Points:

After three months storage, polish the points with a point file before starting up the machine.

(**Reason**) After long storage, the points will be coated with a thin oxidized film.

Do not use emery paper, as residue emery powder will cause rapid wear of the points.

2. Adjustment of Point Gap:

Keep the point gap between 0.3–0.4 mm (0.012~0.018″).

IV. TRANSMISSION OIL:

Fill before starting the machine.
Fill with high grade motor oil.

1. **Quantity of Transmission Oil:**

   1 litre (0.26 U.S. qt.) for BRIDGESTONE 50 and BRIDGESTONE 7 DELUXE & STANDARD.

   0.6 litre (0.158 U.S Gal.) for BRIDGESTONE 90, BRIDGESTONE 90 TRAIL and BRIDGESTONE 90 MOUNTAIN.

   0.5 litre (0.132 U.S. Gal.) for BRIDGESTONE 50 Sport and BRIDGESTONE 60 Sport.

   0.8 litre (0.21 U.S. Gal.) for BRIDGESTONE 175 Dual Twin.

2. **Quality of Oil:**

   SAE No. 30 in summer.

   SAE No. 20 in winter.

   or

   SAE No. 10 W/30 in all seasons may be used, if preferred.

V. FUEL TANK AND OIL TANK:

Fuel tank and oil tank should first be completely drained and all deposits and grit cleaned out.

Then fill fuel tank with gasoline 10 litre (2.6 US gal), oil tank with oil 1.2 litre (1.05 US qt).

SERVICE MEMO

15. TROUBLE SHOOTING:

(1) **Engine is hard to start.**

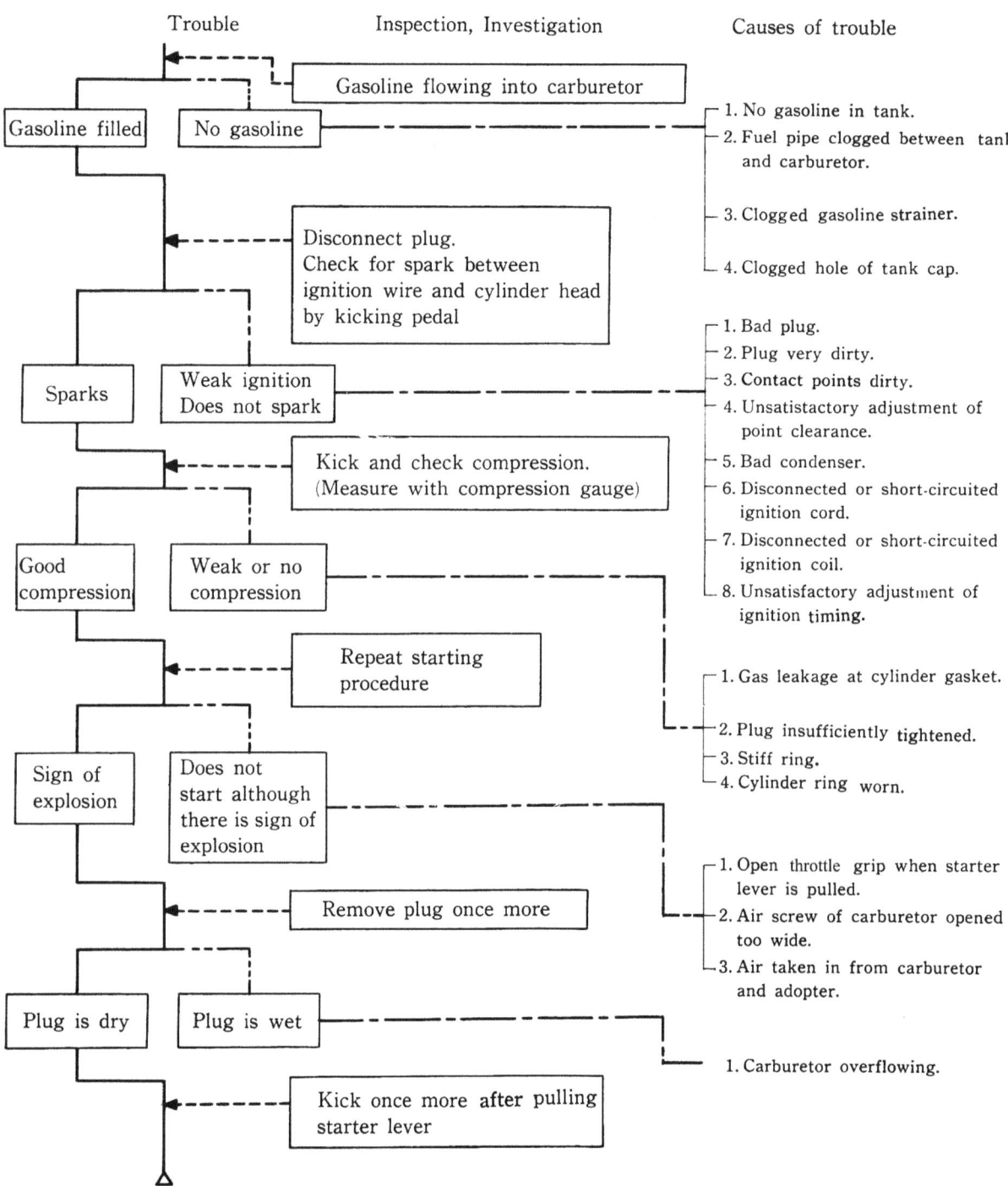

Fuel, spark and compression are basic points for engine operation.
To locate engine trouble first check these points.

(2) **High engine revolution cannot be obtained.**
    Insufficient power.

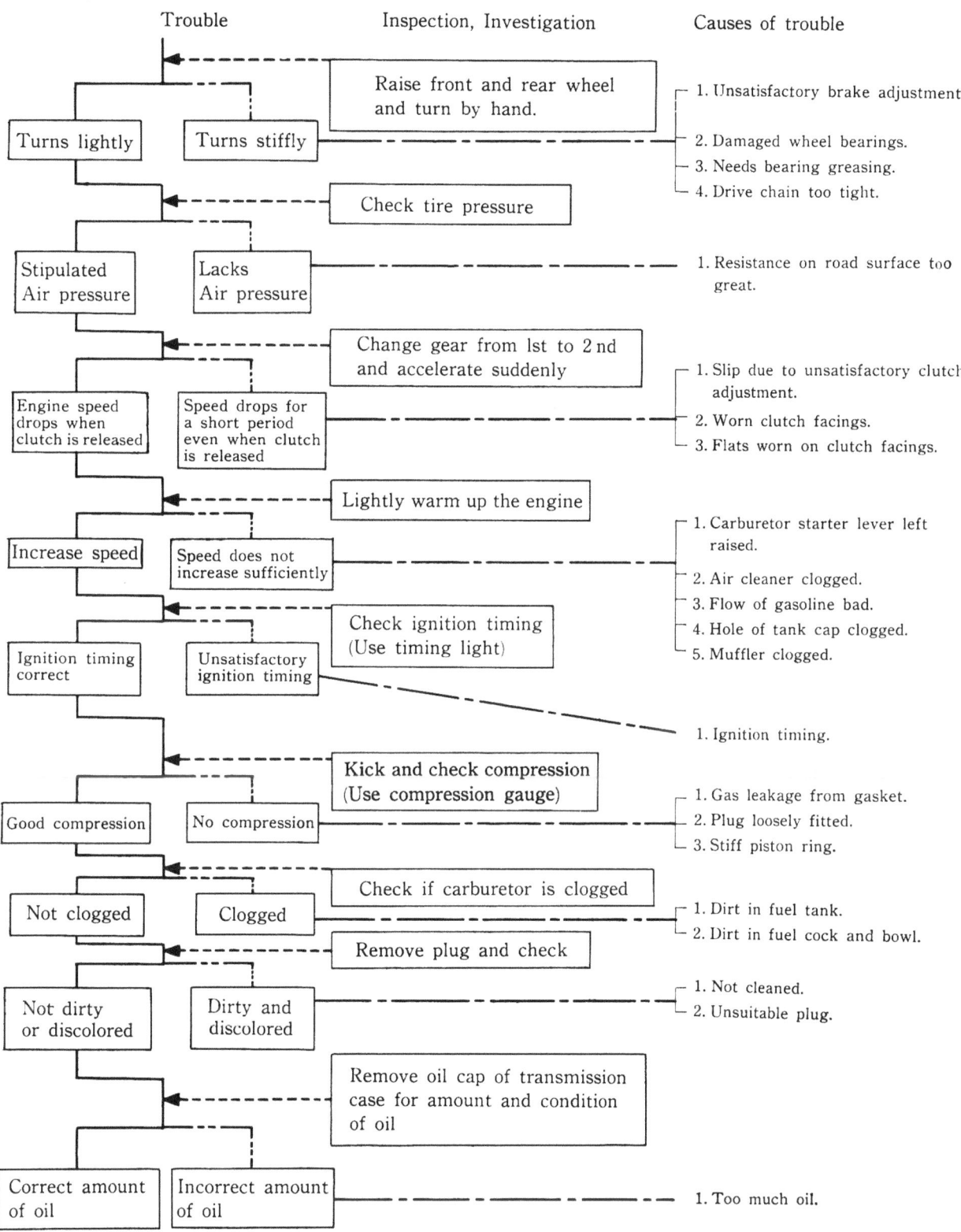

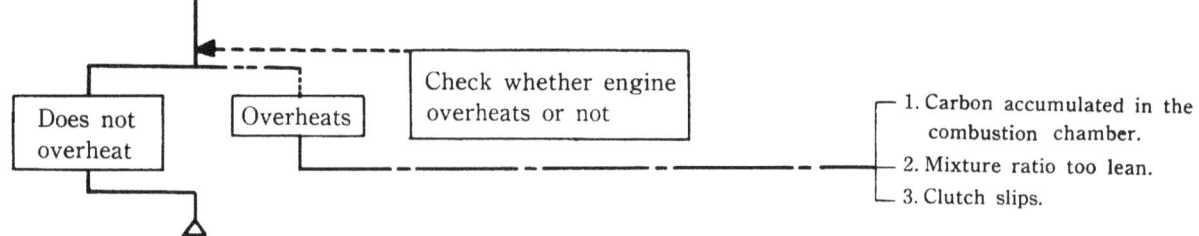

(3) **Unsatisfactory R.P.M. (Chiefly at low speed and idling).**

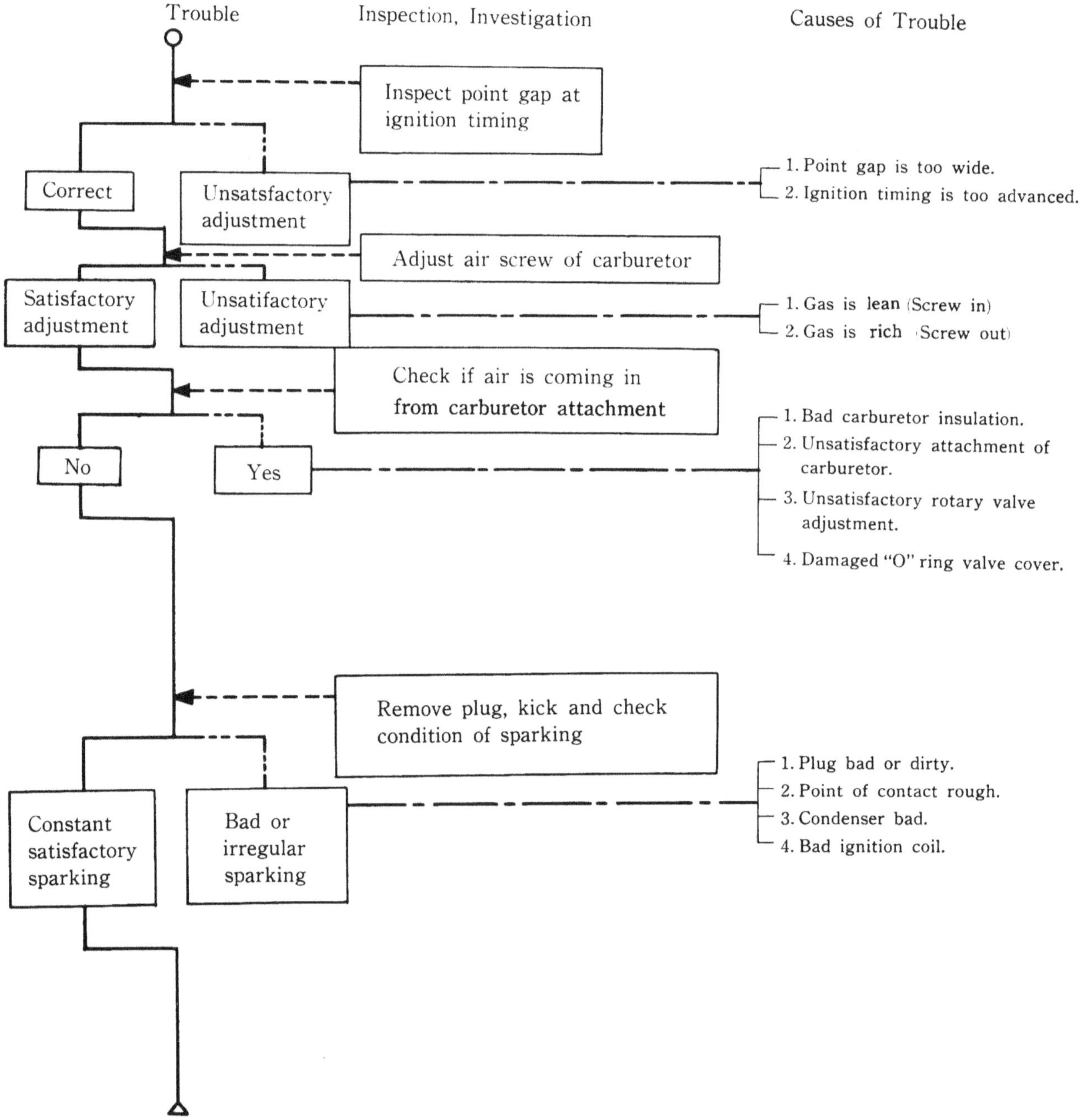

(4) Iregular Revolutions (At medium and high speeds).

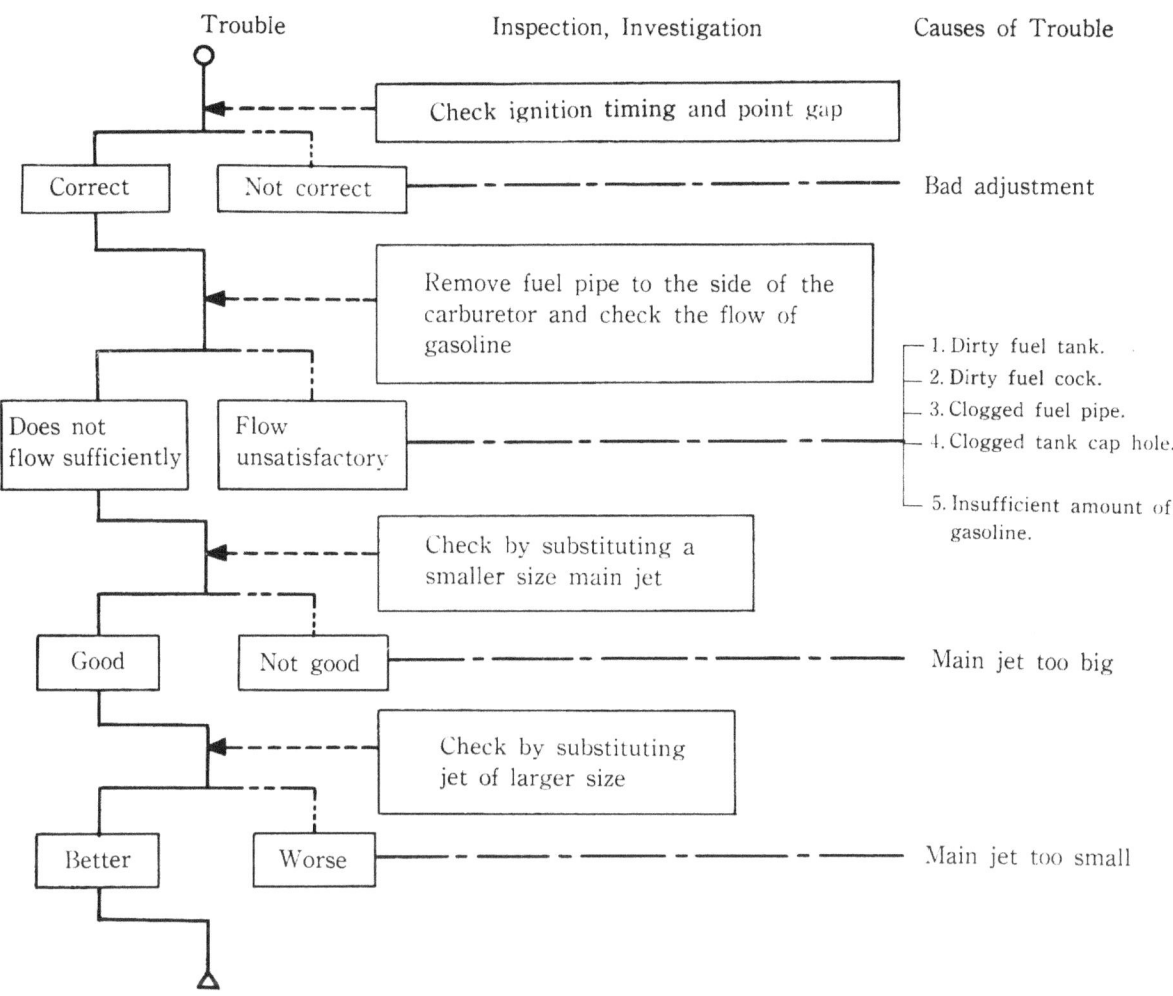

(5) **Unsatisfactory Gear Shifting.**

Trouble · Causes of Trouble

Gears cannot be shifted smoothly
- 1. Improper working gear shift drum.
- 2. Bent shift fork.
- 3. Improper working clutch.
- 4. Worn claws of drum shifter.

Change pedal does not return smoothly
- 1. Broken change return spring.
- 2. Drum shifter touching some part.
- 3. Bent change shaft.

Gears disengage
- 1. Bent and worn out shift fork.
- 2. Worn out claws of drum shifter.
- 3. Worn out drum stopper.

SERVICE MEMO

TUNING-UP
175 DUAL TWIN HURRICANE SCRAMBLER
FOR ROAD RACING

BRIDGESTONE
175 DUAL TWIN HURRICANE SCRAMBLER
For ROAD RACING

4. ENLARGE CYLINDER PORTS

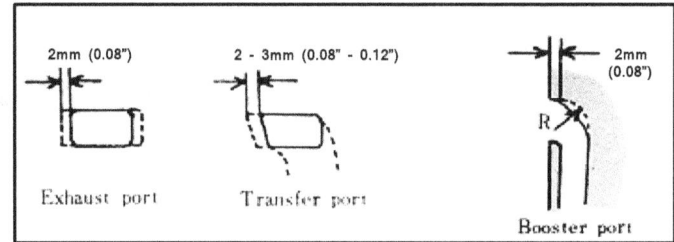

Enlarge the cylinder ports smoothly with a fine electric grinder as shown to eliminate flow friction of gas.

5. INCREASE COMBUSTION CHAMBER COMPRESSION

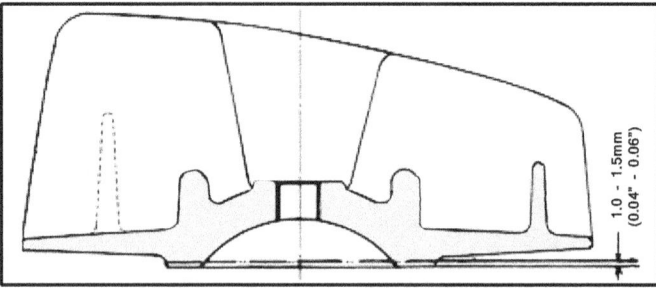

Raise combustion chamber compression by shaving down the cylinder head base as shown.

1. MODIFICATION OF ROTARY DISK VALVES

Enlarge valve gap of the disc as shown. Finish the cut corners (R) carefully to prevent cracking of the disc at high speed.

2. CARBURETOR SETTING

Standard size carburetor will be effective for races, except main jet size from No. 90 (original size) to No. 100.

3. DESIGN OF MUFFLER

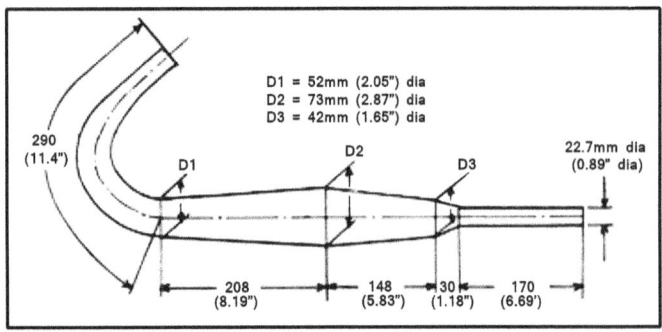

6. MODIFICATION OF ROTARY DISC VALVE COVERS

To suit the carburetor 22.24 mm bore, make and weld the tube by cutting off the original intake tube.

7. IGNITION TIMING

7-1. Ignition Timing: 24° Before Top Dead Center instead of 19° of original timing.

7-2. Piston Displacement Before Top Dead Center: 2.3mm (0.090 inches) instead of 1.44 mm (0.057 inches) of original displacement.

7-3. Point Gap of Contact Breaker: 0.25-0.30mm (0.010-0.012 inches) instead of original gap.

7-4. Spark Plug: NGK B-8HN-B-IIHN

Performance of Standard Engine

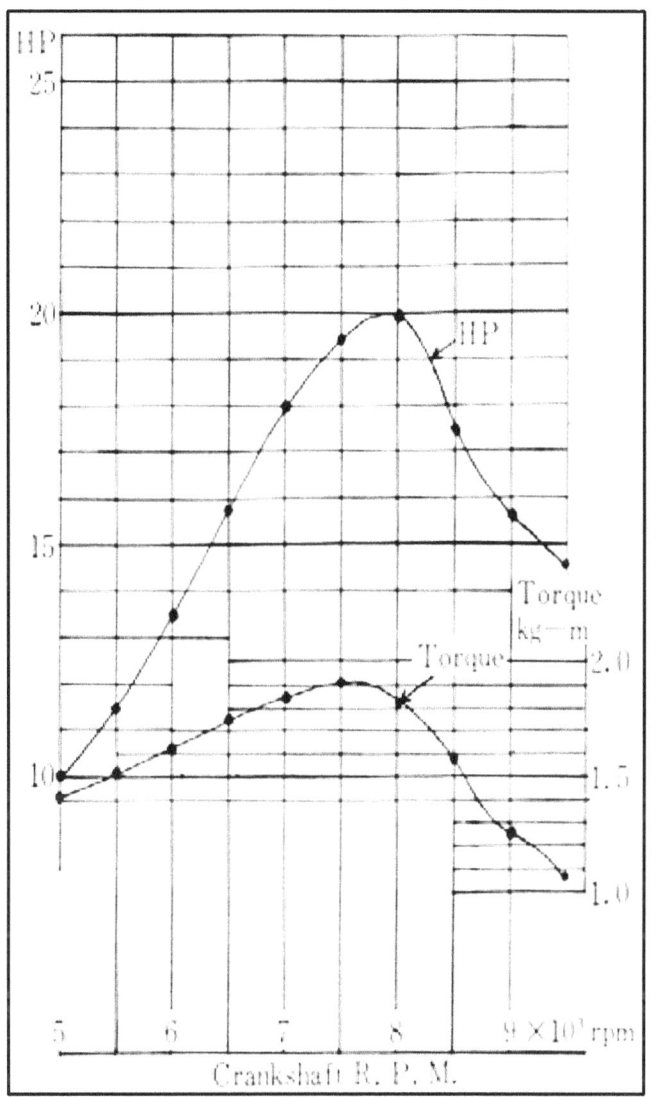

Performance after Tune-up

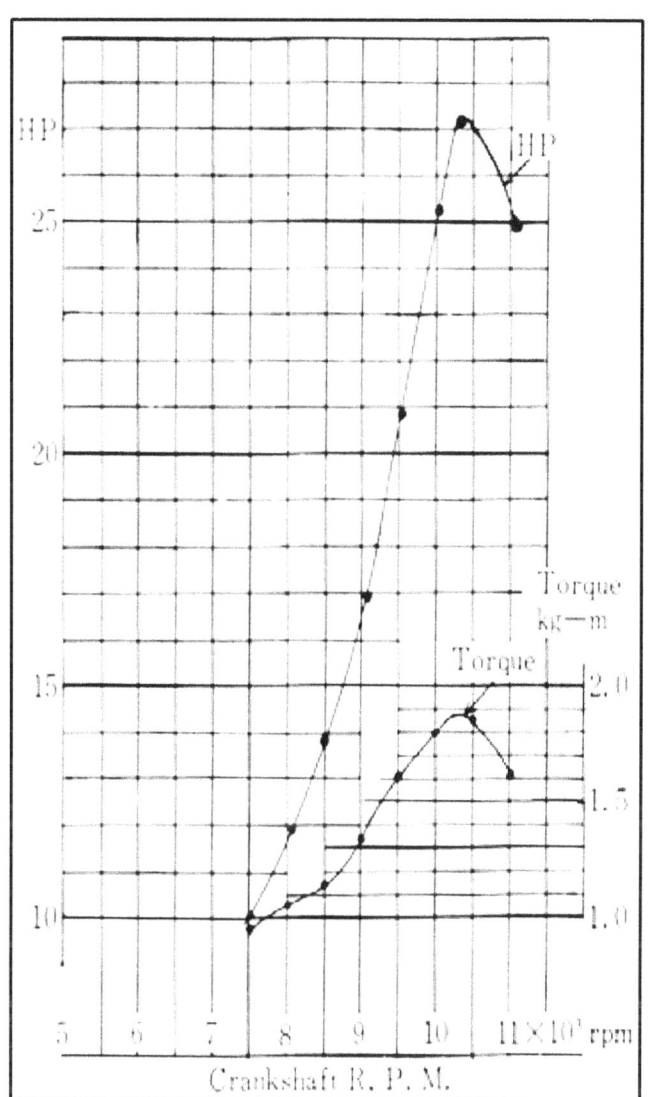

SERVICE MEMO

SERVICE MEMO

TUNING-UP
175 DUAL TWIN HURRICANE SCRAMBLER
FOR SCRAMBLING

BRIDGESTONE
175 DUAL TWIN HURRICANE SCRAMBLER
For SCRAMBLING

1. MODIFICATION OF ROTARY DISC VALVES

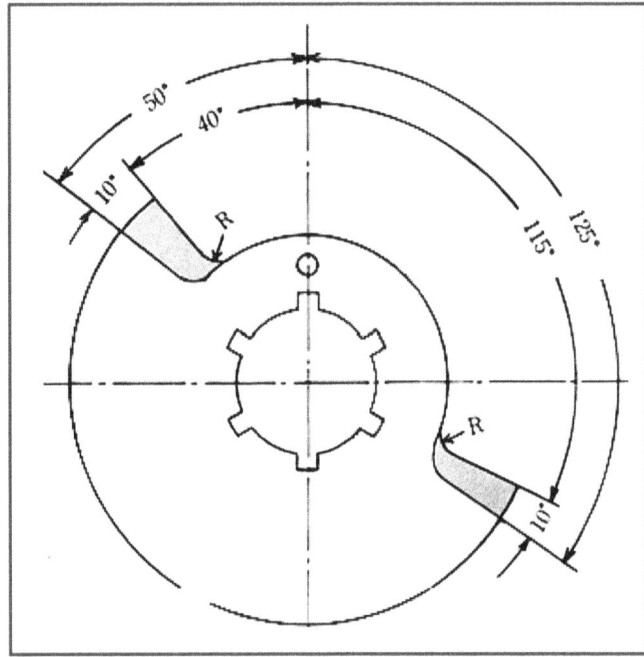

Enlarge valve gap of the disc as shown. Finish the cut corners (R) carefully to prevent cracking of the disc at high speed.

2. CARBURETOR SETTING

To obtain higher power output at high speed, install the AMAL type carburetor VM22-VM24SC and main jet around 270-290.

3. DESIGN OF MUFFLER

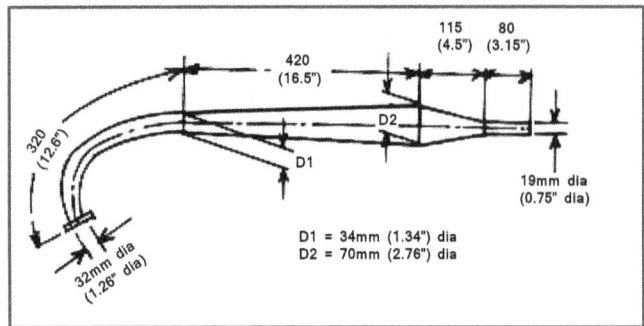

4. ENLARGE BOOSTER PORT (3RD TRANSFER PORT)

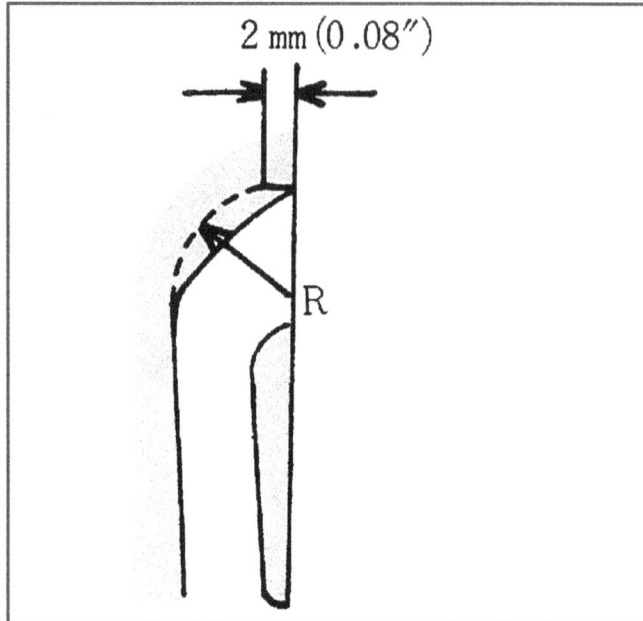

Enlarge the booster port (3rd transfer port) smoothly with a fine electric grinder as shown, for free passage of gas.

5. INCREASE COMBUSTION CHAMBER COMPRESSION

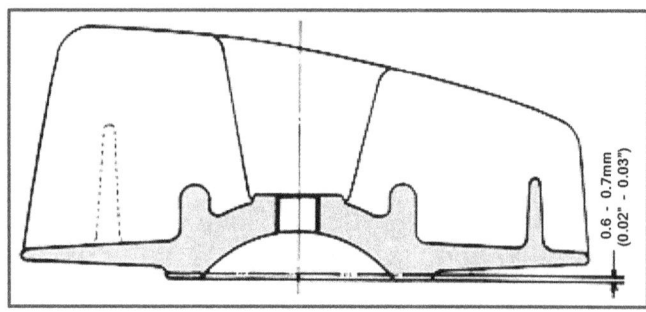

Raise combustion chamber compression by shaving down the cylinder head base as shown.

6. IGNITION TIMING

6-1. Ignition Timing: 24° Before Top Dead Center instead of 19° of original timing.
6-2. Piston Displacement Before Top Dead Center: 2.3 mm (0.090 inches) instead of 1.4mm (0.057 inches) of original displacement.
6-3. Point Gap of Contact Breaker: 0.25-0.30 mm (0.010-0.012 inches) instead of 0.30mm (0.012-0.016 inches) original gap.
6-4. Spark Plug: NGK B-8HN ~ 9HN

Performance of Standard Engine

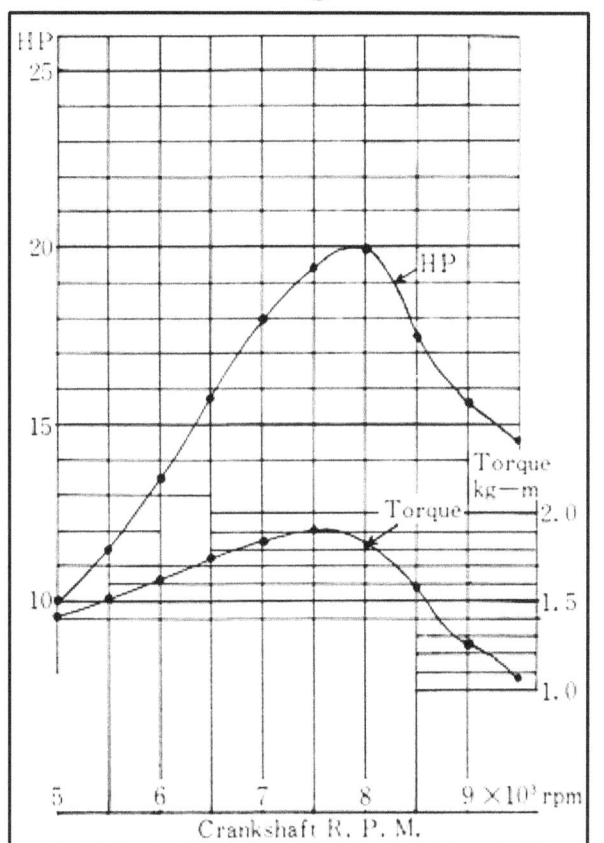

Performance after Tune-up

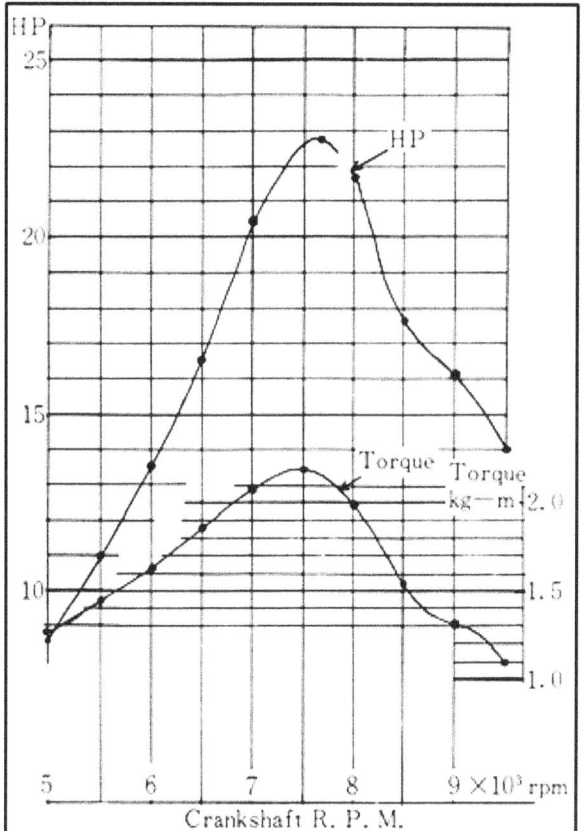

SERVICE MEMO

SERVICE MEMO

BRIDGESTONE 175
Dual Twin

PARTS CATALOGUE

 **BRIDGESTONE TIRE CO., LTD.**

TOKYO, JAPAN

INSTRUCTIONS FOR USING THE PARTS CATALOGUE

1. This catalogue covers all the items of genuine parts and tools of BRIDGESTONE 175 Dual Twin Motorcycle.
2. Please note the following when placing orders.
   a) Be sure to state accurately the Index Number, Part Number and Name of each part (See Note)
   b) All the items recessed (set-back) under individual "assembly items" represent a group of parts comprising the "assembly".
   c) 7D, 7S, HM, 50SP, 60SP, 90 and 90M in the "interchangeability" columns mean respectively BS7 Deluxe model, BS7 Standard model, BS50 Homer model, BS50 Sport model, BS60 Sport model, BS90 and BS90 Mountain models.
   The circles in the "Interchangeability" columns indicate that the parts are interchangeable with those of model BS175 Dual twin.
   d) The numbers shown in the column "Number Required" represent the quantities required for one unit.

Note

For your reference only, we explain below how our part numbers are compiled. These numbers are actually code numbers used by the factory and are of no concern to our dealers, except that they <u>must be</u> distinctly noted against each part ordered, without fail, as the factory bases their production on these <u>numbers</u>, and <u>not</u> on the <u>part names.</u>

Example 1
1) Parts in General (excluding bolts, nuts, washers etc).

Part No.	Part Name
1112 800 0	Left cylinder head

```
       0: In case of Zero, the part is the original
 800~809: show the part is one of BS175 dual twin
 500~509:    "        "        BS90
 320~329:    "        "        BS50SP
 310~319:    "        "        BS50HM
 300~309:    "        "        BS7
    1112: Indicates code No. of Left cylinder head
```

Example 2
2) Bolts and Screws

Part No.	Part Name
0 11 1 0812	Hexagon bolt A

```
 0812: indicates 8mm (nominal diameter) × 12mm (length)
    1: Kind of plating
   11: Code No. of shape
    0: Zero means authorized type of Bolts and screws by Japan Industrial
       Standard regulation (JIS)
```

Example 3
3) Nuts

Part No.	Part Name
0 21 1 0600	Hexagon nut A

```
 0600: 6mm (nominal diameter)
    1: Indicates kinds of plating
   21: Code No.
    0: Zero means authorized type of nut by JIS regulation
```

Example 4
4) Washers
   4)-1

Part No.	Part Name
0 41 1 06 13	Plane washer A

```
   13: Indicates 13mm (Outer diameter)
   06: 6mm (inner diameter)
    1: Indicates kind of plating
   41: Indicates type of washer
    0: Zero indicates type of washer authrized by JIS
```

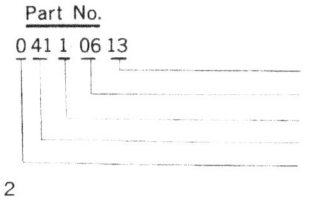

4) 2

Part No.	Part Name
090 41 111	7 plane (Flat) washer

```
  111: Code No. of washer
   41: Indicates shape of washer
  090: 090 indicates the part in used in the category of engine
(095): (095 indicates the part is used in the category of body)
```

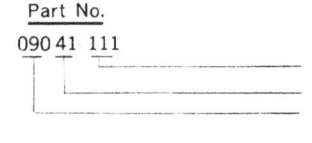

Example 5

Part No.	Part Name
07 6304 03	Ball bearing

```
   03: Shape code No.
 6304: No. of ball bearing by JIS
   07: 07 means Ball bearing
```

Specification of BRIDGESTONE 175 Dual Twin

	Item	Production Model

1. ENGINE

1)	Type:	2-stroke
2)	Piston Displacement:	177cc. (10.8 cu-inch)
3)	Bore and Stroke:	50 × 45mm (1.97 × 1.77 inch)
4)	Compression Ratio:	9.5 : 1
5)	Max. Brake Horse Power:	20HP/8,000 rpm.
6)	Max. Torque:	1.9kg-m/7,500 rpm (13.7 lb-ft/7,500 rpm)
7)	Air Intake System:	Rotary disc valve
8)	Starting System:	Kick Starter
9)	Charging System:	A.C. Generator
10)	Ignition System:	Battery Ignition
11)	Ignition Timing:	BTDC 21
12)	Spark plug:	B-8H
13)	Carburetor:	VM17SC
14)	Engine Lubrication:	Oil
15)	Fuel:	Gasoline
16)	Transmission Oil:	0.8 liter (0.21 US gal.) in transmission case

2. PERFORMANCE

1)	Max. Speed:	Over 130km/h (80 mph)
2)	Climing Ability:	1/3
3)	Fuel Consumption:	55km/L/40km/h (129 mpg/25 mph)
4)	Min. Turning Radius:	1.95m (76.8 inch)
5)	Acceleration (Standing 1/4 mile):	Under 18 sec.
6)	Braking Distance:	6m at 35km/h (20ft. at 22 mph)

3. FRAME AND SUSPENSION

1)	Frame Type:	Pipe frame, Cradle type.
2)	Front Suspension:	Telescopic Fork with Hydraulic Damper
3)	Rear Suspension:	Swing Arm with Hydraulic Damper
4)	Chain case:	Quarter Case (Upper only)

4. TRANSMISSION

1)	Clutch:	Manual, Multiple discs in oil bath.
2)	Transmission:	Adjustable 4-speed constant mesh-rotary. 5-speed constant mesh-return.
3)	Gear Ratio:	Primary (Helical Gear): 1 : 3.41
		Gear box 1st: 1 : 2.61
		2nd: 1 : 1.67
		3rd: 1 : 1.24
		4th: 1 : 1.00
		5th: 1 : 0.85
		Secondary (chain): 1 : 2.37
		Total Gear Ratio 1st: 1 : 21.19
		2nd: 1 : 13.50
		3rd: 1 : 10.03
		4th: 1 : 8.10
		5th: 1 : 6.86
	Tooth of sprockets:	Front (drive)/Rear (driven): 16/38

5. DIMENSION AND WEIGHT

1)	Overall Length:	1,885mm (74.2 inch)
2)	Overall Width:	750mm (29.5 inch) with Standard Handle bar
3)	Overall Height:	1,020mm (40.2 inch)
4)	Saddle Height:	780mm (30.7 inch)
5)	Wheel Base:	1,235mm (48.6 inch)
6)	Ground Clearance:	150mm (59 inch)
7)	Tire Size (Front):	2.50 - 18 4PR
	(Rear):	2.75 - 18 4PR
8)	Tire Pressure (Front):	1.6kg/cm^2 (22.5 lb/in^2)
	(Rear):	2.0kg/cm^2 (28.5 lb/in^2)
9)	Caster:	64
10)	Trail:	83.5mm (3.29 inch)
11)	Braking Angle:	45
12)	Net Weight:	123kg (271 lbs)
13)	Fuel Tank Capacity:	10 litre (2.64 US Gal)
14)	Oil Tank Capacity:	1.8 litre (3.8 pts)
15)	Front Brake:	Right hand operated.
16)	Rear Brake:	Right Foot operated.

6. ELECTRICAL EQUIPMENT

1)	Head Light:	12V - 35/25W
2)	Tail Light:	12V - 8W
3)	Stop Light:	12V - 25W
4)	Battery:	12V - 6AH

7. OTHERS

1)	Main Footrest:	Folding type
2)	Side Stand:	Original Equipment
3)	Oil Injection:	Original Equipment
4)	Luggage carrier:	None

CONTENTS

Engine Group

Index No.	Description	Page
1)	Cylinder · Cylinder head	4~ 5
2)	Crankshaft · Piston · Rotary valve	6~ 7
3)	Oil pump · Pump gear	8~ 9
4)	Carburetor	10~11
5)	A.C. dynamo · Dynamo cover · Neutral switch	12~13
6)	Crank case ass'y	14~15
7)	Left crank case cover	16~17
8)	Right crank case cover · Carburetor cover	18~19
9)	Clutch	20~21
10)	Transmission	22~23
11)	Change pedal · Shift drum · Sportshift lever	24~25
12)	Kick starter shaft · Kick starter arm	26~27

Body Group

Index No.	Description	Page
13)	Frame · Footrest	28~29
14)	Rear fender · Tool box	30~31
15)	Main stand · Side stand · Brake pedal	32~33
16)	Front fender · Handle bar · Back mirror	34~35
17)	Front fork · Steering damper	36~37
18)	Rear fork · Rear cushions	38~39
19)	Fuel tank · Fuel cock · Oil tank	40~41
20)	Left handle grip · Clutch lever · Starter lever	42~43
21)	Right handle grip · Front brake lever	44~45
22)	Speedometer cable · Throttle wire	46~47
23)	Mufflers · Exhaust pipes	48~49
24)	Dual seat · Air cleaner · Covers	50~51
25)	Front wheel	52~53
26)	Rear wheel	54~55
27)	Head lamp · Tail lamp · Speedometer	56~57
29)	Horn · Ignition coil · Main switch · Battery	58~59
28)	Service tool set	60~61

1) CYLINDER—CYLINDER HEAD

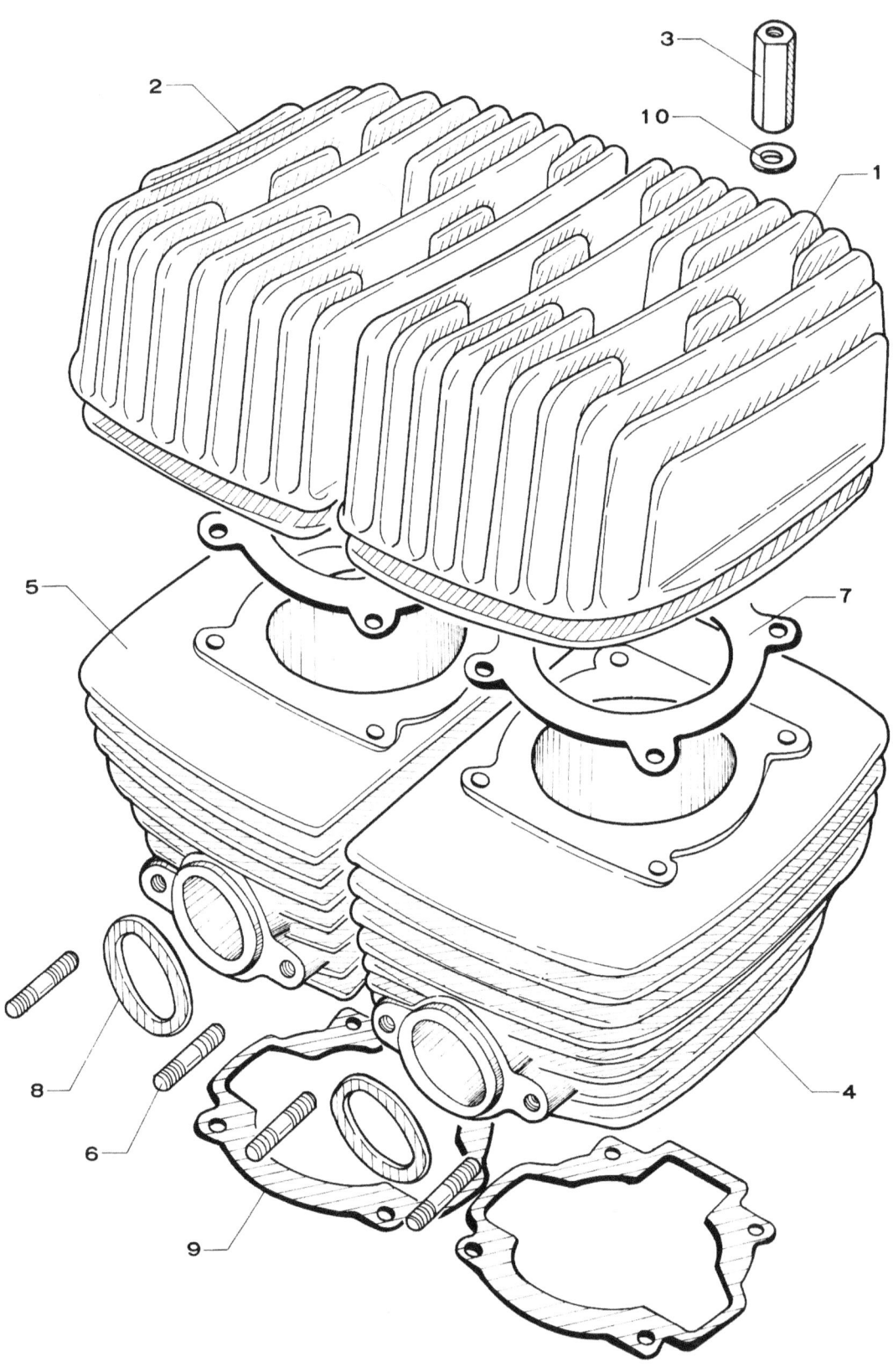

1) CYLINDER—CYLINDER HEAD

Index No.	Part No.	Part Name	No. Req'd	Unit Price		Interchangeability						
				US $	£	7D	7S	HM	50SP	60SP	90	90M
1- 1	1112-8000	Left, Cylinder head	1									
1- 2	1113-8000	Right, Cylinder head	1									
1- 3	1115-8000	Cylinder head nut	8									
1- 4	1122-8000	Left, Cylinder	1									
1- 5	1123-8000	Right, Cylinder	1									
1- 6	09016-101	6×40 stud	4									
1- 7	1141-8000	Cylinder head gasket	2									
1- 8	1142-5000	Exhaust pipe gasket	2									○	○
1- 9	1143-8000	Cylinder base gasket	2									
1-10	09041-111	7 plane washer	8									

Remarks

Interchangeability

Index No.	New Part No.		Old Part No.
1-8	1142-5000	=	EA1-11412......Gasket (exhaust)

2) CRANKSHAFT PISTON ROTARY VALVE

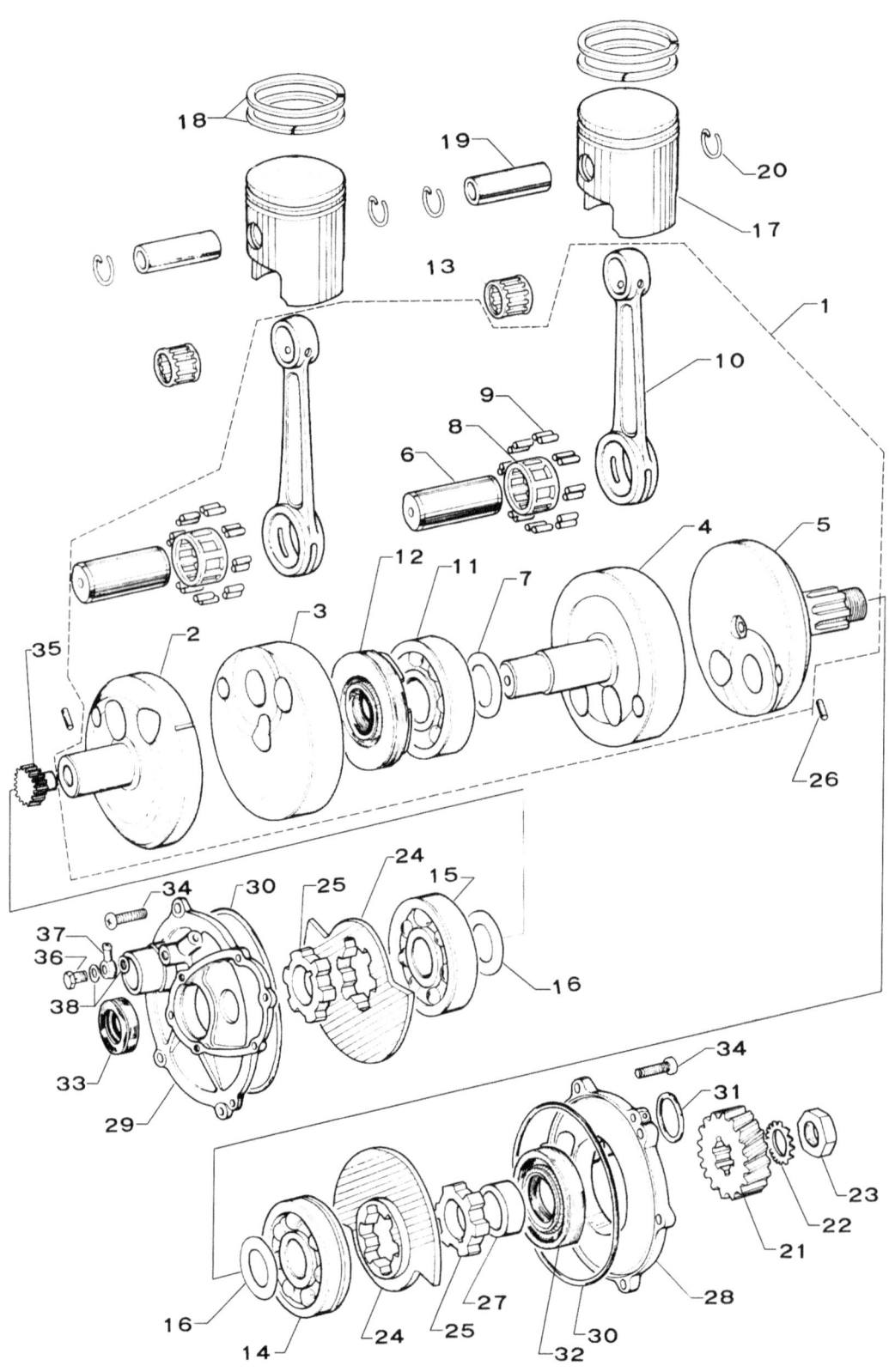

2) CRANKSHAFT—PISTON—ROTARY VALVE

Index No.	Part No.	Part Name	No. Req'd	Unit Price US $	Unit Price £	7D	7S	HM	50SP	60SP	90	90M
2-1	1301-8000	Crankshaft comp.	1									
2-2	1313-8000	Left, crankshaft A	1									
2-3	1314-8000	Left, crankshaft B	1									
2-4	1315-8000	Right, crankshaft A	1									
2-5	1316-8000	Right, crankshaft B	1									
2-6	1321-8000	Crank pin	2									
2-7	09049-106	20×0.3 shim	1								○	○
2-8	1326-5000	Needle roller retainer	2								○	○
2-9	09063-102	3×9.5 Needle roller	32								○	○
2-10	1331-5010	Connecting rod	2									
2-11	09075-101	Ball bearing	1									
2-12	09090-110	20 oil seal	1									
2-13	1333-5010	Needle bearing	2									
2-14	09075-102	Ball bearing	1									
2-15	07-6304-03	Ball bearing	1									
2-16	09049-106	20×0.3 shim	2								○	○
2-17	1341-8000	Piston	2									
2-18	1305-5010	Piston ring kit	2									
2-19	1381-5000	Piston pin	2								○	○
2-20	1382-5000	Piston pin circlip	4								○	○
2-21	1385-8000	Drive pinion	1									
2-22	09045-102	14 external toothed washer	1									
2-23	09029-101	14 left thread nut	1									
2-24	1412-8000	Rotary valve	2									
2-25	1413-8000	Valve guide	2									
2-26	09063-104	3×10 needle roller	2						○	○	○	○
2-27	1451-8000	Crankshaft collar	1									
2-28	1403-8000	Rotary valve cover comp	1									
2-29	1404-8000	Left cover	1									
2-30	09066-103	100 O ring	2								○	○
2-31	09066-104	23 O ring	1								○	○
2-32	09090-109	28 oil seal	1						○	○		
2-33	09090-113	20 oil seal	1									
2-34	0311-0616	Cross rec'd pan head screw	10									
2-35	1551-8000	Pump gear A	1									
2-36	1564-8000	Union bolt	1									
2-37	1565-8000	Union connector	1									
2-38	09064-102	6mm fiber gasket	2			○	○	○	○	○	○	○

Remarks

Index No.	New Part No.		Old Part No.	Index No.	New Part No.		Old Part No.
2-7	09049-106	=	EA1-13411	2-18	1305-5010	=	EA2-13320
2-8	1326-5000	=	EA1-13152	2-26	09063-104	=	GB2-13413
2-9	09063-102	=	EA1-13153	2-30	09066-103	=	EA1-14132
2-10	1331-5010	=	EA2-13211	2-31	09066-104	=	EA1-14133
2-13	1333-5010	=	EA2-13212	2-32	09066-109	=	GB1-14141
2-19	1381-5000	=	EA1-13331	2-38	09064-102	=	E02632
2-20	1382-5000	=	EA1-13332				

3) OIL PUMP — PUMP GEAR

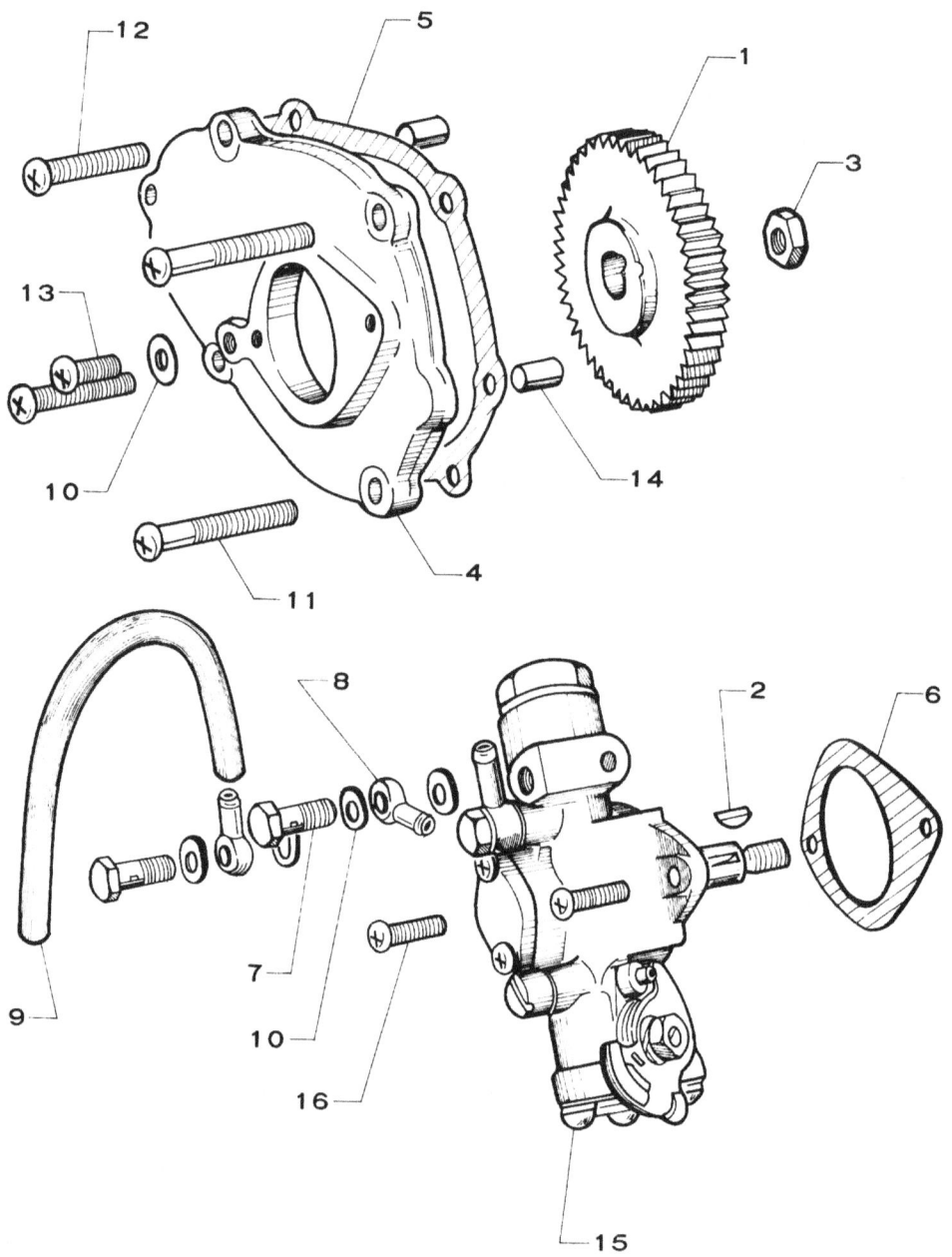

— 8 —

3) OIL PUMP—PUMP GEAR

Index No.	Part No.	Part Name	No. Req'd	Unit Price US $	£	7D	7S	HM	50SP	60SP	90	90M
3- 1	1552-8000	Pump gear B	1									
3- 2	0671-2510	Woodruf key	1									
3- 3	0211-0600	Hex. nut A	1									
3- 4	1561-8000	Pump gear case	1									
3- 5	1562-8000	Gear case gasket	1									
3- 6	1563-8000	Pump gasket	1									
3- 7	1564-8000	Union bolt	2									
3- 8	1565-8000	Union connector	2									
3- 9	1567-8000	Oil tube B	1									
3-10	09064-102	6 fiber gasket	4			○	○	○	○	○	○	○
3-11	0311-0635	Cross rec'd pan head screw	2									
3-12	0311-0616	Cross rec'd pan head screw	2									
3-13	0311-0608	Cross rec'd pan head screw	1									
3-14	09062-104	6×10 roller	2						○	○	○	○
3-15	1501-8000	Oil pump ass'y	1									
3-16	0311-0512	Cross rec'd pan head screw	2									

Remarks

Interchangeability

Index No.	New Part No.		Old Part No.
3-10	09064-102	=	E02632 ....6mm fiber packing
3-14	09062-104	=	EA1-22231......6×10 roller

4) CARBURETOR

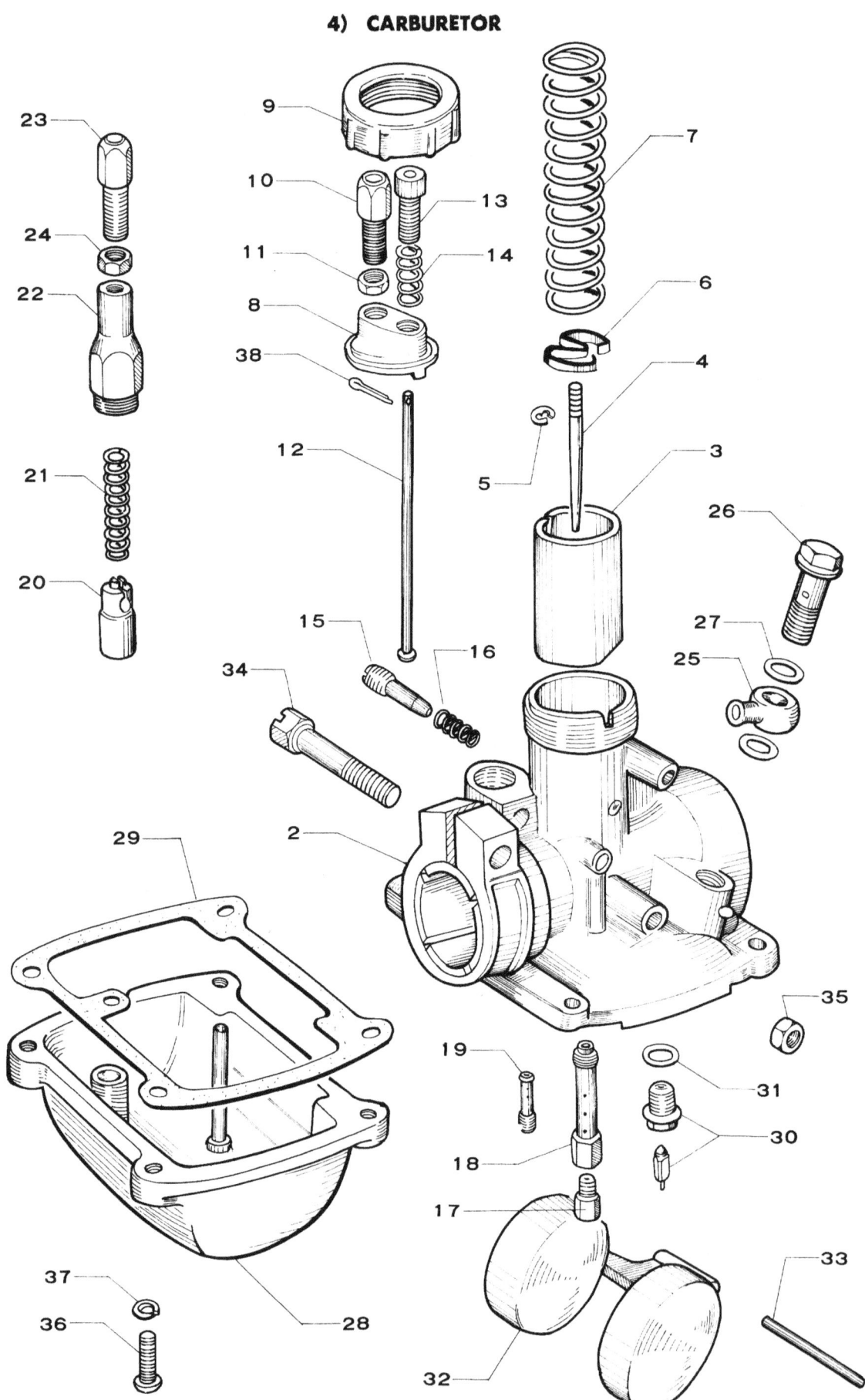

— 10 —

4) CARBURETOR

Index No.	Part No.	Part Name	No. Req'd	Unit Price US $	Unit Price £	7D	7S	HM	50SP	60SP	90	90M
4-1	1600-8000	Carburetor ass'y	2									
4-2	1611-5010	Mixing chamber body	2									
4-3	1614-8000	Throttle valve	2									
4-4	1615-5010	Jet needle	2									
4-5	1616-5010	Needle clip	2									
4-6	1617-5010	Spring seat	2									
4-7	1618-5010	Throttle valve spring	2									
4-8	1619-5010	Mixing chamber top	2									
4-9	1621-5010	Mixing chamber cap	2									
4-10	1622-5000	Cable adjuster	2						○	○	○	○
4-11	1623-5000	Adjuster lock nut	2						○	○	○	○
4-12	1626-5010	Throttle stop rod	2									
4-13	1627-5010	Throttle stop screw	2									
4-14	1628-5010	Stop screw spring	2									
4-15	1631-3010	Pilot air screw	2			○	○	○				
4-16	1632-3010	Air screw spring	2			○	○	○	○	○	○	○
4-17	1635-5010-100	100 main jet	2						○	○	○	○
4-18	1633-8000	Needle jet	2									
4-19	1634-8000	Pilot jet	2									
4-20	1645-5000	Starter plunger	2						○	○	○	○
4-21	1646-5000	Plunger spring	2						○	○	○	○
4-22	1647-5010	Plunger cap	2									
4-23	1622-5000	Cable adjuster	2						○	○	○	○
4-24	1623-5000	Adjuster lock nut	2						○	○	○	○
4-25	1652-5010	Connecting union	2						○	○	○	○
4-26	1651-5000	Union bolt	2					○	○	○	○	○
4-27	1654-3100	Union gasket	4					○	○	○	○	○
4-28	1656-5010	Float chamber body	2									
4-29	1657-5010	Float chamber gasket	2									
4-30	1660-3100	Float valve ass'y	2						○	○	○	○
4-31	1665-3100	Valve seat gasket	2						○	○	○	○
4-32	1666-5010	Float	2									
4-33	1667-3100	Float pin	2						○	○	○	○
4-34	1613-5010	Clamp screw	2									
4-35	0211-0600	Hexagon nut A	2									
4-36	0311-0414	Cross rec'd pan head screw	8						○	○	○	○
4-37	0431-0410	Spring washer	8						○	○	○	○
4-38	0551-1010	Spilit pin	2						○	○	○	○

Remarks

Interchangeability

Index No.	New Part No.		Old Part No.	
3-15	1631-3010	=	E28134	Pilot air screw
3-16	1632-3010	=	E28135	Spring (air screw)
3-17	1682-5000	=	EA1-16141	Main jet (#100)
3-20	1645-5000	=	EA1-16161	Starter planger
3-21	1646-5000	=	EA1-16162	Plunger spring
3-10	1622-5000	=	EA1-16128	Cable adjuster
3-11	1623-5000	=	EA1-16129	Lock nut
3-25	1651-5000	=	EA1-16152	Union connection
3-30	1660-3100	=	GA1-16170	Float needle value ass'y
3-31	1665-3100	=	GA1-16173	Packing (needle seat)
3-33	1667-3100	=	GA1-16182	Float pin
3-26	1651-5000	=	EA1-16151	Union bolt
3-27	1654-3100	=	EA1-16153	Union washer

5) DYNAMO · DYNAMO COVER · NEUTRAL SWITCH

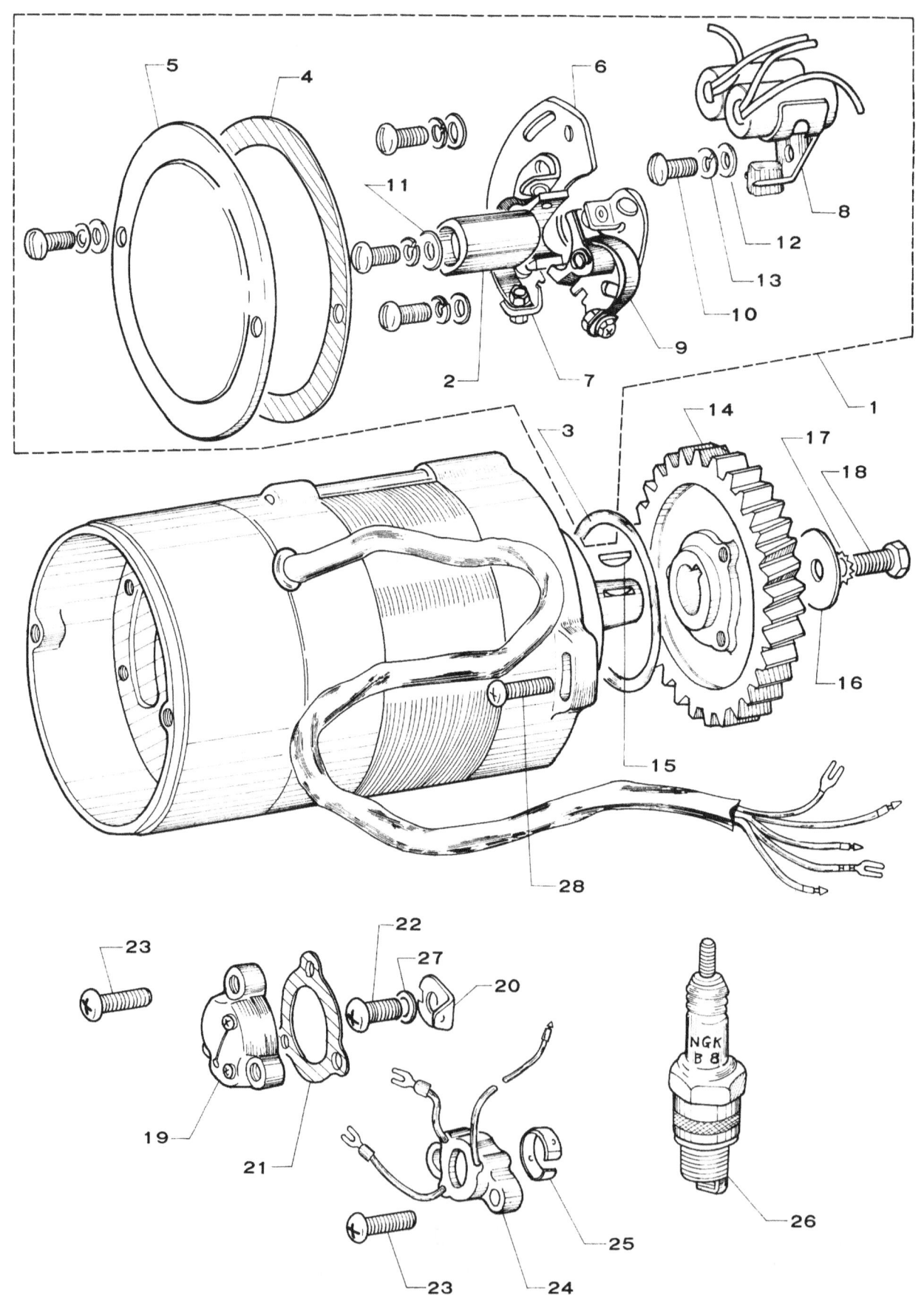

5) DYNAMO · DYNAMO COVER · NEUTRAL SWITCH

Index No.	Part No.	Part Name	No. Req'd	Unit Price US$	£	7D	7S	HM	50SP	60SP	90	90M
5- 1	1703-8000	A · C Dynamo assembly	1									
5- 2	1736-8000	Contact breaker cam	1									
5- 3	1737-8000	O ring	1									
5- 4	1738-8000	Contact breaker cover gasket	1									
5- 5	1739-8000	Contact breaker cover	1									
5- 6	1751-8000	Contact breaker base	1									
5- 7	1752-8000	Left, contact breaker ass'y	1									
5- 8	1753-8000	Condenser	1									
5- 9	1757-8000	Right, contact breaker ass'y	1									
5-10	0361-0408	Pan head screw	10									
5-11	0411-0410	Plane washer A	1									
5-12	0421-0408	Plane washer B	9									
5-13	0431-0410	Spring washer	10									
5-14	1741-8000	Timing gear	1									
5-15	0671-3013	Woodruf key	1			○	○	○	○	○	○	○
5-16	09041-112	6 plane washer	1									
5-17	0451-0611	External toothed washer	1									
5-18	0113-0612	Hexagon bolt A	1									
5-19	1761-8000	Neutral switch case	1									
5-20	1762-8000	Neutral switch contact plate	1									
5-21	1763-8000	Neutral switch gasket	1									
5-22	0311-0610	Cross rec'd pan head screw	1									
5-23	0311-0516	Cross rec'd pan head screw	5									
5-24	1767-8000	Neutral change case	1									
5-25	1768-8000	Neutral change plate	1									
5-26	1781-8000	Spark plug (NGK B-8H)	2									
5-27	0411-0613	Plane washer A	1									
5-28	0311-0520	Cross rec'd pan head screw	1									

Remarks

Interchangeability

Index No.	New Part No.		Old Part No.
5-15	09067-101	=	E03314......3mm woodruf key

6) CRANK CASE ASS'Y

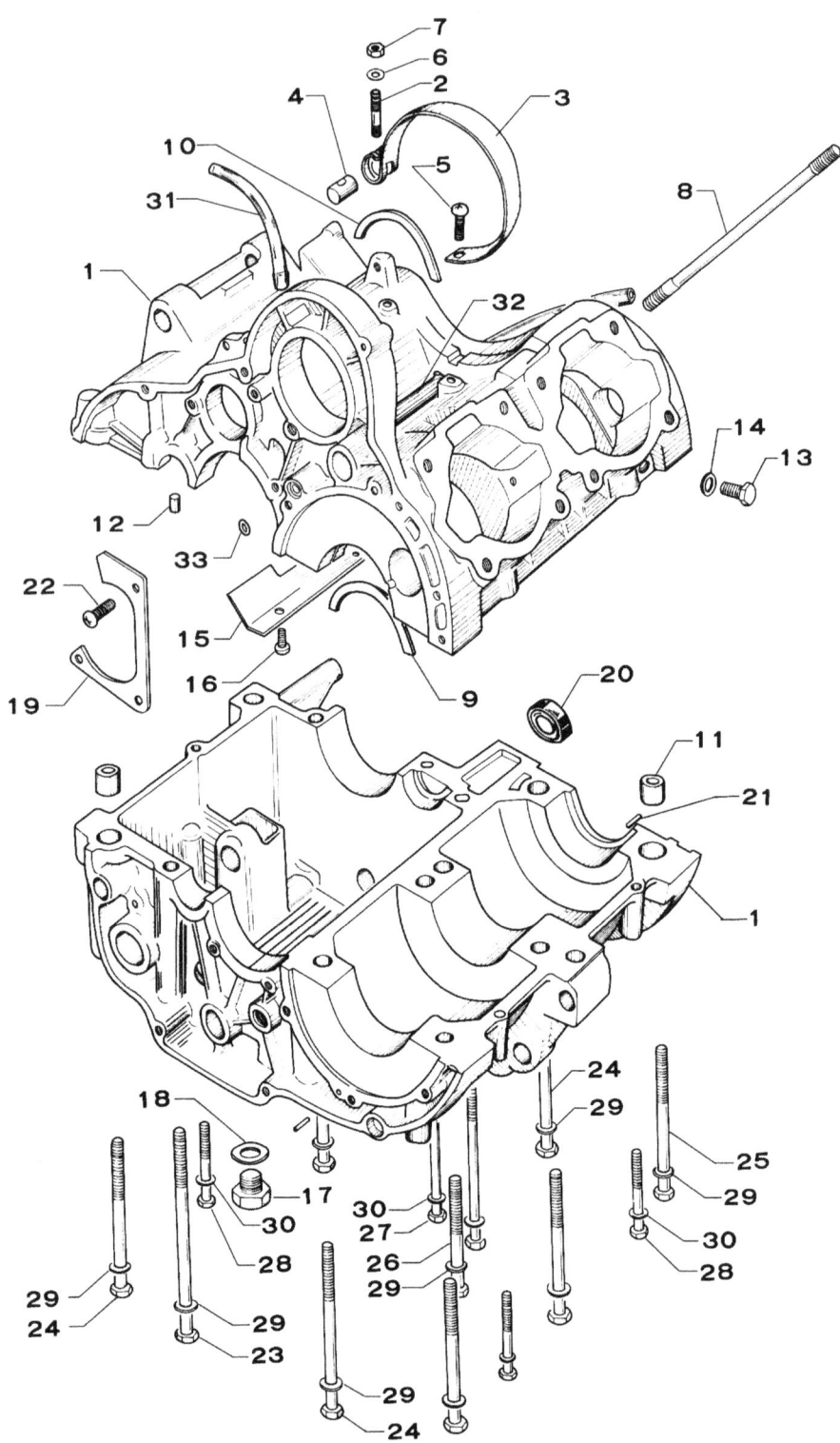

- 14 -

6) CRANK CASE ASS'Y

Index No.	Part No.	Part Name	No. Req'd	Unit Price US $	£	7D	7S	HM	50SP	60SP	90	90M
6- 1	2101-8000	Crank case ass'y	1									
6- 2	09016-101	6×40 stud	1									
6- 3	2117-8000	Dynamo set band	1									
6- 4	2118-8000	Dynamo set pin	1									
6- 5	0311-0610	Cross rec'd pan head screw	1									
6- 6	0411-0613	Plane washer A	1									
6- 7	0211-0600	Hexagon nut A	1									
6- 8	2121-8000	Cylinder mounting stud	8									
6- 9	2122-8000	Bearing retainer A	1									
6-10	2123-8000	Bearing retainer B	1									
6-11	09057-102	8×12×14B Dowel	2									
6-12	09062-104	6×10 roller	1							○	○	○	○
6-13	0111-0812	Hexagon bolt A	1									
6-14	09064-103	8 fiber gasket	1									
6-15	2128-8000	Oil buffle plate	1									
6-16	0311-0510	Cross rec'd pan head screw	2									
6-17	09058-102	16 drain plug	1								○	○
6-18	09065-102	16 alminum gasket	1								○	○
6-19	2145-8000	Counter shaft bearing holder	1									
6-20	09090-101	12 oil seal	1			○	○	○	○	○	○	○
6-21	09056-102	4×8A dowel	2									
6-22	0311-0612	Cross rec'd pan head screw	3									
6-23	09011-102	8×100 hexagon bolt	1									
6-24	0113-0890	Hexagon bolt A	3									
6-25	0113-0880	Hexagon bolt A	4									
6-26	0113-0862	Hexagon bolt A	1									
6-27	09011-103	6×90 hexagon bolt	2									
6-28	0113-0645	Hex. bolt A	3									
6-29	0411-0818	Plane washer A	9									
6-30	0411-0613	Plane washer A	5									
6-31	2135-5000	Breather vinyl tube	1									
6-32	1566-8000	Oil tube A	1									
6-33	09066-106	7 O ring	1									

Remarks

Interchangeability

Index No.	New Part No.		Old Part No.	
6-12	09062-104	=	EA1-22231	6×10 roller
6-17	09058-102	=	EA1-21334	Drain cock
6-18	09065-102	=	EA1 21335	Drain packing
6-20	09090-101	=	E02614	12mm oil seal

7) LEFT CRANK CASE COVER

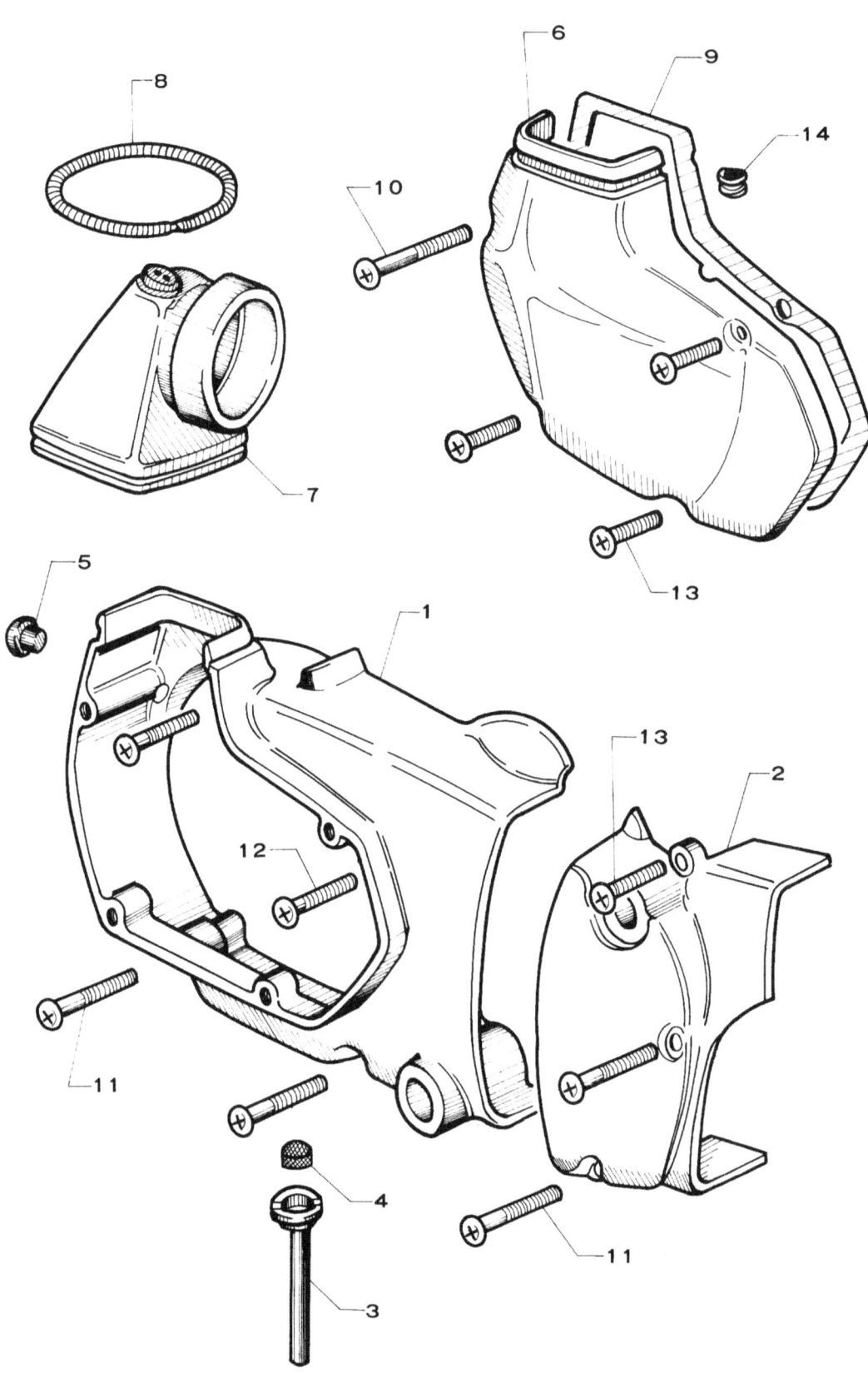

— 16 —

7) LEFT CRANK CASE COVER

Index No.	Part No.	Part Name	No. Req'd	Unit Price		Interchangeability						
				US $	£	7D	7S	HM	50SP	60SP	90	90M
7- 1	2151-8000	Left crank case cover	1									
7- 2	2153-8000	Dust cover A	1									
7- 3	2162-5001	Drain pipe	1						○	○	○	○
7- 4	2163-5001	Drain filter	1						○	○	○	○
7- 5	2168-5000	12 rubber plug	1						○	○	○	○
7- 6	2171-8000	Left carburetor cover	1									
7- 7	2172-8000	Left carburetor cap	1									
7- 8	2178-5010	Carburetor cap ring	1									
7- 9	2185-8000	Carburetor cover gasket	1									
7-10	0311-0635	Cross rec'd pan head screw	1									
7-11	0311-0630	Cross rec'd pan head screw	4									
7-12	0311-0625	Cross rec'd pan head screw	2									
7-13	0311-0620	Cross rec'd pan head screw	4									
7-14	2173-8000	Oil tube grommet	1									

Remarks

Interchangeability

Index No.	New Part No.		Old Part No.
7-3	2162-5001	=	EA1-21321-1......Drain pipe
7-4	2163-5001	=	EA1-21322-1......Filter comp.
7-5	2168-5000	=	EA1-21337.........12mm rubber plug

8) RIGHT CRANK CASE COVER, CARBURETOR COVER

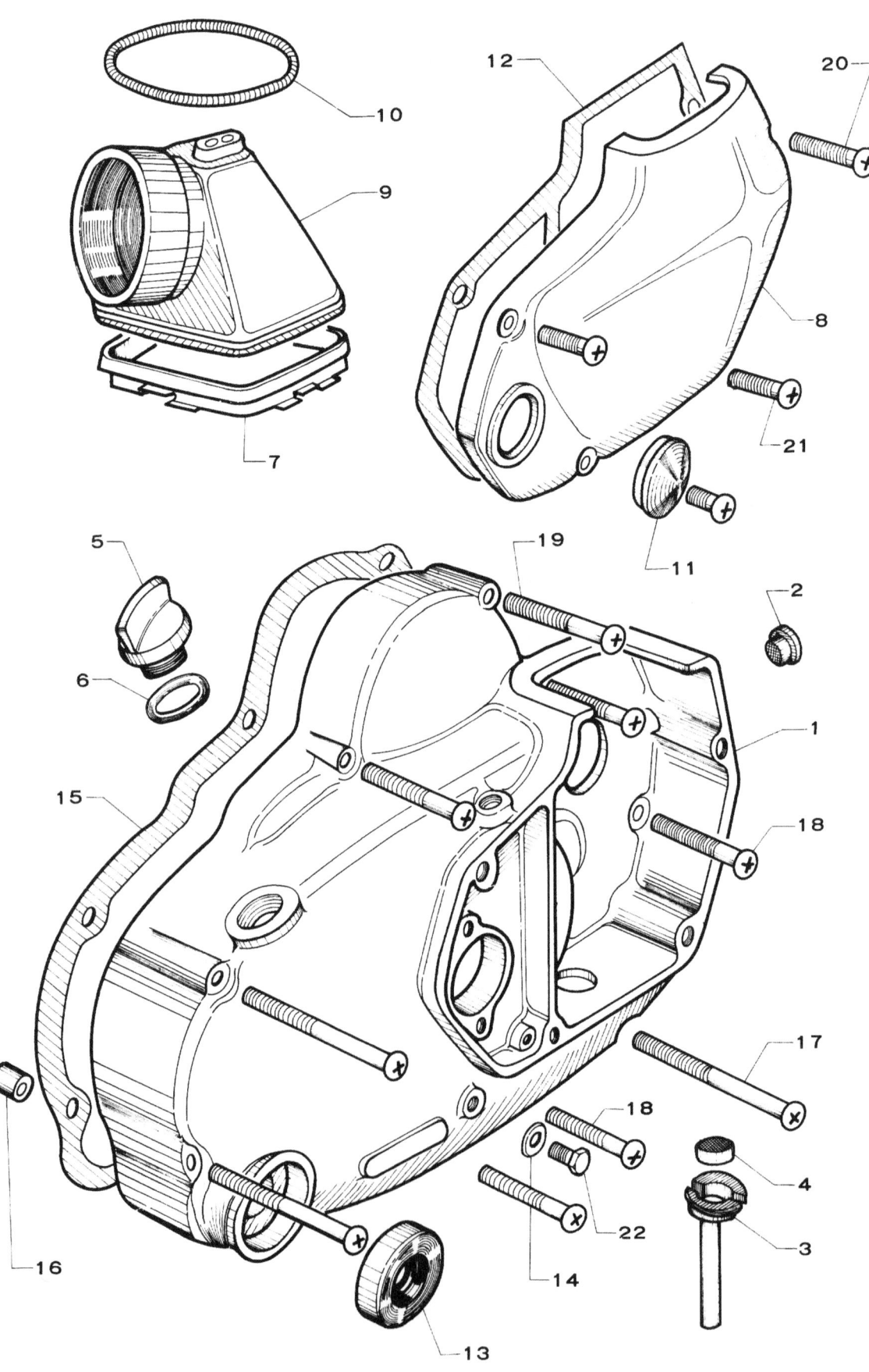

8) RIGHT CRANK CASE COVER, CARBURETOR COVER

Index No.	Part No.	Part Name	No. Req'd	Unit Price US $	£	7D	7S	HM	50SP	60SP	90	90M
8- 1	2161-8000	Right crank case cover	1									
8- 2	2168-5000	12 rubber plug	1						○	○	○	○
8- 3	2162-5001	Drain pipe	1						○	○	○	○
8- 4	2163-5001	Drain filter	1						○	○	○	○
8- 5	2165-8000	Oil filler plug	1									
8- 6	09066-107	21 O ring	1									
8- 7	2174-8000	Carburetor cap guide	1									
8- 8	2176-8000	Carburetor cover	1									
8- 9	2177-8000	Carburetor cap	1									
8-10	2178-5010	Carburetor cap ring	1									
8-11	2179-5000	Release screw cap	1						○	○	○	○
8-12	2185-8000	Carburetor cover gasket	1									
8-13	09090-112	18 oil seal	1									
8-14	09064-102	6 fiber gasket	1			○	○	○	○	○	○	○
8-15	2183-8000	Crank case cover gasket	1									
8-16	09057-101	6×10×10B dewel	2			○	○	○	○	○	○	○
8-17	0311-0665	Cross rec'd pan head screw	3									
8-18	0311-0635	Cross rec'd pan head screw	4									
8-19	0311-0640	Cross rec,d pan head rcrew	2									
8-20	0311-0625	Cross rec'd pan head screw	1									
8-21	0311-0620	Cross rec'd pan head screw	3									
8-22	0111-0610	Hexagon bolt A	1									

Remarks

Interchangeability

Index No.	New Part No.		Old Part No.	
8- 2	2168-5000	=	EA1-21337	12mm rubber plug
8- 3	2162-5001	=	EA1-21321-1	Drain pipe
8- 4	2163-5001	=	EA1-1322-1	Filter comp.
8- 5	2165-5000	=	EA1-21332	Oil cock
8-11	2179-5000	=	EA1-21352	Release cap
8-14	09064-102	=	E02632	6mm fiber gasket
8-16	09057-101	=	E02516	Knock (crank case)

9) CLUTCH

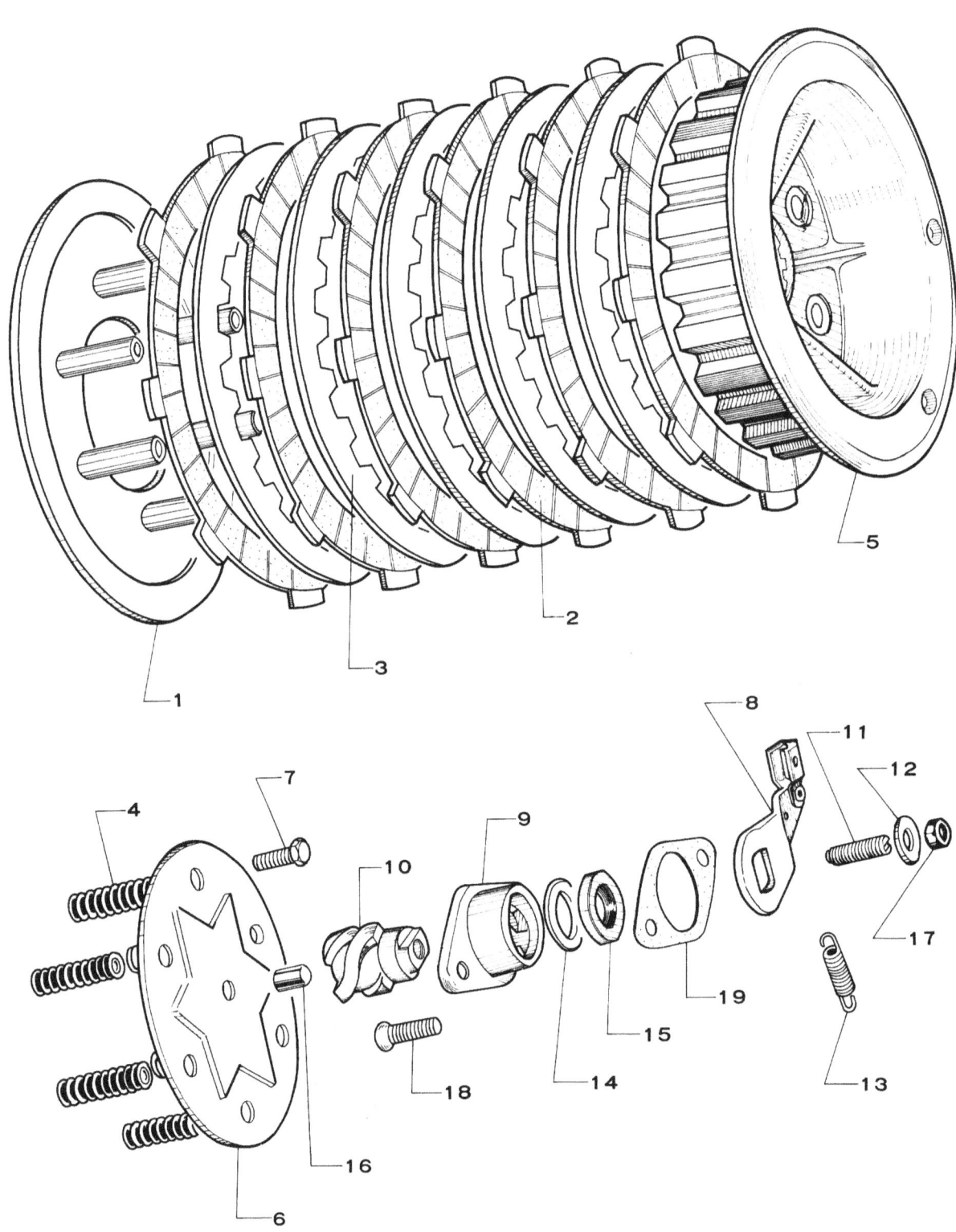

9) CLUTCH

Index No.	Part No.	Part Name	No. Req'd	Unit Price US $	£	Interchangeability 7D	7S	HM	50SP	60SP	90	90M
9- 1	2210-8000	Pressure plate comp.	1									
9- 2	2214-8000	Friction plate	6									
9- 3	2215-8000	Inner plate	5									
9- 4	2218-5010	Clutch spring	6									
9- 5	2221-8000	Clutch hub	1									
9- 6	2227-8000	Set plate comp.	1									
9- 7	0113-0512	Hexagon bolt A	6									
9- 8	2260-5000	Release arm comp.	1						○	○	○	○
9- 9	2264-5000	Release screw	1						○	○	○	○
9-10	2265-5000	Release push screw	1						○	○	○	○
9-11	2267-5000	Release adjust screw	1						○	○	○	○
9-12	2268-5000	Release adjust screw washer	1						○	○	○	○
9-13	2271-5000	Release arm return spring	1						○	○	○	○
9-14	2272-5000	Release guide washer	1									
9-15	09090-102	15 oil seal	1						○	○	○	○
9-16	09062-104	6×10 roller	1						○	○	○	○
9-17	0211-0600	Hexagon nut A	1									
9-18	0331-0614	Cross rec'd flat head screw	2									
9-19	2186-5000	Release screw gasket	1						○	○	○	○

Remarks

Interchangeability

Index No.	New Part No.		Old Part No.
9- 8	2260-5000	=	EA1-22221......Release arm comp.
9- 9	2264-5000	=	EA1-22225......Release screw
9-10	2265-5000	=	EA1-22226......Release push screw
9-11	2267-5000	=	EA1-22227......Adj. screw
9-12	2268-5000	=	EA1-22228......Washer (adjust screw)
9-13	2271-5000	=	EA1-22229......Release return spring
9-14	2272-5000	=	EA1-22232......Guide wasker
9-15	09090-102	=	EA1-22230......15mm oil seal
9-16	09062-104	=	EA1-22231......6×10mm roller
9-19	2186-5000	=	EA1-21515......Packing (release screw)

10) TRANSMISSION

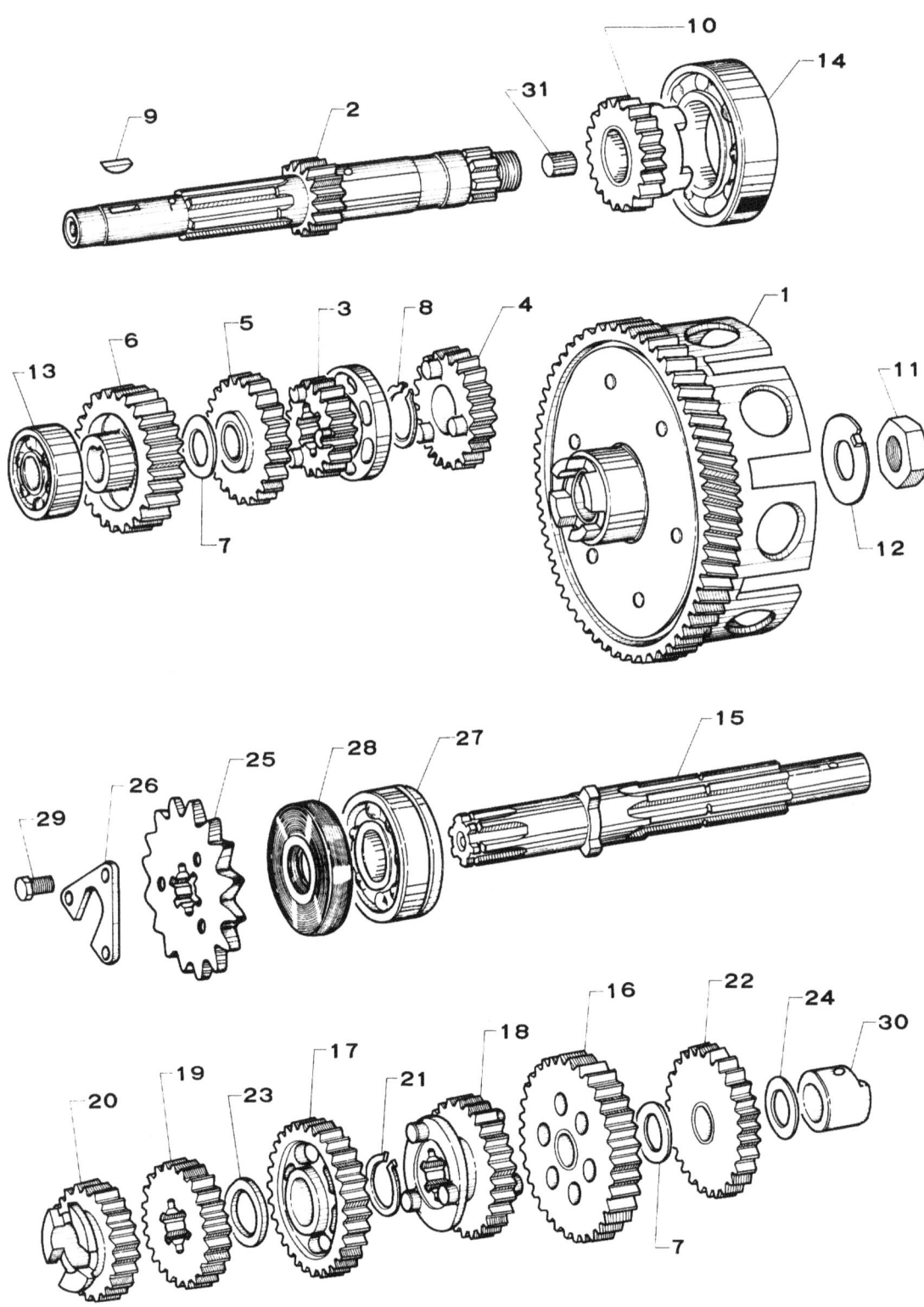

-22-

10) TRANSMISSION

Index No.	Part No.	Part Name	No. Req'd	Unit Price US$	£	7D	7S	HM	50SP	60SP	90	90M
10- 1	2410-8000	Driven gear comp.	1									
10- 2	2421-8000	Counter shaft	1									
10- 3	2426-8000	2nd gear A	1									
10- 4	2431-8000	3rd gear A	1									
10- 5	2436-8000	4th gear A	1									
10- 6	2441-8000	5th gear A	1									
10- 7	09048-104	15 thrust washer	2									
10- 8	09002-105	20B snap ring	1									
10- 9	09067-101	3×15 woodnuf key	1			○	○	○	○	○	○	○
10-10	2611-8000	Kick starter gear A	1									
10-11	09021-102	16 hexagon nut	1								○	○
10-12	09047-104	16 lock washer	1									
10-13	07-6202-41	Ball bearing	1									
10-14	07-6007-01	Ball bearing	1									
10-15	2446-8000	Drive shaft	1									
10-16	2451-8000	1st gear B	1									
10-17	2456-8000	2nd gear B	1									
10-18	2461-8000	3rd gear B	1									
10-19	2466-8000	4th gear B	1									
10-20	2471-8000	5th gear B	1									
10-21	09002-105	20B snap ring	1									
10-22	2616-8000	Kick starter gear B	1									
10-23	2481-8000	Drive shaft spacer	1									
10-24	09048-104	15 thrust washer	1									
10-25	2484-8000	Drive sprocket	1									
10-26	2485-8000	Sprocket set plate	1									
10-27	07-6304-61	Ball bearing	1									
10-28	09090-111	20 oil seal	1									
10-29	0111-0610	Hexagon bolt A	3									
10-30	2133-8000	Drive shaft bush	1									
10-31	2477-8000	Rubber plug	1									

Remarks

Interchangeability

Index No.	New Part No.		Old Part No.
10- 9	09067-101	=	E03314-0 ......3mm woodruf key
10-11	09021-102	=	EA1-23231......16mm hex. nut

11) CHANGE PEDAL—SHIFT DRUM—SPORTSHIFT LEVER

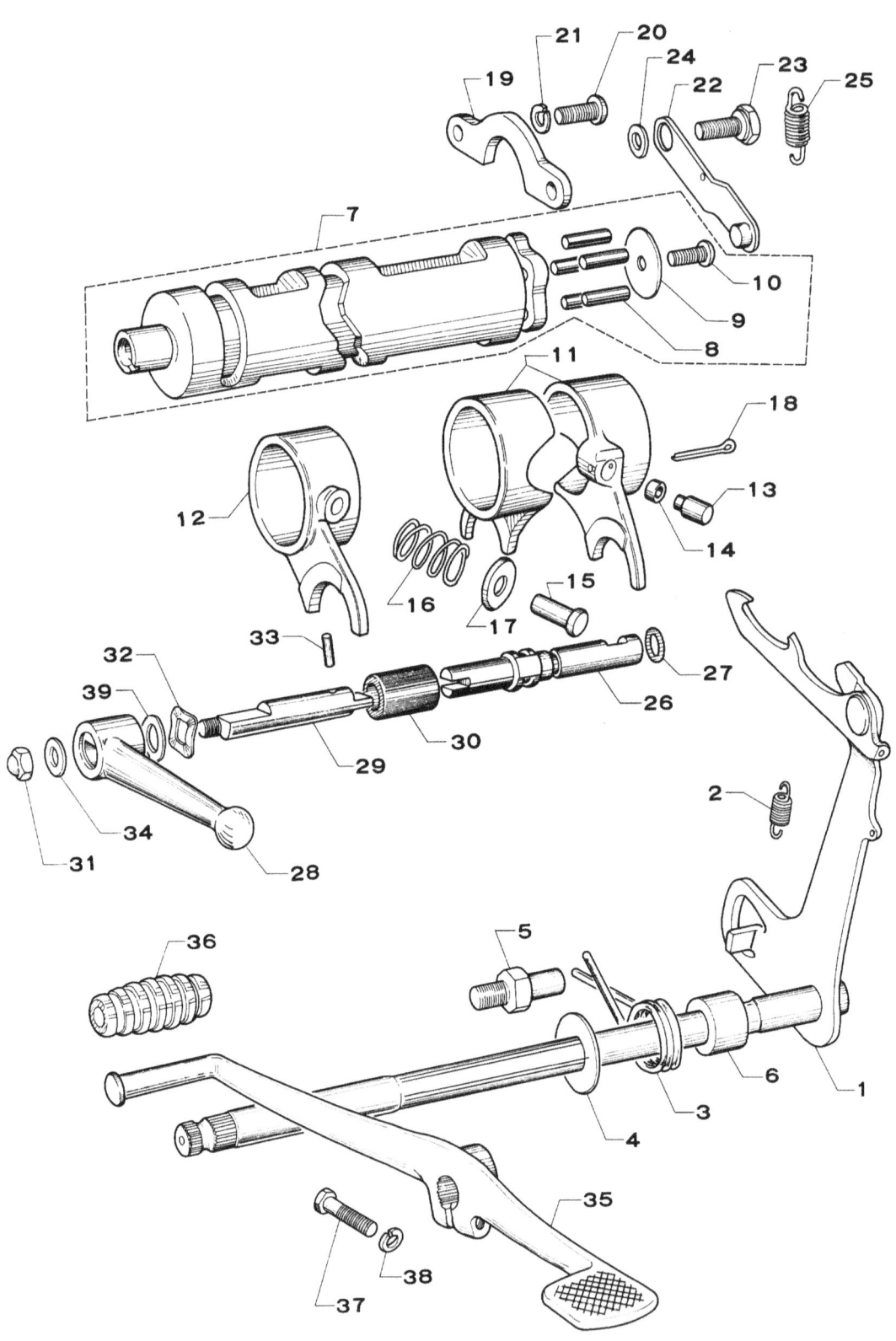

11) CHANGE PEDAL—SHIFT DRUM—SPORTSHIFT LEVER

Index No.	Part No.	Part Name	No. Req'd	Unit Price US $	£	7D	7S	HM	50SP	60SP	90	90M
11- 1	2510-8000	Change arm comp.	1									
11- 2	2517-5000	Drum shifter spring	1						○	○	○	○
11- 3	2551-5000	Change shaft return spring	1						○	○	○	○
11- 4	2552-3001	Change shaft spring seat	1			○	○	○	○	○	○	○
11- 5	2553-5000	Change arm stopper pin	1						○	○	○	○
11- 6	2557-8000	Change shaft spacer	1									
11- 7	2502-8000	Shift drum ass'y	1									
11- 8	2522-3001	Shift pin	5									
11- 9	2524-8000	Shift pin holder	1									
11-10	0311-0512	Cross rec'd pan head screw	1									
11-11	2541-8000	Shift fork A	2									
11-12	2542-8000	Shift fork B	1									
11-13	2544-8000	Fork guide A	2									
11-14	2545-8000	Fork guide roller	2									
11-15	2546-8000	Fork guide B	1									
11-16	2547-8000	Fork guide spring	1									
11-17	2548-8000	Spring holder	1									
11-18	0551-2525	Spilit pin	2									
11-19	2549-5001	Drum guide plate	1								○	○
11-20	0311-0614	Cross rec'd pan head screw	2									
11-21	0432-0615	Spring washer	2									
11-22	2531-8000	Drum stopper arm	1									
11-23	2536-8000	Drum stopper bolt	1									
11-24	09041-112	6 plane washer	1									
11-25	2538-5000	Drum stopper spring	1						○	○	○	○
11-26	2571-8000	Sportshifts shaft	1									
11-27	09066-106	7 O ring	1									
11-28	2574-8000	Sportshift lever	1									
11-29	2575-8000	Sportshift lever shaft	1									
11-30	2576-8000	Sportshift shaft rubber	1									
11-31	09525-104	6 cap nut	1					○				
11-32	09046-102	10 wave washer	1									
11-33	09063-104	3×10 needle roller	1						○	○		
11-34	0411-0613	Plane washer A	1									
11-35	2581-8001	Gear change pedal	1									
11-36	2582-5000	Change pedal rubber	1						○	○	○	○
11-37	0113-0620	Hexagon bolt A	1									
11-38	0432-0615	Spring washer	1									
11-39	09041-113	10 plane washer	1									

Remarks

Interchangeability

Index No.	New Parts No.		Old Parts No.
11- 2	2517-5000	=	EA1-24115...Drum
11- 3	2551-5000	=	EA1-24117...Return spring
11- 4	2552-3001	=	E06114-2 ...Washer 12mm
11- 5	2553-5000	=	EA1-24118...Stopper pin

Interchangeability

Index No.	New Parts No.		Old Parts No.
11-19	2549-5001	=	EA1-24221...Thrust receiver
11-25	2538-5000	=	EA1-24235...Drum stopper spring
11-36	2582-5000	=	EA1-24312...Gear change pedal rubber
11-31	09525-104	=	GA1-31439...Blind nut 6mm

12) KICK STARTER SHAFT — KICK STARTER ARM

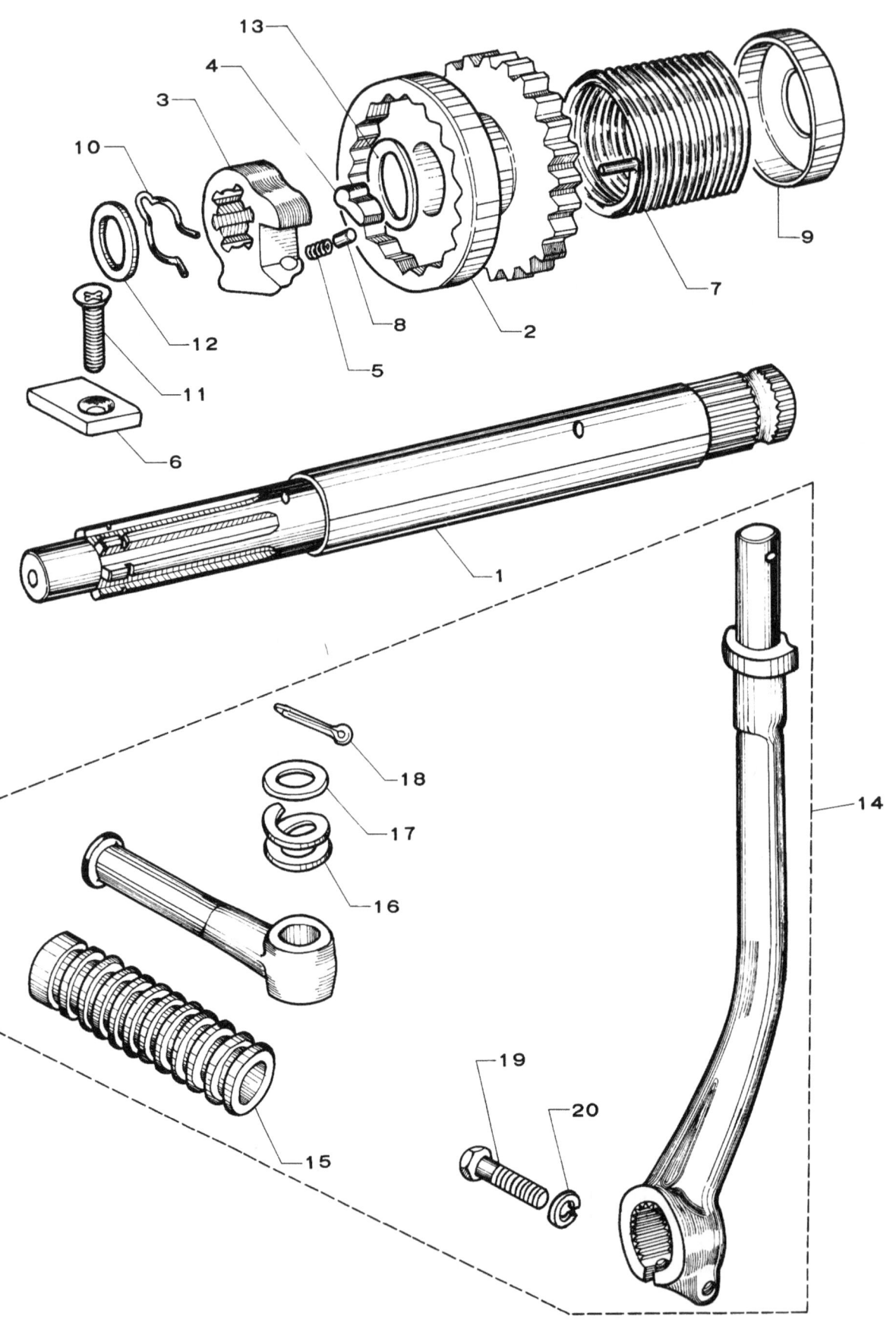

12) KICK STARTER SHAFT—KICK STARTER ARM

Index No.	Part No.	Part Name	No. Req'd	Unit Price US $	£	7D	7S	HM	50SP	60SP	90	90M
12- 1	2621-8000	Kick starter shaft	1									
12- 2	2631-8000	Kick starter gear C	1									
12- 3	2632-8000	Kick starter ratchet arm	1									
12- 4	2633-8000	Kick starter ratchet	1									
12- 5	2634-8000	Kick starter ratchet spring	1									
12- 6	2635-8000	Kick starter ratchet stepper	1									
12- 7	2636-8000	Kick starter return spring	1									
12- 8	2642-8000	Kick starter ratchet pole	1									
12- 9	2643-8000	Return spring holder	1									
12-10	09008-101	16B circlip	1									
12-11	0331-0612	Cross rec'd flat head screw	1									
12-12	09048-103	12 thrust washer	1									
12-13	09048-105	16 thrust washer	1									
12-14	2680-8000	Kick starter arm ass'y	1									
12-15	2683-3011	Kick starter pedal rubber	1							○	○	○	○
12-16	2684-5000	Kick starter pedal spring	1							○	○	○	○
12-17	09041-107	10 plane washer	1							○	○	○	○
12-18	0551-3018	Spilit pin	1									
12-19	0113-0625	Hexagon bolt A	1									
12-20	0431-0615	Spring washer	1									

Remarks
Interchangeability

Index No.	New Part No.		Old Part No.
12-15	2683-3011	=	E18513-1 ......Pedal rubber
12-16	2684-5000	=	EA1-25214......Kick pedal spring washer
12-17	09041-107	=	E18515 ....Washer (kick pedal)

13) FRAME—FOOT RESTS

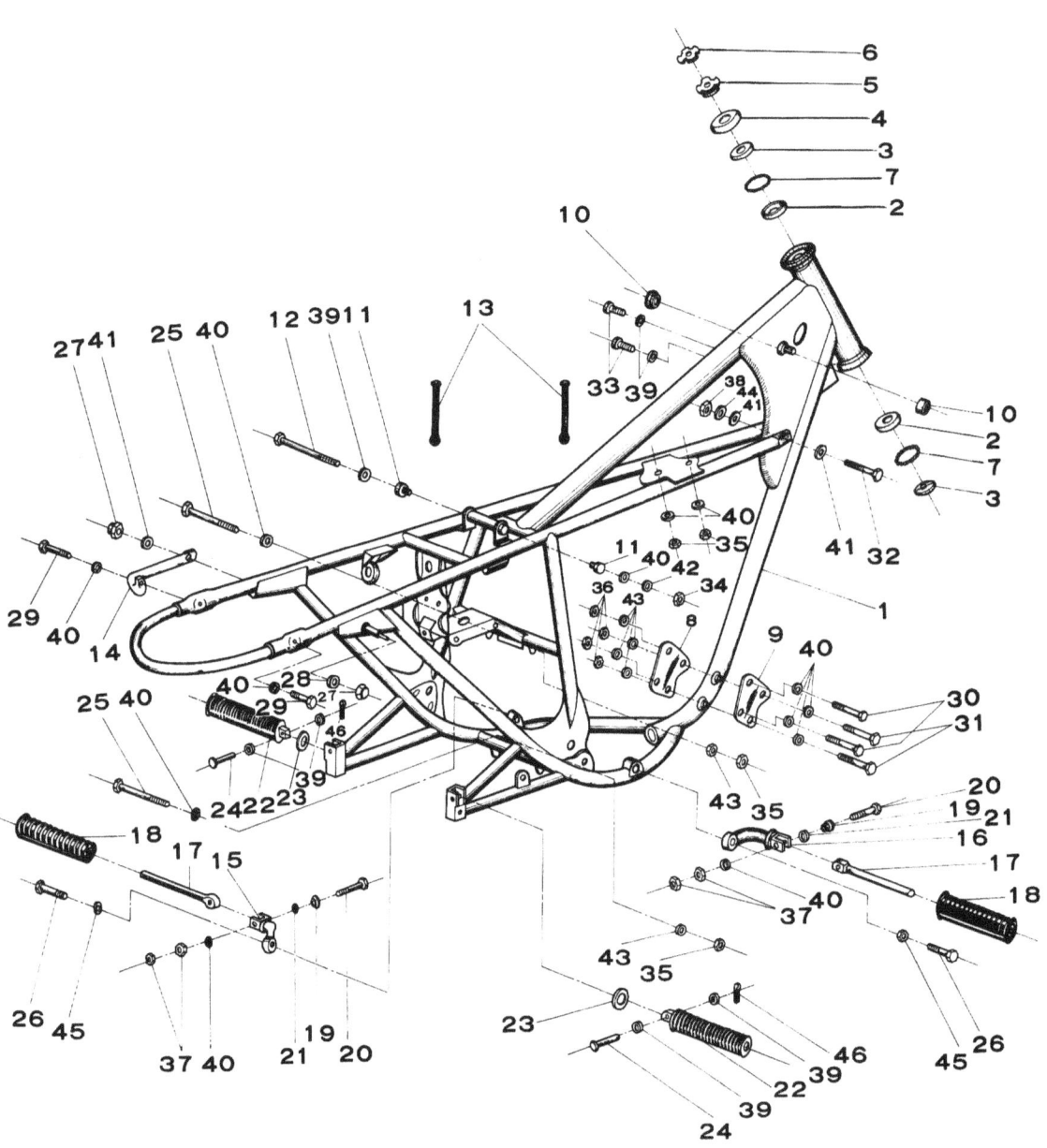

13) FRAME—FOOT RESTS

Index No.	Part No.	Part Name	No. Req'd	Unit Price US$	£	7D	7S	HM	50SP	60SP	90	90M
13- 1	3110-8000	Frame comp.	1									
13- 2	3311-8000	Outer race	2									
13- 3	3313-8000	Inner race	2									
13- 4	3319-8000	Race cap	1									
13- 5	3322-5000	Race adjuster	1								○	○
13- 6	3321-5000	Race lock nut	1								○	○
13- 7	0611-0104	Ball (1/4")	38									
13- 8	3365-8000	Left engine bracket	1									
13- 9	3366-8000	Right engine bracket	1									
13-10	3416-8000	Front tank cushion rubber	2									
13-11	3417-5000	Rear tank cushion rubber	2							○	○	○	○
13-12	3419-5000	Tank mounting bolt	1							○	○	○	○
13-13	3424-3010	Wire harness strap	2										
13-14	3428-8000	Frame handle	1										
13-15	3715-8000	Left foot rest	1										
13-16	3716-8000	Right foot rest	1										
13-17	3711-5010	Foot rest bar	2										
13-18	3721-3002	Foot rest rubber	2			○	○	○	○	○	○	○
13-19	3722-5010	Foot rest mounting spacer	2									○
13-20	3723-5010	Foot nest mounting bolt	2									○
13-21	09546-104	10 wave washer	2									○
13-22	3702-5000	Tandem foot rest comp.	2									○	
13-23	3762-5000	Tandem foot rest washer	2									○	
13-24	3763-5000	Tandem foot rest pin	2									○	
13-25	09511-101	8×108 Hexagon bolt	2										
13-26	09511-127	12×50 Hexagon bolt	2										
13-27	09525-105	10 cap nut	2										
13-28	09541-107	10 plane washer	1							○	○	○	○
13-29	0132-0816	Hexagon bolt C	2										
13-30	0122-0845	Hexagon bolt B	2										
13-31	0122-0856	Hexagon bolt B	2										
13-32	0122-1065	Hexagon bolt B	1										
13-33	0311-0610	Cross rec'd pan head screw	2										
13-34	0211-0600	Hexagon nut A	1										
13-35	0211-0800	Hexagon nut A	4										
13-36	0212-0800	Hexagon nut A	4										
13-37	0231-0800	Hexagon nut C	4										
13-38	0212-1000	Hexagon nut A	1										
13-39	0411-0613	Plane washer A	7										
13-40	0411-0818	Plane washer A	13										
13-41	0411-1022	Plane washer A	3										
13-42	0431-0615	Spring washer	1										
13-43	0431-0820	Spring washer	6										
13-44	0431-1025	Spring washer	1										
13-45	0431-1230	Spring washer	2										
13-46	0552-1612	Spilit pin	2										

Remarks

Interchangeability

Index No.	New Part No.		Old Part No.	
13- 6	3321-5000	=	EA1-31414	......Lock nut
13- 5	3322-5000	=	EA1-31415	......Adjusting nut
13-11	3417-5000	=	EA1-31424	......Rear set rubber (tank)
13-12	3419-5000	=	EA1-31425	......Tank set bolt
13-27	09525-105	=	EA1-31428	......10mm Blind nut
13-28	09541-107	=	EA1-31432	......Washer 10mm
13-17	3711-5010	=	EA13-67121	......Rubber shaft
13-18	3721-3002	=	M08421-2	......Foot rest rubber
13-19	3722-5010	=	EA13-67122	......Space washer
13-20	3723-5010	=	EA13-67124	......Bolt
13-21	09546-104	=	EA13-67123	......Wave washer
13-22	3702-5000	=	EA1-67300	......Tandem foot rest comp.
13-23	3762-5000	=	EA1-67322	......Washer
13-24	3763-5000	=	EA1-67323	......Pin

14) REAR FENDER—TOOL BOX

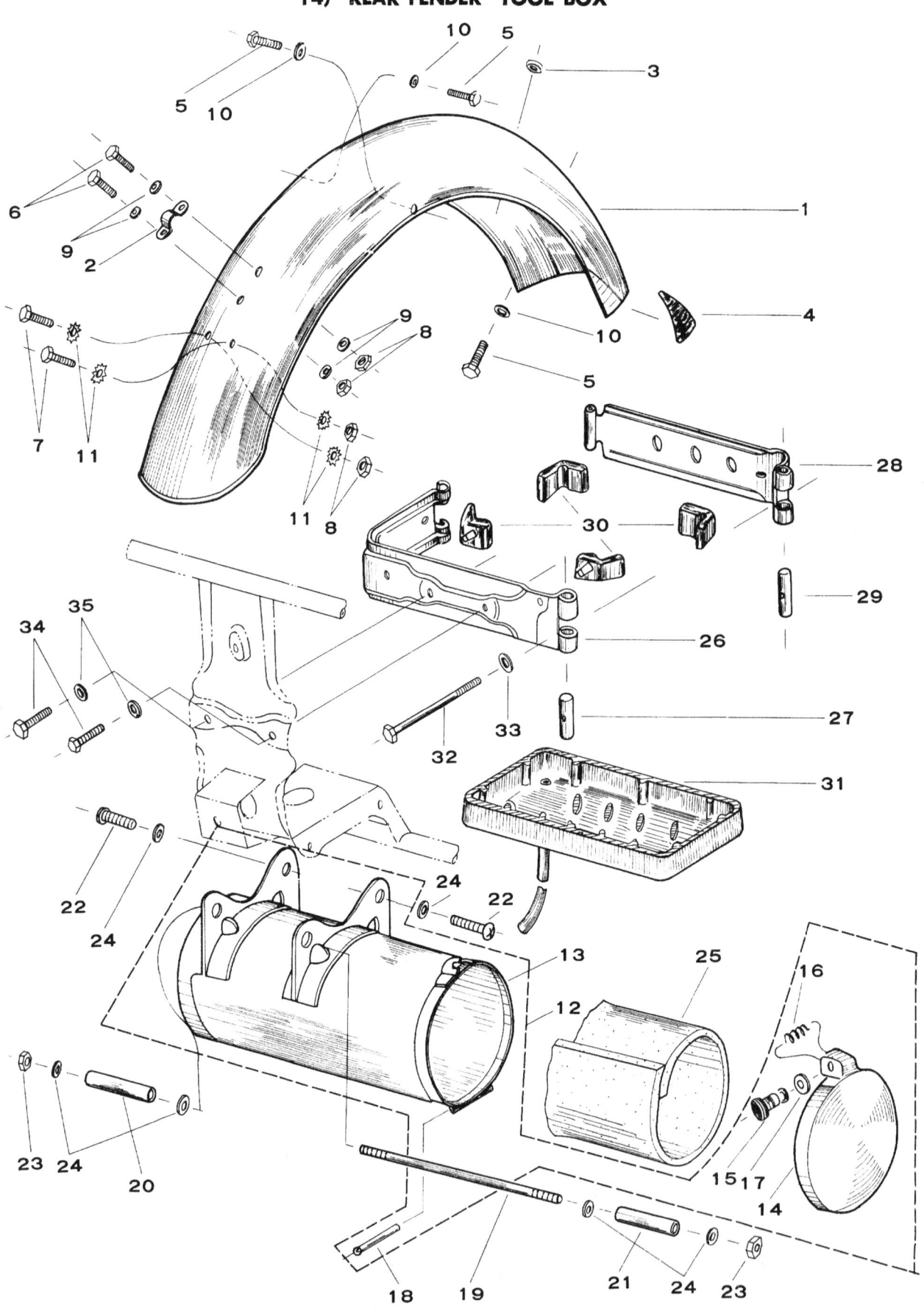

—30—

14) REAR FENDER—TOOL BOX

Index No.	Part No.	Part Name	No. Req'd	Unit Price US $	£	7D	7S	HM	50SP	60SP	90	90M
14- 1	3260-8000	Rear fender comp.	1									
14- 2	3388-8000	Rear fender clamp.	1									
14- 3	3412-3000	Rear fender grommet	1			◯	◯	◯	◯	◯	◯	◯
14- 4	3426-8000	Rear fender protector	1									
14- 5	0111-0812	Hexagon bolt A	3									
14- 6	0112-0614	Hexagon bolt A	2									
14- 7	0111-0614	Hexagon bolt A	2									
14- 8	0211-0600	Hexagon nut A	4									
14- 9	0411-0613	Plane washer A	4									
14-10	0411-0818	Plane washer A	3									
14-11	0451-0611	External toothed washer	4									
14-12	3301-8000-FAR	Tool box ass'y	1									
14-13	3352-8000-FAR	Tool box	1									
14-14	3347-8000-FAR	Tool box cap	1									
14-15	3348-8000	Tool box button	1									
14-16	3349-8000	Tool box spring	1									
14-17	6832-3001	Circlip	1			◯	◯	◯	◯	◯	◯	◯
14-18	0552-2540	Spilit pin	1									
14-19	3444-8000	Cover bolt	1									
14-20	3445-8000	Left cover spacer	1									
14-21	3446-8000	Right cover spacer	1									
14-22	0311-0610	Cross rec'd pan head screw	2									
14-23	0211-0600	Hexagon nut	2									
14-24	0411-0613	Plane washer A	6									
14-25	3427-8000	Tool set pad	1									
14-26	3342-8000	Battery bracket	1									
14-27	3343-8000	Battery bracket pin	1									
14-28	3353-8000	Battery band	1									
14-29	3344-8000	Battery band pin	1									
14-30	3345-8000	Battery pad	4									
14-31	3346-8000	Battery seat	1									
14-32	09511-128	6×71 hexagon bolt	1									
14-33	0411-0613	Plane washer A	2									
14-34	0111-0610	Hexagon bolt A	2									
14-35	0431-0615	Spring washer	2									

Remarks

Interchangeability

Index No.	New Part No.		Old Part No.
14- 3	3412-3000	=	M01831 ………Grommet
14-17	6832-3001	=	M08633-1……Circlip (knob)

15) MAIN STAND—SIDE STAND—BRAKE PEDAL

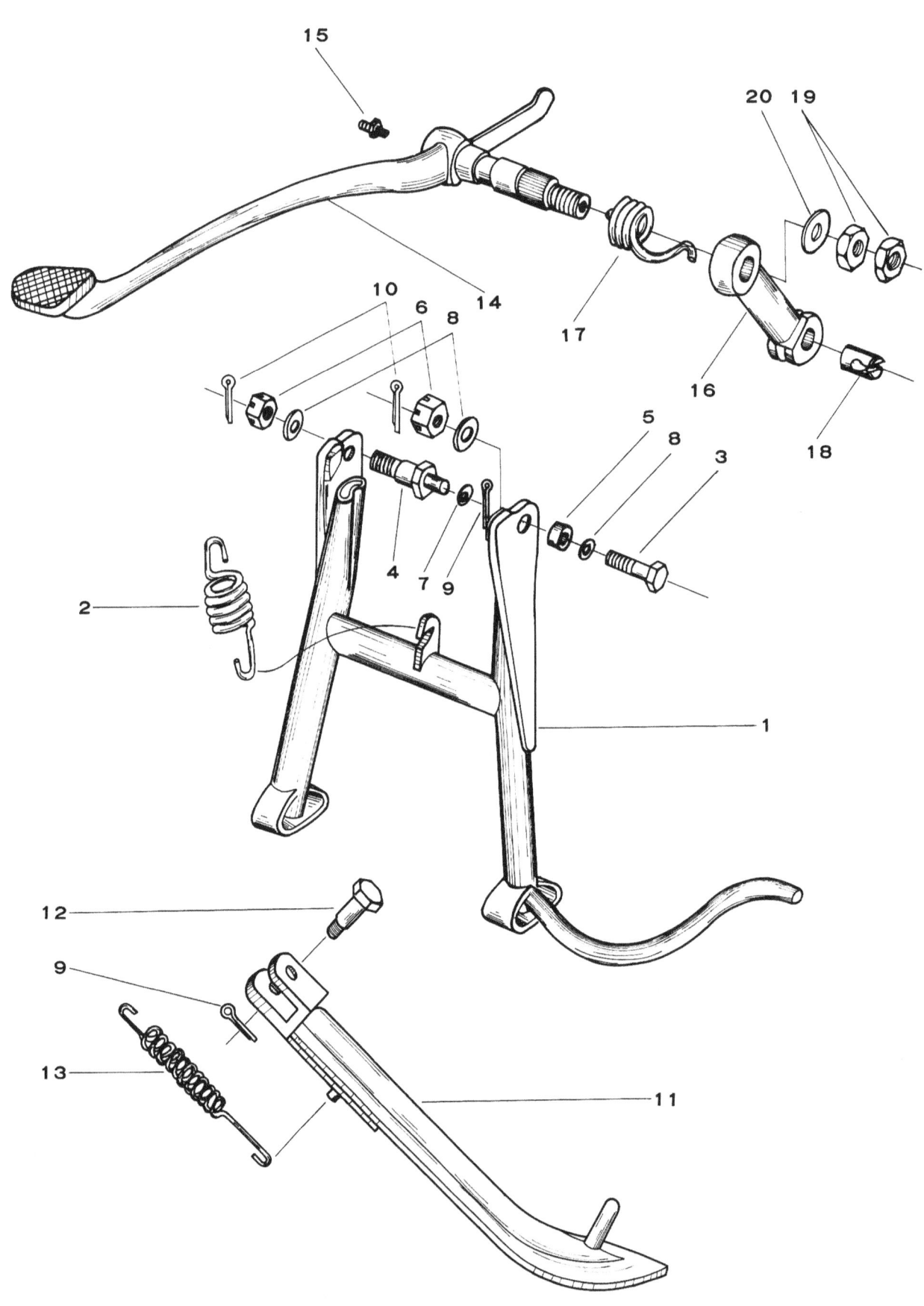

15) MAIN STAND—SIDE STAND—BRAKE PEDAL

Index No.	Part No.	Part Name	No. Req'd	Unit Price US $	£	7D	7S	HM	50SP	60SP	90	90M
15- 1	3610-8000	Main stand comp.	1									
15- 2	3624-8000	Main stand spring	1									
15- 3	3625-8000	Left stand bolt	1									
15- 4	3626-8000	Right stand bolt	1									
15- 5	3627-8000	Main stand spacer	1									
15- 6	09522-103	10 hexagon sloted nut	2									
15- 7	0411-0818	Plane washer A	1									
15- 8	0411-1022	Plane washer A	3									
15- 9	0551-2018	Spilit pin	1									
15-10	0551-2025	Spilit pin	2									
15-11	3650-8000	Side stand comp.	1									
15-12	3662-8000	Side stand bolt	1									
15-13	3663-8000	Side stand spring	1									
15-14	3810-8000	Brake pedal comp.	1									
15-15	4224-3110	Grease nipple	1									
15-16	3811-8000	Brake pedal arm	1									
15-17	3821-8000	Brake pedal spring	1									
15-18	3822-8000	Brake pedal pin	1									
15-19	0231-1000	Hexagon nut C	2									
15-20	0411-1022	Plane washer A	1									

Remarks

16) FRONT FENDER—HANDLE BAR—BACK MIRROR

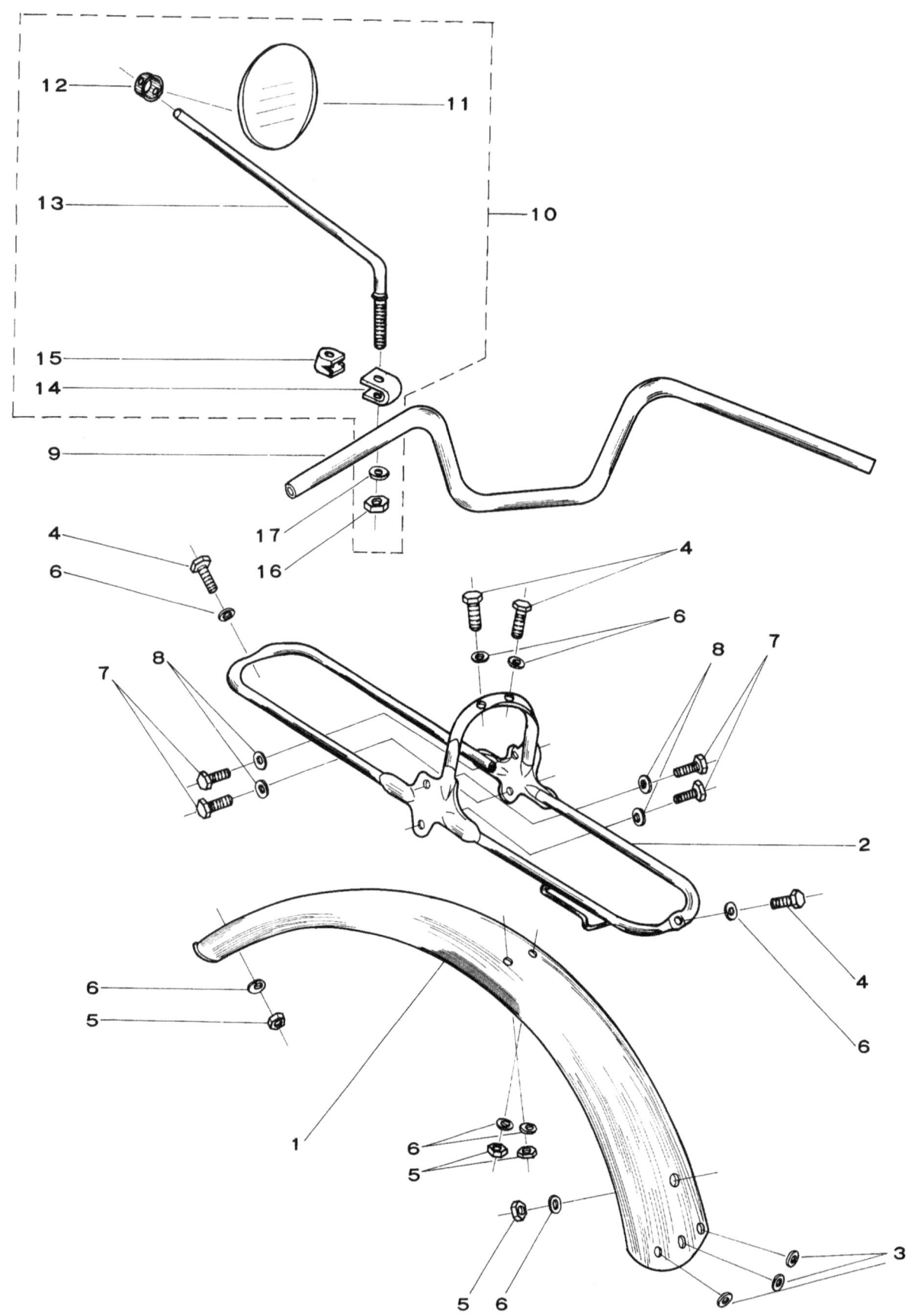

—34—

16) FRONT FENDER—HANDLE BAR—BACK MIRROR

Index No.	Part No.	Part Name	No. Req'd	Unit Price		Interchangeability						
				US $	£	7D	7D	HM	50SP	60SP	90	90M
16- 1	4411-8000	Front fender	1									
16- 2	4425-8000	Front fender stay	1									
16- 3	4435-5010	Front fender plug	3									
16- 4	0112-0614	Hexagon bolt A	4									
16- 5	0211-0600	Hexagon nut A	4									
16- 6	0411-0613	Plane washer A	8									
16- 7	0111-0812	Hexagon bolt A	4									
16- 8	0431-0820	Spring washer	4									
16- 9	4511-8000	Up handle bar	1									
16-10	4601-8000	Back mirror ass'y	1									
16-11	4610-8000	Back mirror comp.	1									
16-12	4611-8000	Mirror set cap	1									
16-13	4621-8000	Back mirror stay	1									
16-14	4622-8000	Back mirror clamp.	1									
16-15	4624-8000	Clamp spacer	1									
16-16	0211-0800	Hexagon nut A	1									
16-17	0421-0816	Plane washer B	1									

17) FRONT FORK—STEERING DAMPER

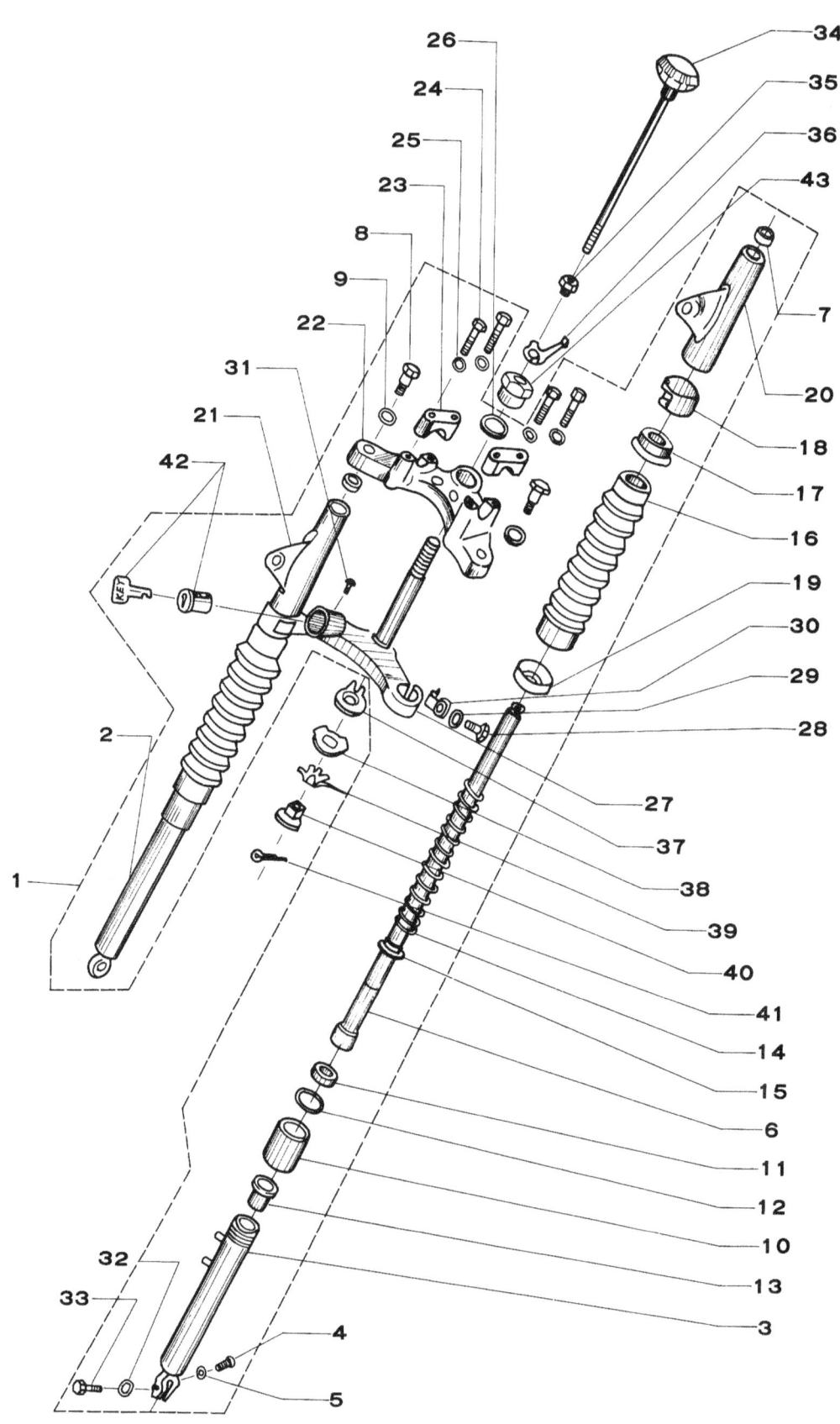

17) FRONT FORK—STEERING DAMPER

Index No.	Part No.	Part Name	No. Req'd	Unit Price US $	£	7D	7S	HM	50SP	60SP	90	90M
17- 1	4100-8000	Front fork ass'y	1									
17- 2	4111-8000	Outer tube A	1									
17- 3	4131-8000	Outer tube B	1									
17- 4	09531-101	4×8 cross rec'd pan head screw	2								○	○
17- 5	4118-5000	Drain plug gasket	2								○	○
17- 6	4113-8000	Inner tube A	2									
17- 7	4123-8000	Inner tube packing	2									
17- 8	4124-8000	Upper bridge bolt	2									
17- 9	4125-8000	Upper bridge washer	2									
17-10	4114-8000	Outer tube nut	2									
17-11	09590-115	32 oil seal	2									
17-12	09566-107	40 O ring	2									
17-13	4116-8000	Cushion slide metal	2									
17-14	4121-8000	Front cushion main spring	2									
17-15	4122-8000	Main spring guide	2									
17-16	4177-8000	Front fork boot	2									
17-17	4178-8000	Boot holder upper	2									
17-18	4174-8000	Fork cover guide	2									
17-19	4179-8000	Boot holder lower	2									
17-20	4171-8000-FAR	Left fork cover	1									
17-21	4181-8000-FAR	Right fork cover	1									
17-22	4161-8000	Upper bridge	1									
17-23	4162-8000	Handle holder	2									
17-24	0133-0836	Hexagon bolt C	4									
17-25	0421-0612	Plane washer B	4									
17-26	4165-5000	Steering head washer	1								○	○
17-27	4151-8000	Lower bridge	1									
17-28	0131-1032	Hexagon bolt C	2									
17-29	0431-1025	Spring washer	2									
17-30	4153-8000	Wire clamp	2									
17-31	09535-102	3.5×4.8 drive screw	1									
17-32	0431-0820	Spring washer	1									
17-33	09511-116	8×25 hexagon bolt	1						○	○	○	○
17-34	4311-8000	Steering damper knob	1									
17-35	4312-8000	Damper knob guide	1									
17-36	4313-8000	Damper lock spring	1									
17-37	4316-8000	Damper retaining plate	1									
17-38	4318-8000	Damper pressure plate	1									
17-39	4319-8000	Steering damper spring	9									
17-40	4321-8000	Damper spring guide	1									
17-41	0551-1612	Spilit pin	1									
17-42	3433-8000	Handle lock	1									
17-43	4164-8000	Steering head nut	1									

Remarks

Interchangeability

Index No.	New Part No.		Old Part No.	
17- 4	09531-101	=	EA1-41161	Drain plug
17- 5	4118-5000	=	EA1-41162	Prain plug packing
17-33	09511-116	=	EA1-41251	Axle bracket bolt
17-26	4165-5000	=	EA1-41552	Cap nut washer

18) REAR FORK—REAR CUSHIONS

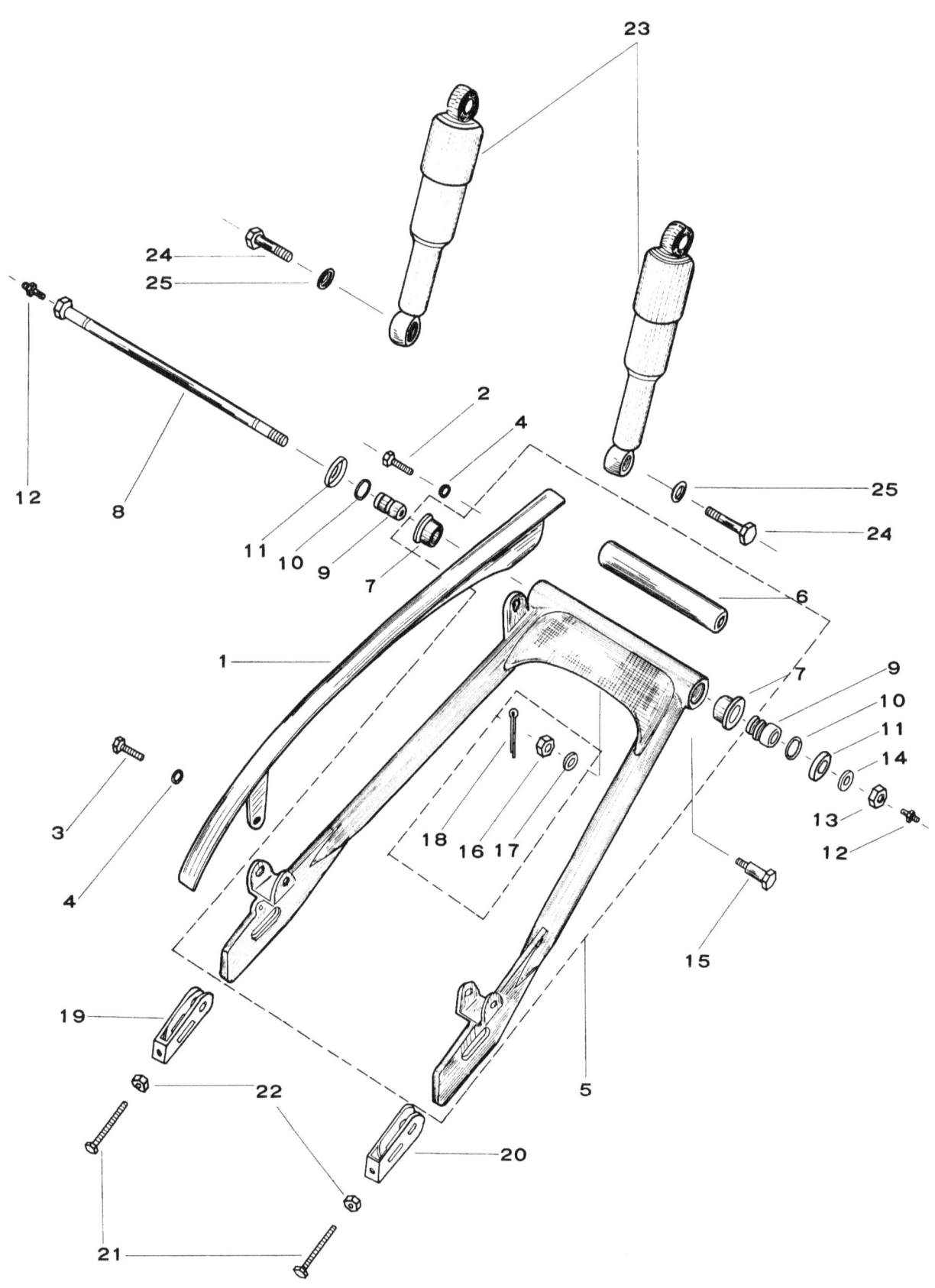

18) REAR FORK—REAR CUSHIONS

Index No.	Part No.	Part Name	No. Req'd	Unit Price US $	£	7D	7S	HM	50SP	60SP	90	90M
18- 1	4751-8000	Half chain case	1									
18- 2	0112-0608	Hexagon bolt A	1									
18- 3	0112-0614	Hexagon bolt A	1									
18- 4	0411-0613	Plane washer A	2									
18- 5	4810-8000	Rear fork comp.	1									
18- 6	4857-8000	Rear fork spacer	1									
18- 7	4851-8000	Rear fork bush	2									
18- 8	3414-8000	Pivot shaft	1									
18- 9	4856-8000	Rear fork collar	2									
18-10	09566-106	18 O ring	2									
18-11	4858-8000	Fork pivot cap	2									
18-12	4224-3110	Grease nipple	2									
18-13	0252-1400	Hexagon nut E	1									
18-14	09541-109	14 plane washer	1									
18-15	4855-8000	Torque rod bolt	1									
18-16	09522-101	8 hexagon sloted nut	1									
18-17	0411-0818	Plane washer A	1									
18-18	0551-2018	Spilit pin	1									
18-19	4862-8000	Left chain adjuster	1									
18-20	4863-8000	Right chain adjuster	1									
18-21	4864-8000	Chain adjuster bolt	2									
18-22	0222-0600	Hexagon nut B	2									
18-23	4901-8000-FAR	Rear cushion ass'y	2									
18-24	0122-1032	Hexagon bolt B	2									
18-25	0411-1022	Plane washer A	2									

Remarks

19) FUEL TANK—FUEL COCK—OIL TANK

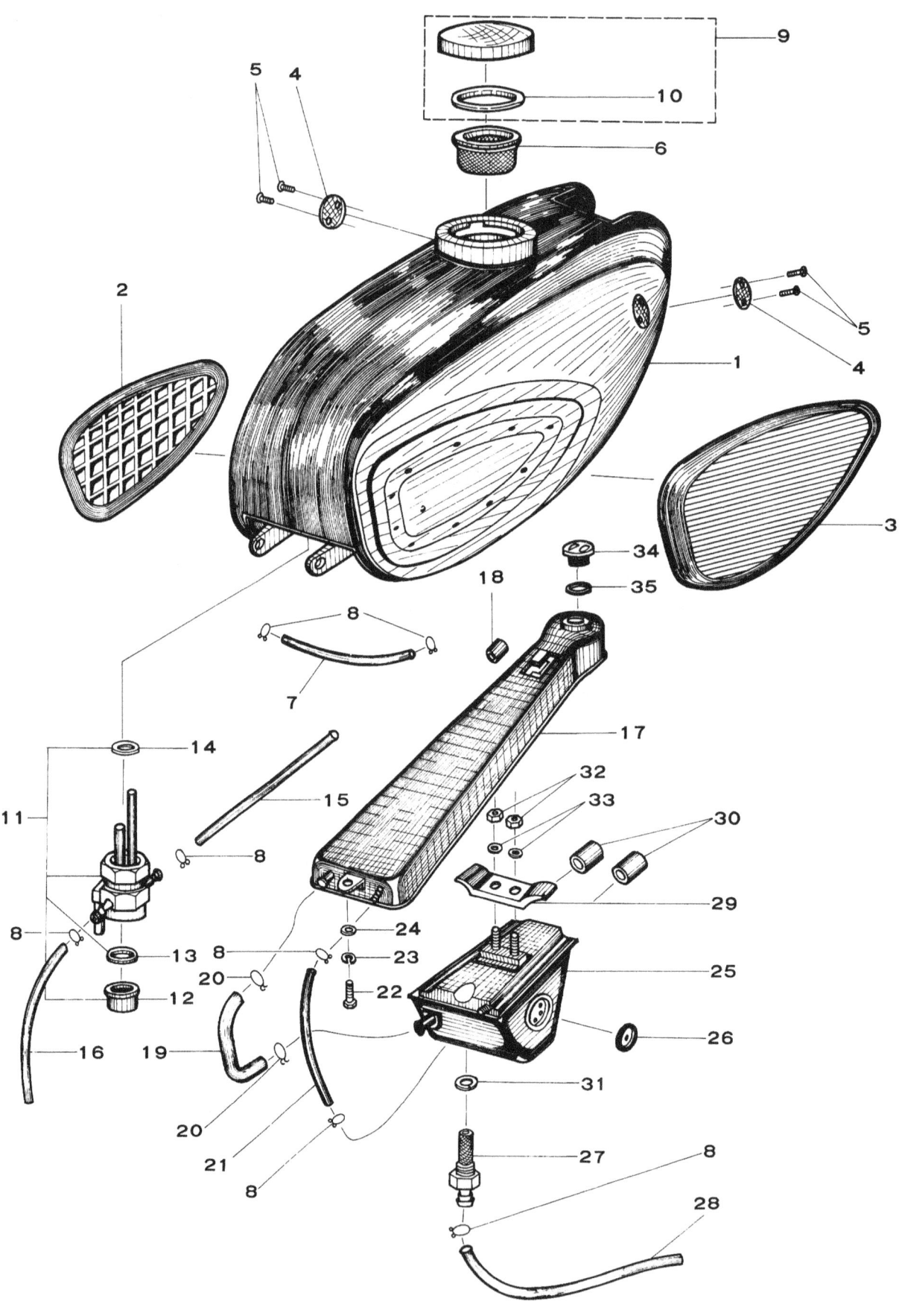

— 40 —

19) FUEL TANK—FUEL COCK—OIL TANK

Index No.	Part No.	Part Name	No. Req'd	Unit Price US$	£	Interchangeability 7D	7S	HM	50SP	60SP	90	90M
19- 1	5110-8000-FAR	Fuel tank comp.	1									
19- 2	5141-8000	Left knee grip	1									
19- 3	5142-8000	Right knee grip	1									
19- 4	5143-5000	Fuel tank emblem	2						○	○	○	○
19- 5	0311-0306	Cross rec'd pan head screw	4			○	○	○	○	○	○	○
19- 6	5145-8000	Fuel tank filter	1									
19- 7	5186-8000	Tank connecting tube	1									
19- 8	5187-3004	Fuel tube clip	8			○	○	○	○	○	○	○
19- 9	5102-8000	Tank cap ass'y	1									
19-10	5171-8000	Tank cap gasket	1									
19-11	5103-8000	Fuel cock ass'y	1									
19-12	5182-8000	Fuel strainer cup	1									
19-13	5183-8000	Strainer cup gasket	1									
19-14	5184-8000	Fuel cock gasket	1									
19-15	5173-8000	Left fuel tube	1									
19-16	5174-8000	Right fuel tube	1									
19-17	5510-8000	Oil tank comp.	1									
19-18	5511-8000	Oil tank pad	1									
19-19	5512-8000	Oil tank connecting tube	1									
19-20	5513-8000	Oil connecting tube clip	2									
19-21	5514-8000	Breather tube	1									
19-22	0111-0610	Hexagon bolt A	1									
19-23	0431-0615	Spring washer	1									
19-24	0411-0613	Plane washer A	1									
19-25	5530-8000	Sub oil tank	1									
19-26	5531-8000	Oil gauge	1									
19-27	5532-8000	Oil tank filter	1									
19-28	5533-8000	Oil tube C	1									
19-29	5536-8000	Sub oil tank bracket	1									
19-30	5537-8000	Sub oil tank pad	2									
19-31	09564-101	10 fiber gasket	1									
19-32	0211-0600	Hexagon nut A	2									
19-33	0411-0613	Plane washer A	2									
19-34	5560-8000	Oil tank cap comp.	1									
19-35	09566-108	27 O ring	1									

Remarks

Interchangeability

Index No.	New Part No.	Old Part No.
19-4	5143-5000	= EA1-51213......Side mark (tank)
19-8	5187-3004	= M07183-4 ......Clip (fuel pipe)
19-5	0311-0306	= PNK-3×6 ......3×6mm small cross rec'd screw

20) LEFT HANDLE GRIP - CLUTCH LEVER - STARTER LEVER

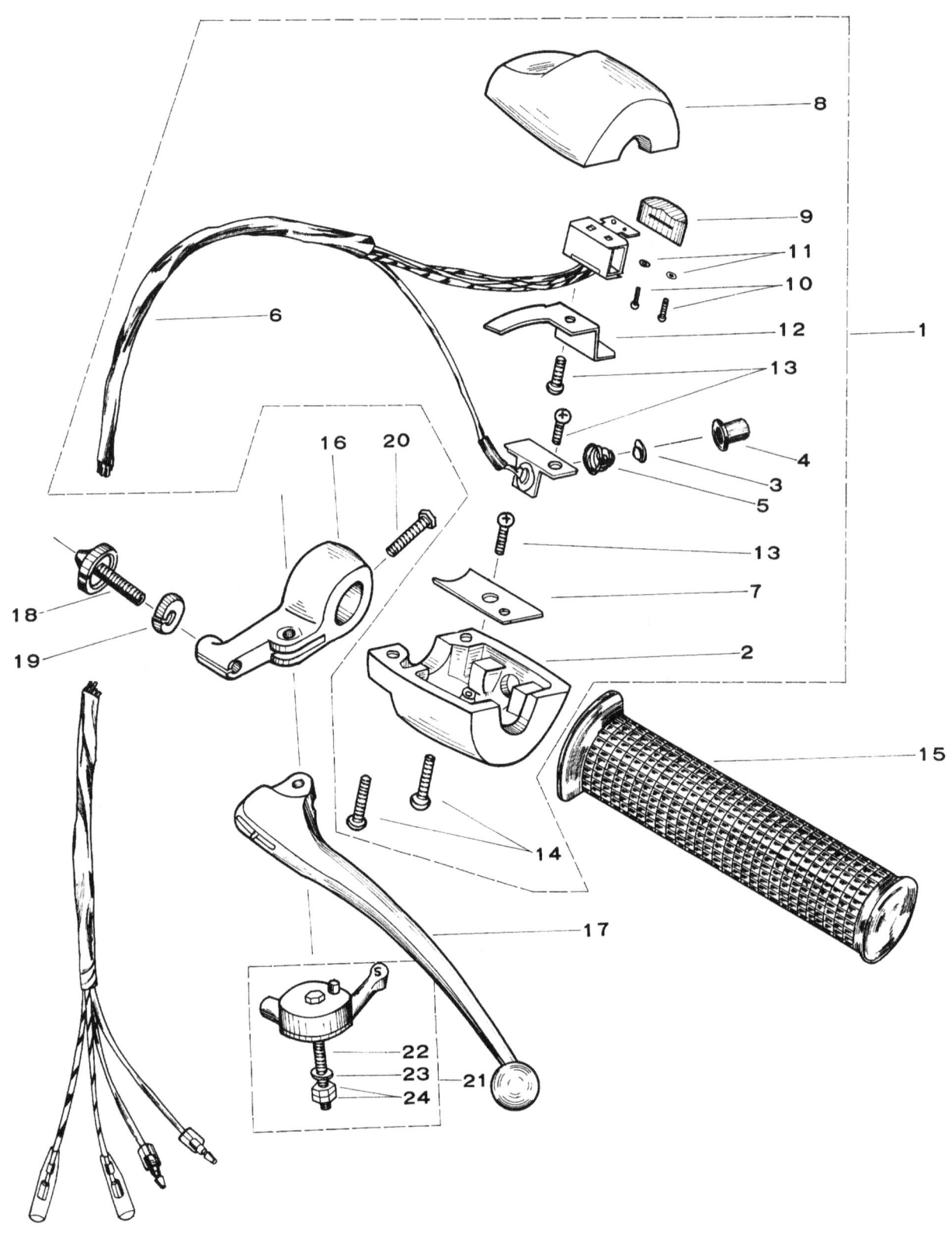

20) LEFT HANDLE GRIP-CLUTCH LEVER-STARTER LEVER

Index No.	Part No.	Part Name	No. Req'd	Unit Price US $	£	Interchangeability 7D	7S	HM	50SP	60SP	90	90M
20- 1	6105-8000	Left case ass'y	1									
20- 2	6111-8000	Left switch case	1									
20- 3	6112-3100	Horn switch contact plate	1					○				
20- 4	6113-3100	Horn switch button	1			○	○	○	○	○	○	○
20- 5	6114-3100	Horn switch spring	1			○	○	○	○	○	○	○
20- 6	6115-8000	Left handle wire	1									
20- 7	6116-8000	Left wire clamp	1									
20- 8	6121-8000	Left switch case cover	1									
20- 9	6119-8000	Handle switch knob	1									
10-10	0361-0206	Pan head screw	2									
10-11	0431-0205	Spring washer	2									
10-12	6117-8000	Dipper switch clamp	1									
10-13	0311-0306	Cross rec'd pan head screw	3									
10-14	0311-0614	Cross rec'd pan head screw	2									
10-15	6123-8000	Left handle grip	1									
10-16	6125-8000	Left lever holder	1									
17-17	6122-8000	Clutch lever	1									
17-18	6126-8000	Wire adjuster	1									
17-19	6127-8000	Wire adjuster lock nut	1									
20-20	0111-0625	Hexagon bolt A	1									
20-21	6103-8000	Starter lever ass'y	1									
20-22	09511-131	6×45 hexagon bolt	1									
20-23	0421-0612	Plane washer B	1									
20-24	0231-0600	Haxagon nut C	2									

Remarks

Interchangeability

index No.	New Part No.		Old Part No.	
20-4	6113-3100	=	GA1-61113	Horn button
20-5	6114-3100	=	GA1-61114	Horn spring
20-3	6112-3100	=	GA1-61112	Contact plate

21) RIGHT HANDLE GRIP—FRONT BRAKE LEVER

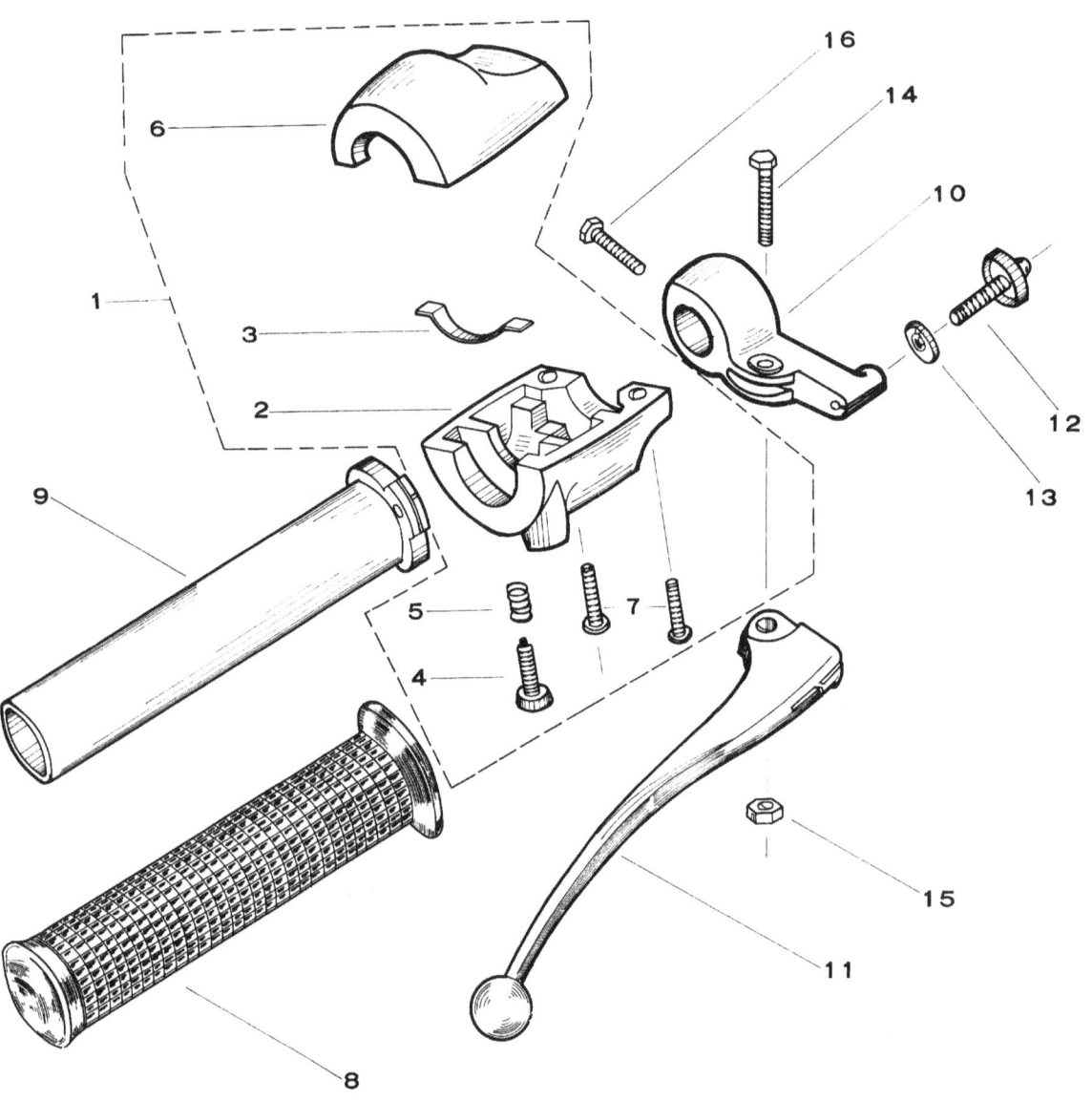

21) RIGHT HANDLE GRIP—FRONT BRAKE LEVER

Index No.	Part No.	Part Name	No. Req'd	Unit Price US $	£	7D	7S	HM	50SP	60SP	90	90M
21- 1	6107-8000	Right case ass'y	1									
21- 2	6141-8000	Right switch case	1									
21- 3	6161-8000	Throttle grip adjust spring	1									
21- 4	6158-8000	Throttle grip adjust screw	1									
21- 5	6165-8000	Screw retaining spring	1									
21- 6	6151-8000	Right switch case cover	1									
21- 7	0311-0614	Cross rec'd pan head screw	2									
21- 8	6153-8000	Right handle grip	1									
21- 9	6154-8000	Throttle grip pipe	1									
21-10	6149-8000	Right lever holder	1									
21-11	6152-8000	Front brake lever	1									
21-12	6126-8000	Wire adjuster	1									
21-13	6127-8000	Wire adjuster lock nut	1									
21-14	09511-132	6×25 hexagon bolt	1									
21-15	0221-0600	Hexagon nut B	1									
21-16	0111-0625	Hexagon bolt A	1									

Remarks

22) SPEEDOMETER CABLE—THROTTLE WIRE

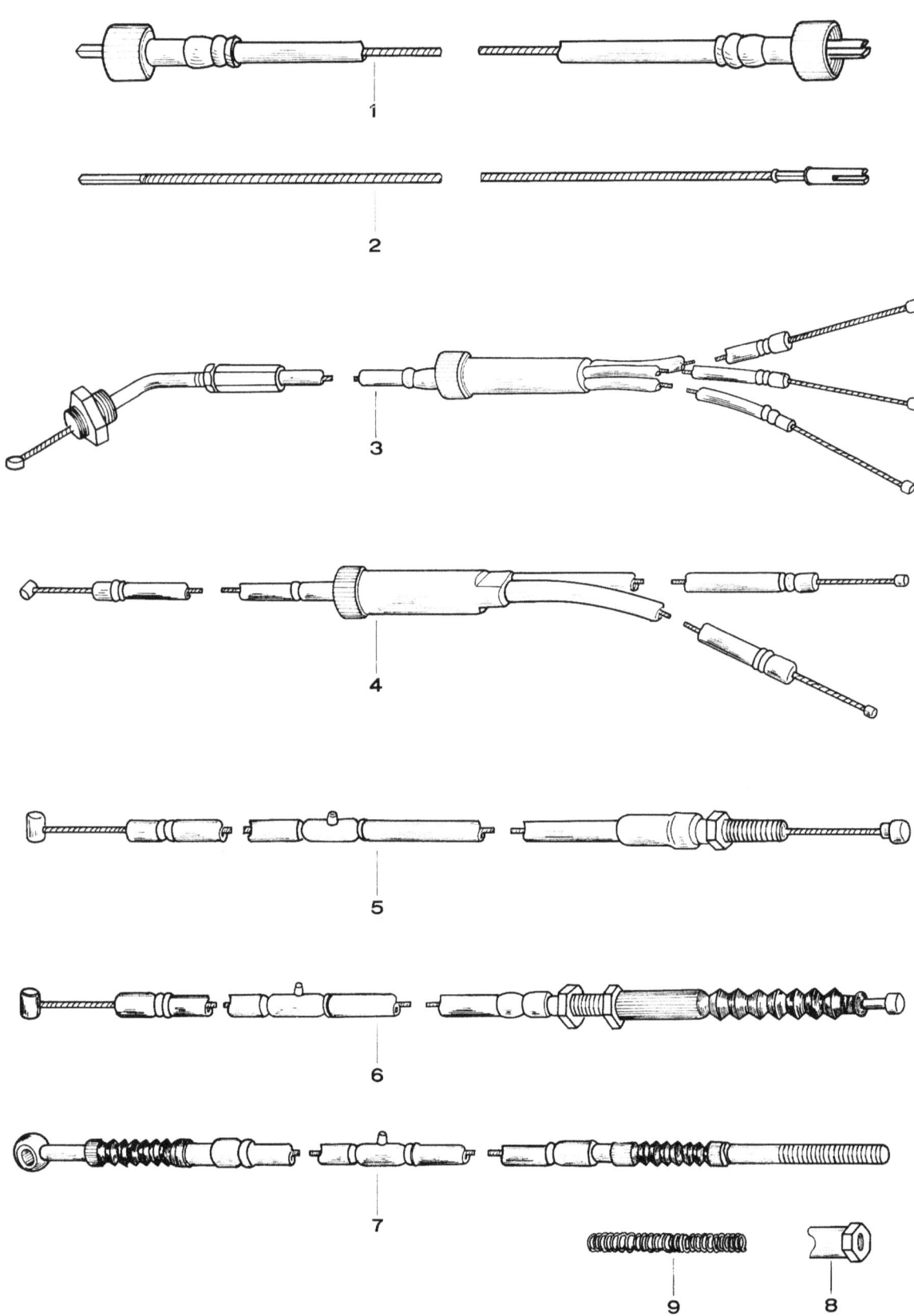

22) SPEEDOMETER CABLE—THROTTLE WIRE

Index No.	Part No.	Part Name	No. Req'd	Unit Price		Interchangeability						
				US $	£	7D	7S	HM	50SP	60SP	90	90M
22-1	6171-8000	Speedometer cable	1									
22-2	9411-8000	Speedometer inner cable	1									
22-3	6176-8000	Throttle wire	1									
22-4	6178-8000	Carburetor starter wire	1									
22-5	6186-8000	Clutch wire	1									
22-6	6181-8000	Front brake wire	1									
22-7	3841-8000	Rear brake wire	1									
22-8	3832-3000	Brake rod adjuster	1			○	○	○	○	○	○	○
22-9	3833-8000	Brake rod spring	1									

Remarks

Interchangeability

Index No.	New Part No.		Old Part No.
22-8	3832-3000	=	M04332-0......Adjusting nut

23) MUFFLERS—EXHAUST PIPES

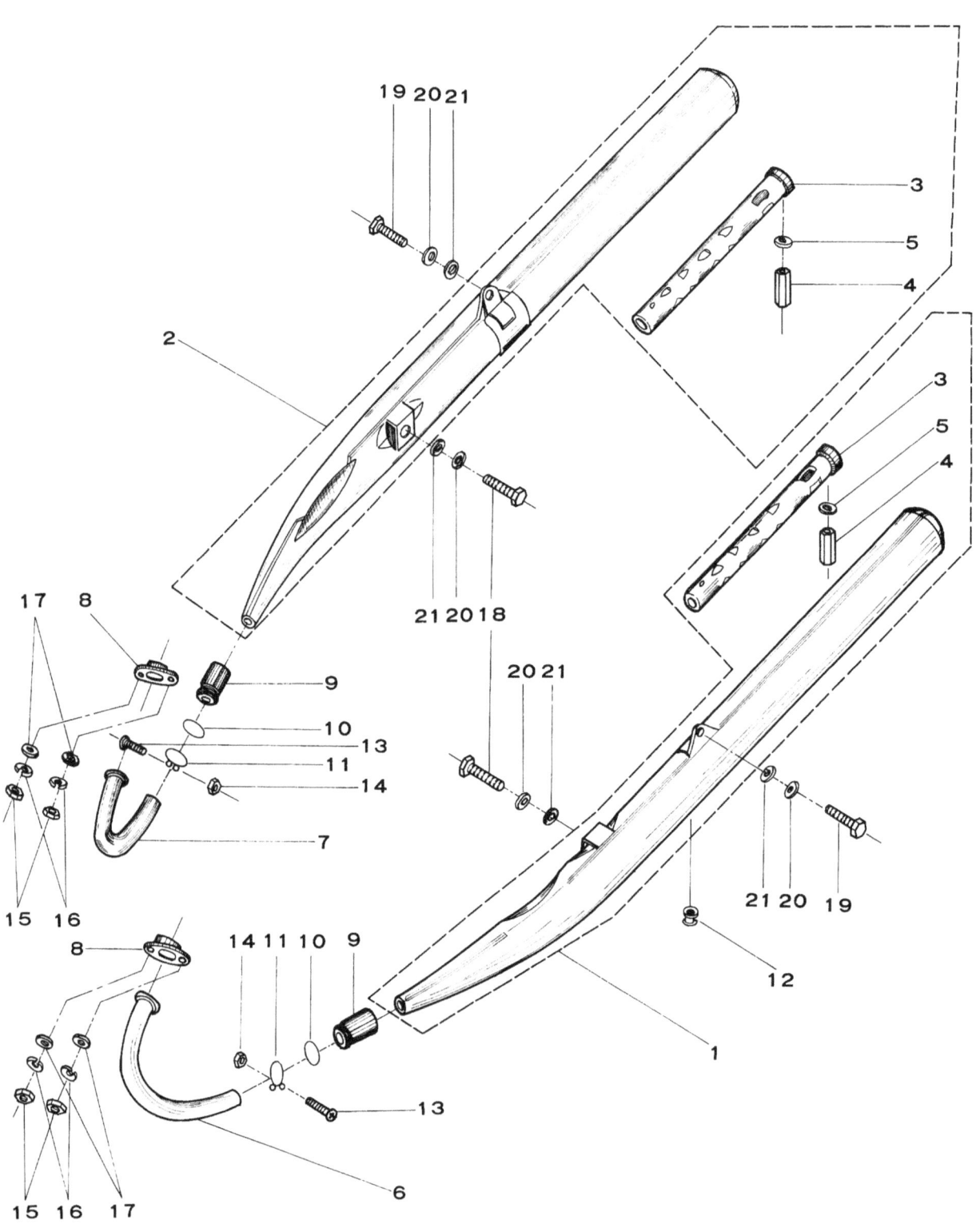

—48—

23) MUFFLERS—EXHAUST PIPES

Index No.	Part No.	Part Name	No. Req'd	Unit Price US $	£	7D	7S	HM	50SP	60SP	90	90M
23- 1	6302-8000	Left muffler ass'y	1									
23- 2	6303-8000	Right muffler ass'y	1									
23- 3	6320-8000	Diffuser pipe	2									
23- 4	6321-8000	Diffuser pipe nut	2									
23- 5	0411-0512	Plane washer A	2									
23- 6	6352-8000	Left exhaust pipe	1									
23- 7	6353-8000	Right exhaust pipe	1									
23- 8	6361-8000	Exhaust pipe clamp	2									
23- 9	6362-5000	Muffler joint rubber	2						○	○	○	○
23-10	6364-5000	Muffler joint ring	2						○	○	○	○
23-11	6363-5000	Muffler joint stopper	2						○	○	○	○
23-12	3335-8000	Stand rubber stopper	1									
23-13	0311-0412	Cross rec'd pan head screw	2									
23-14	0211-0400	Hexagon nut A	2									
23-15	0211-0600	Hexagon nut A	4									
23-16	0431-0615	Spring washer	4									
23-17	0411-0613	Plane washer A	4									
23-18	0111-0816	Hexagon bolt A	2									
23-19	0122-0832	Hexagon bolt B	2									
23-20	0431-0820	Spring washer	4									
23-21	0411-0818	Plane washer A	4									

Remarks

Interchangeability

Index No.	New Part No.		Old Part No.
23 -9	6362-5000	−	EA1-63121......Rubber joint (muffler)
23-11	6363-5000	=	EA1-63124......Stopper (rubber joint)
23-10	6364-5000	=	EA1-63122......Ring (rubber joint)

24) DUAL SEAT—AIR CLEANER—COVERS

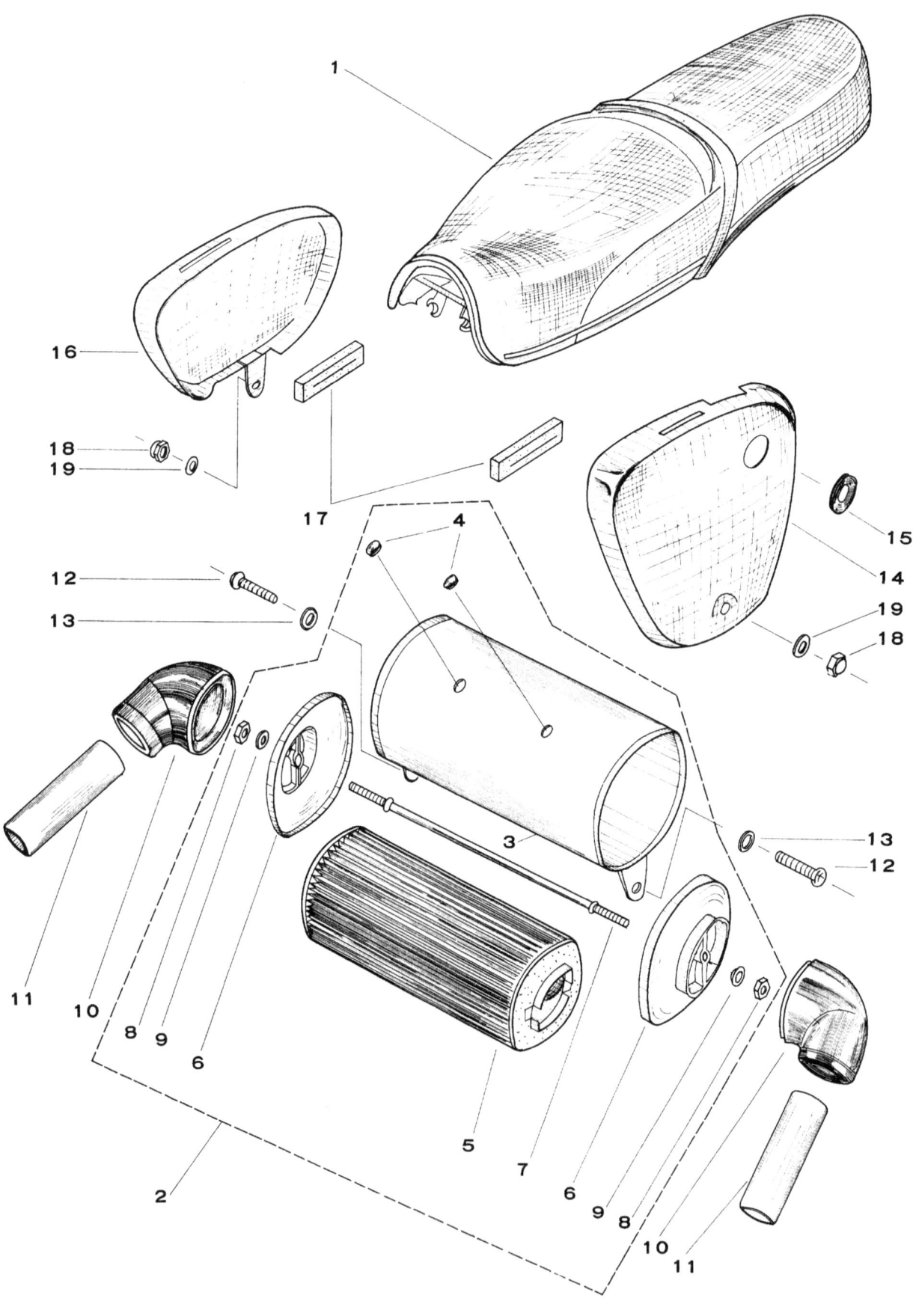

— 50 —

24) DUAL SEAT – AIR CLEANER – COVERS

Index No.	Part No.	Part Name	No. Req'd	Unit Price US $	£	7D	7S	HM	50SP	60SP	90	90M
24- 1	6402-8000	Dual seat ass'y	1									
24- 2	6201-8000	Air cleaner ass'y	1									
24- 3	6221-8000	Air cleaner case	1									
24- 4	4435-5010	Front fender plug	2									
24- 5	6211-8000	Air cleaner element	1									
24- 6	6222-8000	Air cleaner cover	2									
24- 7	6223-8000	Air cleaner bolt	1									
24- 8	0211-0500	Hexagon nut A	2									
24- 9	0411-0512	Plane washer A	2									
24-10	6242-8000	Air pipe joint	2									
24-11	6241-8000	Air pipe	2									
24-12	0311-0614	Cross rec'd pan head screw	2									
24-13	0411-0613	Plane washer A	2									
24-14	6811-8000-FAR	Left cover	1									
24-15	6812-8000	Main switch grommet	1									
24-16	6821-8000-FAR	Right cover	1									
24-17	3447-8000	Cover pad	2									
24-18	09525-104	6 cap nut	2					○				
24-19	0411-0613	Plane washer A	2									

Remarks

25) FRONT WHEEL

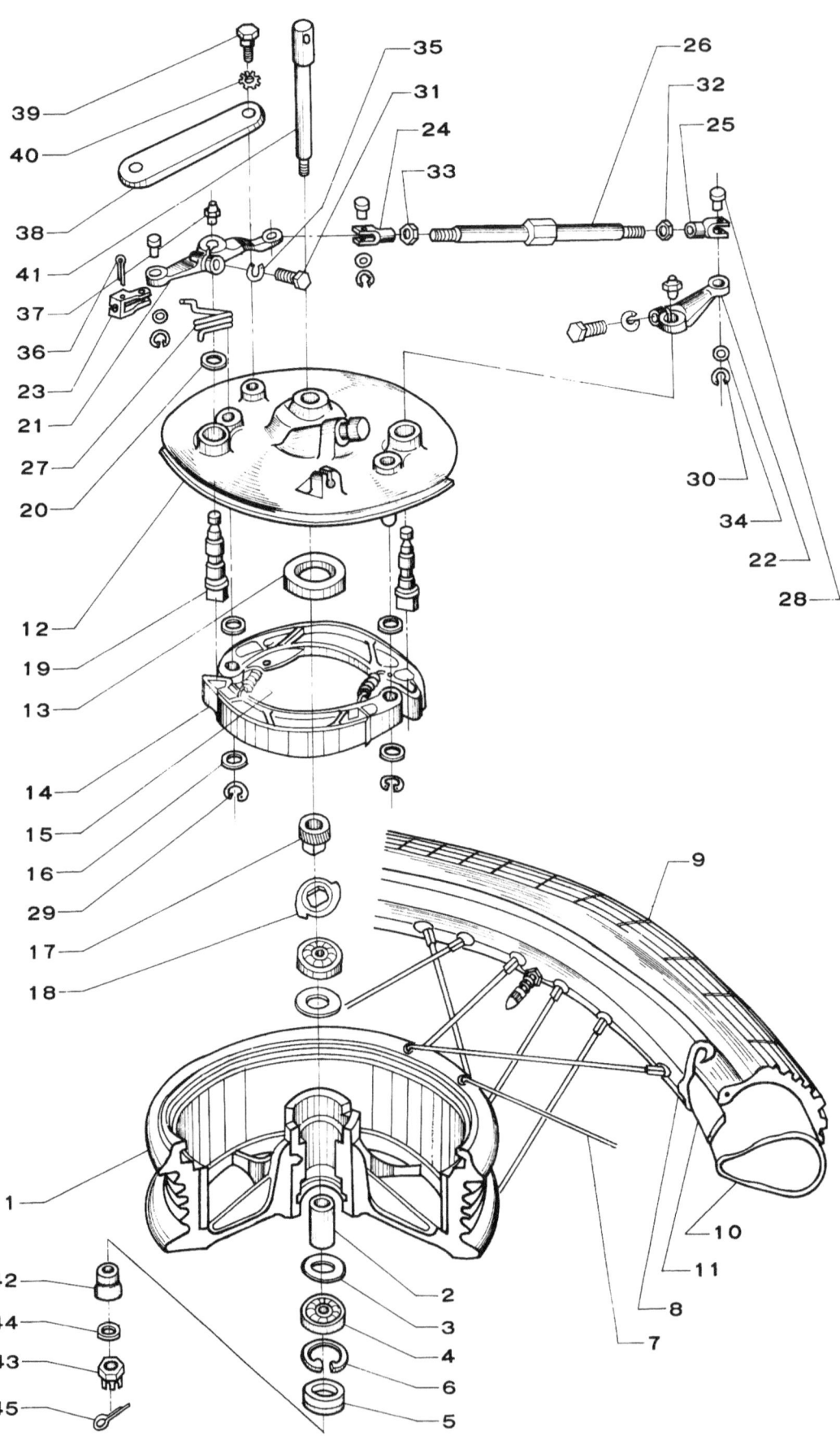

25) FRONT WHEEL

Index No.	Part No.	Part Name	No. Req'd	Unit Price US$	£	7D	7S	HM	50SP	60SP	90	90M
25- 1	7111-8000	Front brake drum	1									
25- 2	7114-8000	Front drum collar	1									
25- 3	7115-8000	Collar supporter	2									
25- 4	07-6302-43	Ball bearing	2									
25- 5	09590-110	22 oil seal	1									
25- 6	09501-101	42A snap ring	1									
25- 7	7108-8000	Front spoke ass'y	1									
25- 8	7241-8000	Wheel rim	1									
25- 9	7251-8000	Front wheel tire	1									
25-10	7252-8000	Front wheel tube	1									
25-11	7253-8000	Tire flap	1									
25-12	7130-8000	Front panel comp.	1									
25-13	09590-111	48 oil seal	1									
25-14	7140-8000	Brake shoe comp.	2									
25-15	7145-8000	Brake shoe spring	2									
25-16	09548-101	14 thrust washer	4									
25-17	7148-8000	Speedometer gear	1									
25-18	7149-8000	Speedometer gear connector	1									
25-19	7151-8000	Front brake cam	2									
25-20	7152-8000	Cam dust seal	2									
25-21	7153-8000	Brake arm A	1									
25-22	7154-8000	Brake arm B	1									
25-23	7155-8000	Wire connector	1									
25-24	7156-8000	Rod end A	1									
25-25	7157-8000	Rod end B	1									
25-26	7158-8000	Brake arm rod	1									
25-27	7159-8000	Front arm return spring	1									
25-28	7161-8000	Brake arm pin	3									
25-29	09502-101	14B snap ring	2									
25-30	09504-101	5D snap ring	3									
25-31	0112-0620	Hexagon bolt A	2									
25-32	0232-0500	Hexagon nut C	1									
25-33	09529-101	5 left thread nut	1									
25-34	0421-0612	Plane washer B	3									
25-35	0431-0615	Spring washer	2									
25-36	0551-2020	Spilit pin	1									
25-37	7134-3002	Grease nipple	2			○	○	○	○	○	○	○
25-38	7166-8000	Front torque link	1									
25-39	7167-8000	Front link bolt	1									
25-40	0441-1018	Internal toothed washer	1									
25-41	7221-8000	Front wheel axle	1									
25-42	7226-8000	Front axle collar	1									
25-43	09522-102	14 hexagon sloted nut	1									
25-44	09541-109	14 plane washer	1									
25-45	0551-3025	Spilit pin	1									

Remarks

Interchangeability

Index No.	New Part No.		Old Part No.
25-37	7134-3002	=	M04137A-1......Grease nipple

26) REAR WHEEL

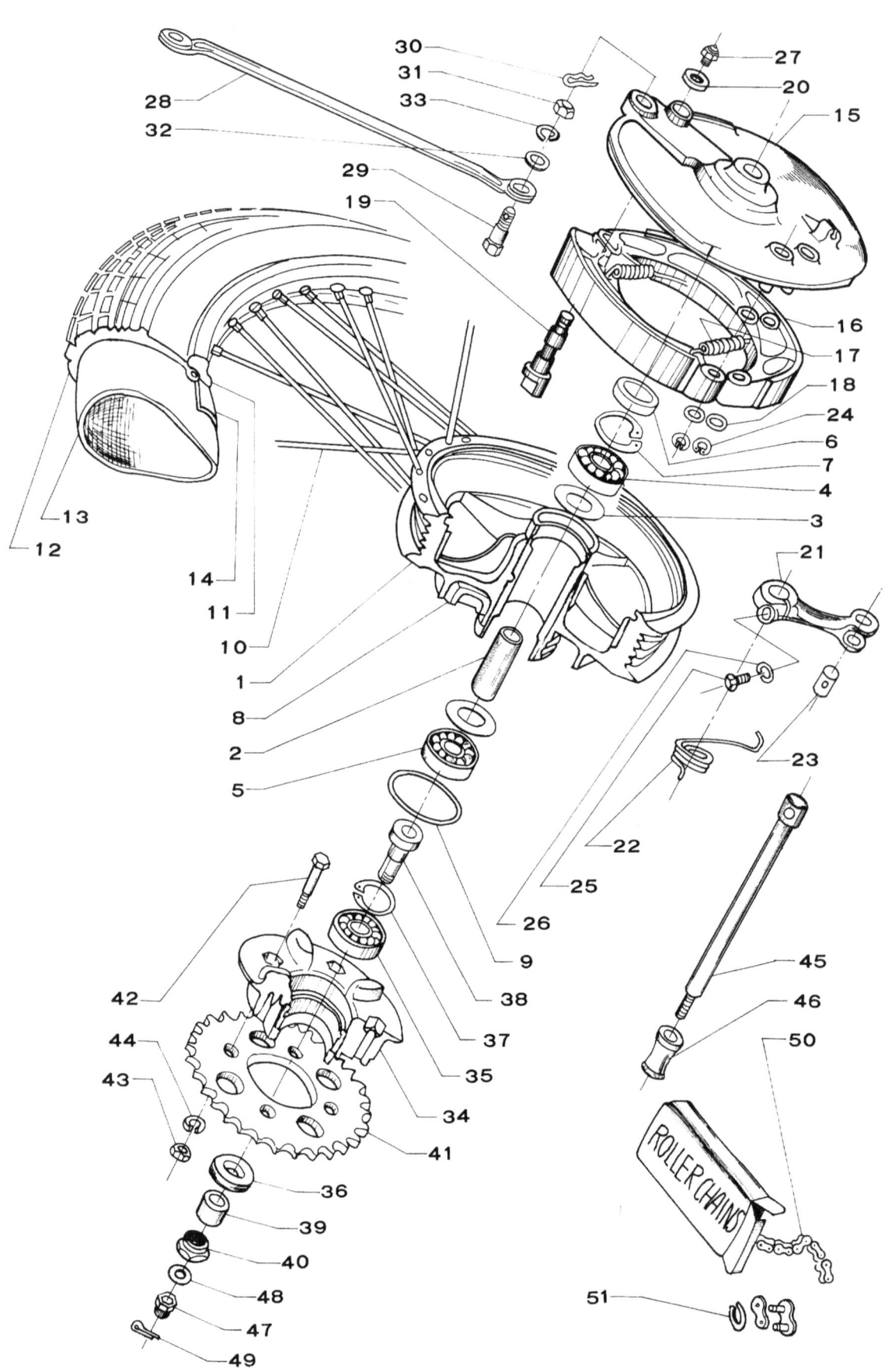

− 54 −

26) REAR WHEEL

Index No.	Part No.	Part Name	No. Req'd	Unit Price US$	£	7D	7S	HM	50SP	60SP	90	90M
26- 1	7311-8000	Rear brake drum	1									
26- 2	7314-8000	Rear drum collar	1									
26- 3	7115-8000	Collar supporter	2									
26- 4	07-6302-03	Ball bearing	1									
26- 5	07-6302-43	Ball bearing	1									
26- 6	09590-112	22 oil seal	1									
26- 7	09501-101	42A snap ring	1									
26- 8	7319-8000	Rear wheel damper	4									
26- 9	09566-105	50 O ring	1									
26-10	7308-8000	Rear spoke ass'y	1									
26-11	7241-8000	Wheel rim	1									
26-12	7451-8000	Rear wheel tire	1									
26-13	7452-8000	Rear wheel tube	1									
26-14	7453-8000	Tire flap	1									
26-15	7330-8000	Rear panel comp.	1									
26-16	7140-8000	Brake shoe comp.	1									
26-17	7145-8000	Brake shoe spring	2									
26-18	09548-101	14 thrust washer	4									
26-19	7351-8000	Rear brake cam	1									
26-20	7152-8000	Cam dust seal	1									
26-21	7353-8000	Brake arm C	1									
26-22	7359-8000	Rear arm return spring	1									
26-23	7361-3003	Brake arm pin	1			○	○	○	○	○	○	○
26-24	09502-101	14B snap ring	2									
26-25	0112-0620	Hexagon bolt A	1									
26-26	0431-0615	Spring washer	1									
26-27	7134-3002	Grease nipple	1			○	○	○	○	○	○	○
26-28	7366-8000	Rear torque link	1									
26-29	7367-8000	Rear link bolt	1									
26-30	7369-8000	Latch clip	1									
26-31	0211-0800	Hexagon nut A	1									
26-32	0411-0818	Plane washer A	1									
26-33	0431-0820	Spring washer	1									
26-34	7371-8000	Drive flange	1									
26-35	07-6204-23	Ball bearing	1									
26-36	09590-113	28 oil seal	1									
26-37	09501-102	47A snap ring	1									
26-38	7376-8000	Drive flange collar	1									
26-39	7377-8000	Oil seal collar	1									
26-40	7379-8000	Flange collar nut	1									
26-41	7381-8000	Driven sprocket	1									
26-42	7386-3110	Sprocket bolt	4						○	○	○	○
26-43	0231-0800	Hexagon nut C	4									
26-44	0431-0820	Spring washer	4									
26-45	7421-8000	Rear wheel axle	1									
26-46	7426-8000	Rear axle collar	1									
26-47	09522-102	14 hexagon sloted nut	1									
26-48	09541-109	14 plane washer	1									
26-49	0551-3025	Spilit pin	1									
26-50	7501-8000	Roller chain ass'y	1									
26-51	7520-8000	Chain joint comp.	1									

Remarks

Interchangeability

Index No.	New Part No.		Old Part No.
26-23	7361-3003	=	M04252-3 ......Auchor pin
26-27	7134-3002	=	M04137A-1......Grease nipple
26-42	7386-3110	=	GA3-72153......Bolt (sprocket)

27) HEAD LAMP—TAIL LAMP—SPEEDOMETER

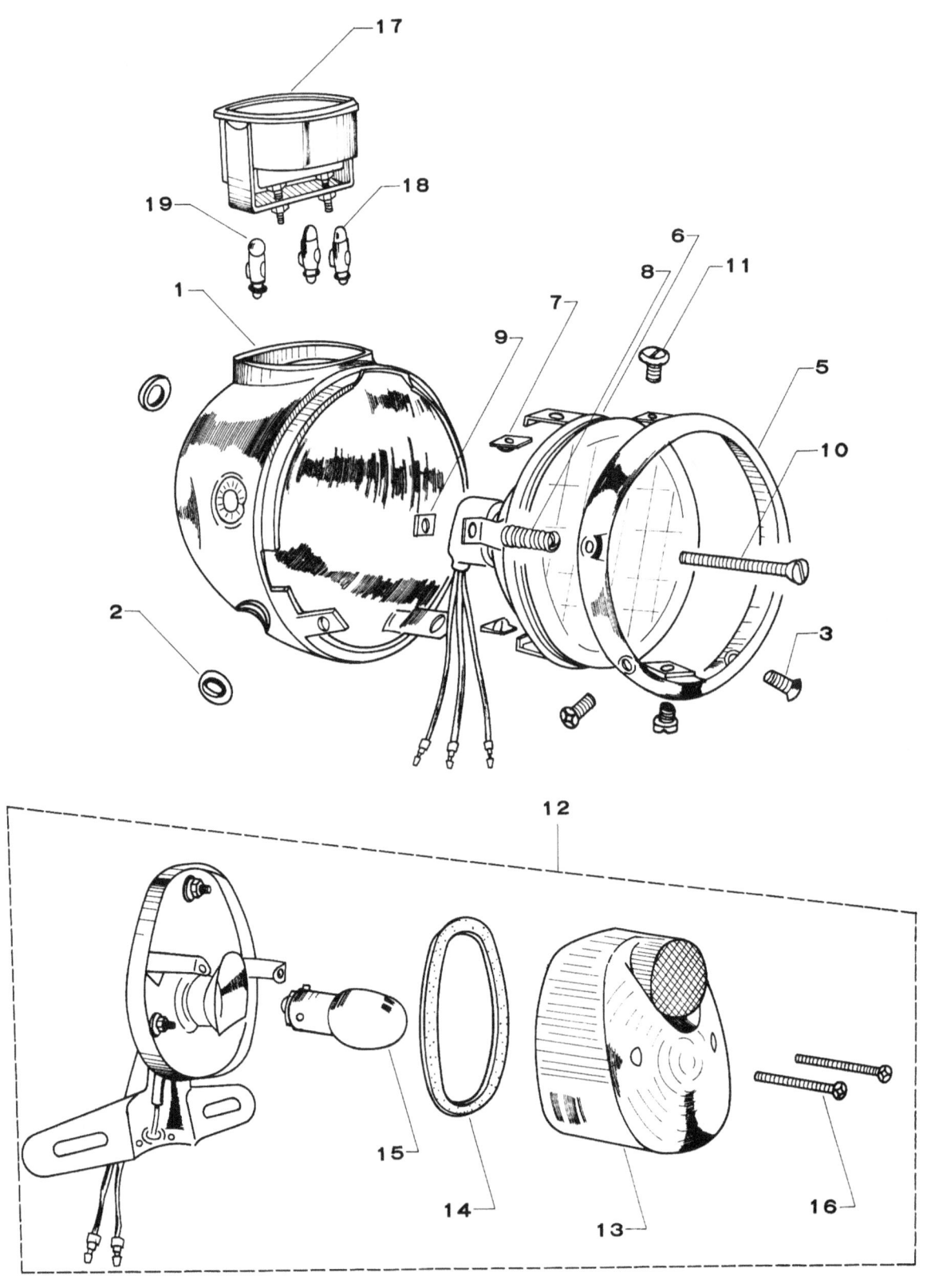

27) HEAD LAMP — TAIL LAMP — SPEEDOMETER

Index No.	Part No.	Part Name	No. Req'd	Unit Price US$	£	Interchangeability 7D	7S	HM	50SP	60SP	90	90M
27- 1	8111-8000-FAR	Head lamp body	1									
27- 2	8125-8000	Head lamp grommet	2									
27- 3	0342-0510	Cross rec'd oval head screw	2									
27- 4	8102-8000	Head lamp ass'y	1									
27- 5	8140-8000	Head lamp rim comp.	1									
27- 6	8150-8000	Head lamp lens comp.	1									
27- 7	8173-8000	Quick acting nut	2									
27- 8	8174-8000	Adjusting spring	1									
27- 9	8175-8000	Square nut	1									
27-10	8176-8000	Adjusting screw	1									
27-11	8177-8000	Holder screw	2									
27-12	8205-8000	Tail lamp ass'y	1									
27-13	8251-8000	Tail lamp lens	1									
27-14	8253-8000	Tail lamp gasket	1									
27-15	8252-3040	Tail lamp bulb	1			○						
27-16	0372-0330	Round head screw	2									
27-17	8401-8000	Speedometer ass'y	1									
27-18	8424-3000	Speedometer bulb	2			○						
27-19	8424-8000	Speedometer bulb	1									

Remarks

Interchangeability

Index No.	New Part No.		Old Part No.
27-19	8252-3040	=	M4516......Bulb (taillight) C.H.P.

28) HORN—IGNITION COIL—MAIN SWITCH—BATTERY

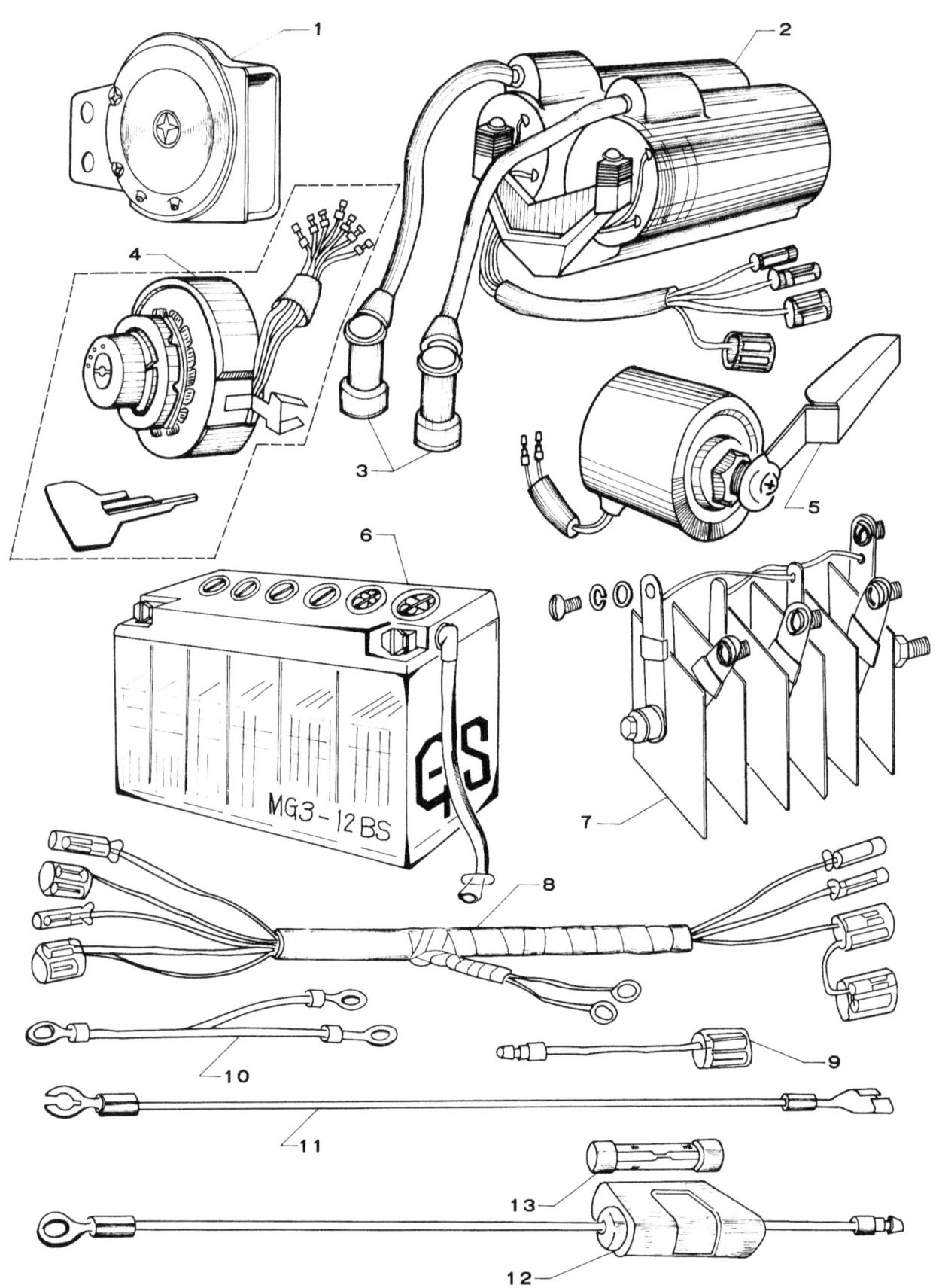

— 58 —

28) HORN—IGNITION COIL—MAIN SWITCH—BATTERY

Index No.	Part No.	Part Name	No. Req'd	Unit Price US$	£	Interchangeability 7D	7S	HM	50SP	60SP	90	90M
28- 1	8402-8000	Horn ass'y	1									
28- 2	8501-8000	Ignition coil ass'y	1									
28- 3	8520-5000	Plug cap ass'y	2						○	○	○	○
28- 4	8601-8000	Main switch ass'y	1									
28- 5	8602-8000	Stop switch ass'y	1									
28- 6	8701-3002	Battery	1			○						
28- 7	8702-8000	Rectifier ass'y	1									
28- 8	8811-8000	Wire harness	1									
28- 9	8824-5010	High beam wire	1								○	○
28-10	8831-8000	Body earth wire	1									
28-11	8835-5000	Speedometer earth wire	1								○	○
28-12	8802-8000	Fuse ass'y	1									
28-13	8861-3000	Fuse	1			○					○	○

Remarks

Interchangeability

Index No.	New Part No.		Old Part No.	
28- 6	8701-3002	=	M06600A-1	Battery
28- 9	8824-5010	=	EAE88121	High beam connector
28-11	8835-5000	=	EA1-61321-1	Speedometer earth wire
28-13	8861-3000	=	M06811-0	Fuse
28- 3	8520-5000	=	EA1-89320	Plug cap

29) SERVICE TOOL SET

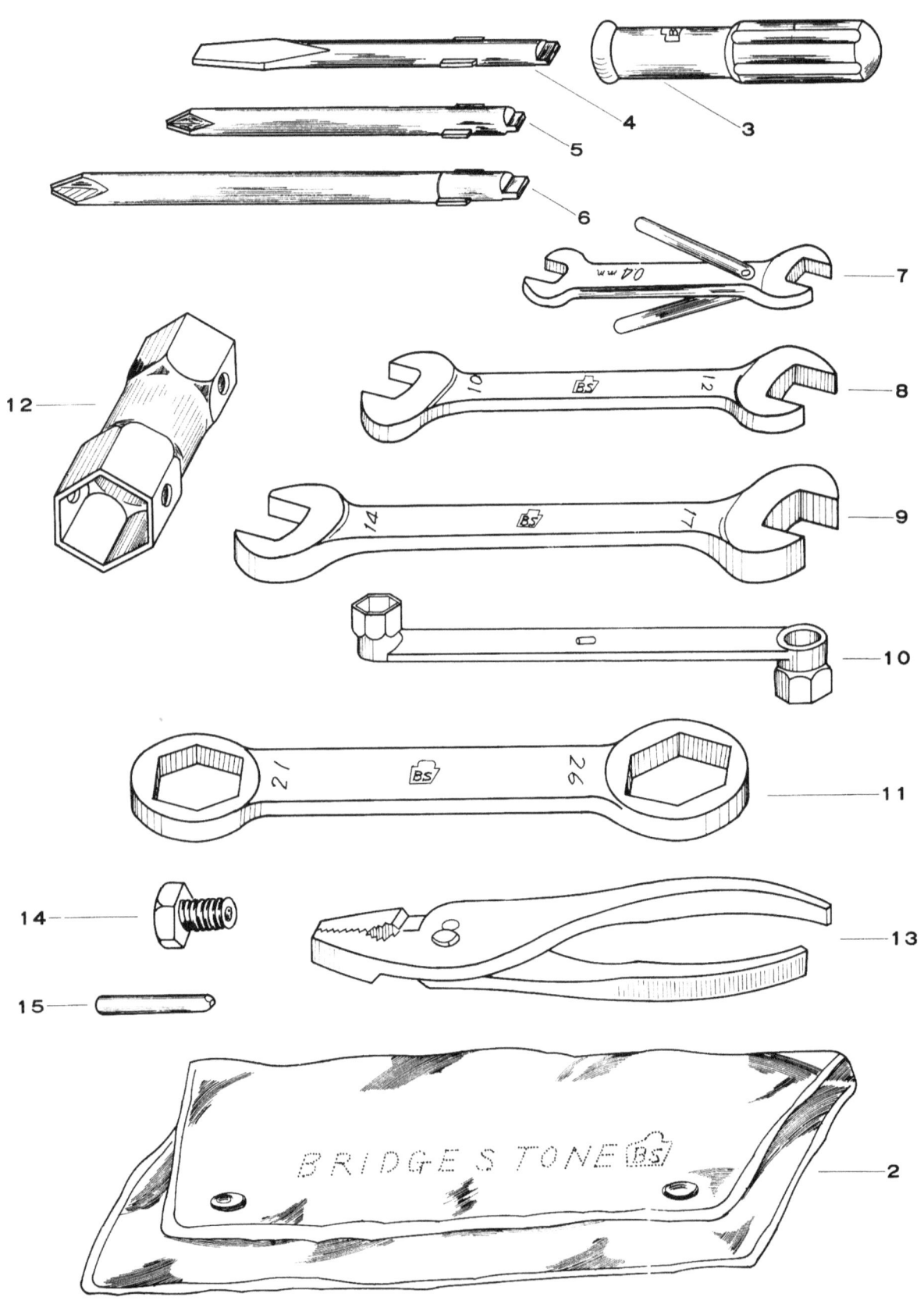

29) SERVICE TOOL SET

Index No.	Part No.	Part Name	No. Req'd	Unit Price US$	£	Interchangeability 7D	7S	HM	50SP	60Sp	90	90M
29- 1	9201-8000	Service tool set	1									
29- 2	9211-5000	Tool bag	1								○	○
29- 3	9231-3000	Driver grip	1			○	○	○	○	○	○	○
29- 4	9228-5000	Screw driver C	1			○	○	○	○	○	○	○
29- 5	9226-5000	Screw driver A	1								○	○
29- 6	9227-3000	Screw driver B	1									
29- 7	9212-3001	Double spanner 8×9	1			○	○	○	○	○	○	○
29- 8	9215-5000	Double spanner 10×12	1								○	○
29- 9	9217-5000	Double spanner 14×17	1								○	○
29-10	9219-8000	Box wrench 10×12	1									
29-11	9221-8000	Axle wrench	1									
29-12	9218-5000	Plug box spanner	1								○	○
29-13	9225-5000	Plier	1								○	○
29-14	9236-8000	Timing bolt	1									
29-15	9237-8000	Timing bar	1									

Remarks

Interchangeability

Index No.	New Part No.		Old Part No.	
29- 2	9211-5000	=	EA1-69111	Tool bag
29- 7	9212-3001	=	M08714-1	8×9 double head spanner
29- 8	9215-5000	=	EA1-69115	10×12mm double head spanner
29- 9	9217-5000	=	EA1-69114	14×17mm double head spanner
29-12	9218-5000	=	EA1-69113	Box spanner
29-13	9225-5000	=	EA1-69112	Plier
29- 5	9226-5000	=	EA1-69117	⊕ driver No. 1
29- 4	9228-3000	=	M08717-0	⊖ driver
29- 3	9231-3000	=	M08713-0	Driver grip

VELOCEPRESS MANUALS - MOTORCYCLE

1930'S BRITISH MOTORCYCLE CARBS & ELEC COMPONENTS (BOOK OF)
1930'S BRITISH MOTORCYCLE ENGINES (OVERHAUL & MAINTENANCE)
1930'S BRITISH MOTORCYCLE GEARBOXES & CLUTCHES (BOOK OF)
AJS 1932-1948 SINGLES & TWINS 250cc THRU 1000cc (BOOK OF)
AJS 1945-1960 SINGLES 350cc & 500cc MODELS 16 & 18 (BOOK OF)
AJS 1955-1965 SINGLES 350cc & 500cc (BOOK OF)
ARIEL 1932-1939 PREWAR MODELS (BOOK OF)
ARIEL 1933-1951 (WORKSHOP MANUAL)
ARIEL 1939-1960 4 STROKE SINGLES (BOOK OF)
ARIEL 1958-1964 LEADER & ARROW (BOOK OF)
BMW R26 R27 (1956-1967) FACTORY WORKSHOP MANUAL
BMW R50 R50S R60 R69S (1955-1969) FACTORY WORKSHOP MANUAL
BRIDGESTONE 90 SERIES FACTORY WSM & PARTS CATALOGUE
BRIDGESTONE 175 SERIES FACTORY WSM & PARTS CATALOGUE
BSA BANTAM ALL MODELS FROM 1948 ONWARDS (BOOK OF)
BSA SINGLES & V-TWINS UP TO 1927 (BOOK OF)
BSA SINGLES & V-TWINS UP TO 1935 (BOOK OF)
BSA SINGLES & V-TWINS 1936-1939 (BOOK OF)
BSA SINGLES & V-TWINS 1936-1952 (BOOK OF)
BSA OHV & SV SINGLES 250-600cc 1945-1954 (BOOK OF)
BSA OHV & SV SINGLES 250cc 1954-1970 (BOOK OF)
BSA OHV SINGLES 350 & 500cc 1955-1967 (BOOK OF)
BSA TWINS 1948-1962 (BOOK OF)
BSA TWINS 1962-1969 (SECOND BOOK OF)
DOUGLAS 1929-1939 PREWAR ALL MODELS (BOOK OF)
DOUGLAS 1948-1957 POSTWAR ALL MODELS FACTORY SHOP MANUAL
DUCATI 160cc, 250cc & 350cc OHC MODELS FACTORY SHOP MANUAL
HONDA 50 ALL MODELS UP TO 1970 INC MONKEY & TRAIL (BOOK OF)
HONDA 90 ALL MODELS UP TO 1966 (BOOK OF)
HONDA 125-150cc TWINS C/CS/CB/CA FACTORY WORKSHOP MANUAL
HONDA 250-305 TWINS C/CS/CB FACTORY WORKSHOP MANUAL
HONDA C100 SUPER CUB FACTORY WORKSHOP MANUAL
HONDA C110 SPORT CUB 1962-1969 FACTORY WORKSHOP MANUAL
HONDA TWINS & SINGLES 50cc THRU 305cc 1960-1966 (BOOK OF)
HONDA TWINS ALL MODELS 125cc THRU 450cc UP TO 1968 (BOOK OF)
J.A.P. ENGINES 1927-1952 & MOTORCYCLES 1934-1952 (BOOK OF)
LAMBRETTA 1947-1957 ALL 125 & 150cc MODELS (BOOK OF)
LAMBRETTA 1957-1970 LI & TV MODELS (SECOND BOOK OF)
MATCHLESS 1931-1939 ALL MODELS 250cc THRU 990cc (BOOK OF)
MATCHLESS 1945-1956 350 & 500cc SINGLES (BOOK OF)
MATCHLESS 1955-1966 350 & 500cc SINGLES (BOOK OF)
NEW IMPERIAL ALL SV & OHV FROM 1935 ONWARDS (BOOK OF)
NORTON 1932-1939 PREWAR MODELS (BOOK OF)
NORTON 1932-1947 (BOOK OF)
NORTON 1938-1956 (BOOK OF)
NORTON 1955-1963 MODELS 19, 50 & ES2 (BOOK OF)
NORTON 1955-1965 DOMINATOR TWINS (BOOK OF)
NORTON 1957-1970 TWINS FACTORY WORKSHOP MANUAL
NSU PRIMA 1956-1964 ALL MODELS (BOOK OF)
NSU QUICKLY 1953-1963 ALL MODELS (BOOK OF)
PANTHER 1932-1958 LIGHTWEIGHT MODELS 250 & 350cc (BOOK OF)
PANTHER 1938-1966 HEAVYWEIGHT MODELS 600 & 650cc (BOOK OF)
RALEIGH MOPEDS 1960-1969 (BOOK OF)
RALEIGH MOTORCYCLES 1919-1933 (BOOK OF)
ROYAL ENFIELD 1934-1946 SINGLES & V TWINS (BOOK OF)
ROYAL ENFIELD 1937-1953 SINGLES & V TWINS (BOOK OF)
ROYAL ENFIELD 1946-1962 SINGLES (BOOK OF)
ROYAL ENFIELD 1958-1966 250cc & 350cc SINGLES (SECOND BOOK OF)
ROYAL ENFIELD 736cc INTERCEPTOR FACTORY WORKSHOP MANUAL
RUDGE 1933-1939 (BOOK OF)
SUNBEAM 1928-1939 (BOOK OF)
SUNBEAM 1946-1957 S7 & S8 (BOOK OF)
SUZUKI 50cc & 80cc UP TO 1966 (BOOK OF)
SUZUKI T10 1963-1967 FACTORY WORKSHOP MANUAL
SUZUKI T20 & T200 1965-1969 FACTORY WORKSHOP MANUAL
TRIUMPH 1935-1939 PREWAR MODELS (BOOK OF)
TRIUMPH 1935-1949 (BOOK OF)
TRIUMPH 1937-1951 (WORKSHOP MANUAL)
TRIUMPH 1945-1955 FACTORY WORKSHOP MANUAL
TRIUMPH 1945-1958 TWINS (BOOK OF)
TRIUMPH 1956-1969 TWINS (BOOK OF)
VELOCETTE 1925-1970 ALL SINGLES & TWINS (BOOK OF)
VESPA 1951-1961 (BOOK OF)
VESPA 1955-1963 125 & 150cc & GS MODELS (SECOND BOOK OF)
VESPA 1955-1968 GS & SS (BOOK OF)
VESPA 1963-1972 90, 125 & 150cc (THIRD BOOK OF)
VILLIERS ENGINE UP TO 1959 INC. 3 WHEELERS (BOOK OF)
VILLIERS ENGINE UP TO 1969 (BOOK OF)
VINCENT 1935-1955 (WORKSHOP MANUAL)

VELOCEPRESS TECHNICAL BOOKS – MOTORCYCLE

CATALOG OF BRITISH MOTORCYCLES (1951 MODELS)
INDIAN PONYBIKE, BOY RACER & PAPOOSE ILL PARTS LIST & SALES LIT
MOTORCYCLE ENGINEERING (P.E. Irving)
SPEED AND HOW TO OBTAIN IT (Motor Cycle Magazine UK)
TUNING FOR SPEED (P.E. Irving)

VELOCEPRESS MANUALS - THREE WHEELER'S

BSA THREE WHEELER (BOOK OF)
VINTAGE MORGAN THREE WHEELER (BOOK OF)

VELOCEPRESS MANUALS - AUTOMOBILE

AUSTIN-HEALEY 6-CYLINDER WORKSHOP MANUAL
AUSTIN-HEALEY SPRITE & MG MIDGET WORKSHOP MANUAL 1958-1971
BMW 600 LIMOUSINE FACTORY WORKSHOP MANUAL
BMW 600 LIMOUSINE OWNERS HAND BOOK & SERVICE MANUAL
BMW 2000 & 2002 1966-1976 WORKSHOP MANUAL
BMW ISETTA FACTORY WORKSHOP MANUAL
CORVAIR 1960-1969 WORKSHOP MANUAL
CORVETTE V8 1955-1962 WORKSHOP MANUAL
FIAT 500 FACTORY WORKSHOP MANUAL 1957-1973
JAGUAR E-TYPE 3.8 & 4.2 SERIES 1 & 2 WORKSHOP MANUAL
JAGUAR MK 7, 8, 9 & XK120, 140, 150 WORKSHOP MANUAL 1948-1961
METROPOLITAN FACTORY WORKSHOP MANUAL
MGA & MGB OWNERS HANDBOOK & WORKSHOP MANUAL
MG MIDGET TC, TD, TF & TF1500 WORKSHOP MANUAL
PORSCHE 356 1948-1965 WORKSHOP MANUAL
PORSCHE 912 WORKSHOP MANUAL
TRIUMPH TR2, TR3, TR4 1953-1965 WORKSHOP MANUAL
VOLKSWAGEN TRANSPORTER, TRUCKS & WAGONS 1950-1979 WSM
VOLVO 1944-1968 ALL MODELS WORKSHOP MANUAL

VELOCEPRESS TECHNICAL BOOKS - AUTOMOBILE

FERRARI 250/GT SERVICE AND MAINTENANCE
FERRARI GUIDE TO PERFORMANCE
FERRARI OWNER'S HANDBOOK
FERRARI TUNING TIPS & MAINTENANCE TECHNIQUES
HOW TO BUILD A FIBERGLASS CAR
HOW TO BUILD A RACING CAR
HOW TO RESTORE THE MODEL 'A' FORD
MASERATI OWNER'S HANDBOOK
OBERT'S FIAT GUIDE
PERFORMANCE TUNING THE SUNBEAM TIGER
SOUPING THE VOLKSWAGEN
SOLEX CARBURETORS (EMPHASIS ON UK & EU AUTOMOBILES)
SU CARBURETORS (EMPHASIS ON UK AUTOMOBILES)
WEBER CARBURETORS (EMPHASIS ON ALFA & FIAT)

VELOCEPRESS BOOKS & GUIDES - AUTOMOBILE

ABARTH BUYERS GUIDE
COMPLETE CATALOG OF JAPANESE MOTOR VEHICLES
FERRARI 308 SERIES BUYER'S AND OWNER'S GUIDE
FERRARI BERLINETTA LUSSO
FERRARI BROCHURES AND SALES LITERATURE 1946-1967
FERRARI BROCHURES AND SALES LITERATURE 1968-1989
FERRARI OPP, MAINTENANCE & SERVICE H/BOOKS 1948-1963
FERRARI SERIAL NUMBERS PART I - ODD NUMBERS TO 21399
FERRARI SERIAL NUMBERS PART II - EVEN NUMBERS TO 1050
FERRARI SPYDER CALIFORNIA
HENRY'S FABULOUS MODEL "A" FORD
MASERATI BROCHURES AND SALES LITERATURE

VELOCEPRESS BOOKS – RACING

CARRERA PANAMERICANA - MEXICAN ROAD RACE (BOOK OF)
DIALED IN - THE JAN OPPERMAN STORY
IF HEMINGWAY HAD WRITTEN A RACING NOVEL
LE MANS 24 (THE BOOK THAT THE FILM WAS BASED ON)
VEDA ORR'S NEW REVISED HOT ROD PICTORIAL

AUTOBOOKS WORKSHOP MANUALS & BROOKLANDS ROAD TEST PORTFOLIOS

FOR A COMPLETE LISTING OF THE AUTOBOOKS & BROOKLANDS TITLES THAT WE CURRENTLY HAVE AVAILABLE, PLEASE VISIT OUR WEBSITE.